D0507346

Glorious Fish
IN THE MICROWAVE

IN THE MICROWAVE

PATRICIA TENNISON

CB

CONTEMPORARY
BOOKS

CHICAGO · NEW YORK

Library of Congress Cataloging-in-Publication Data

Tennison, Patricia.
    Glorious fish in the microwave / Patricia Tennison.
        p.   cm.
    ISBN 0-8092-4480-2 : $12.95
      1. Cookery (Fish)   2. Cookery (Seafood)   3. Microwave cookery.
  I. Title.
  TX747.T46   1989
  641.6'92—dc20   89-22067
                                                            CIP

Copyright © 1989 by Patricia Tennison
All rights reserved
Published by Contemporary Books, Inc.
180 North Michigan Avenue, Chicago, Illinois 60601
Manufactured in the United States of America
International Standard Book Number: 0-8092-4480-2

Published simultaneously in Canada by Beaverbooks, Ltd.
195 Allstate Parkway, Valleywood Business Park
Markham, Ontario L3R 4T8 Canada

CONTENTS

PART II • THE RECIPES

ACKNOWLEDGMENTS

I always suspected that I might write a book about fish. But I'm constantly amazed at how many people are needed and are willing to help produce just one book.

Editor Nancy Crossman provided constant encouragement to keep our standards high; Georgene Sainati directed the artwork with her usual flair; photographer Bill Hogan and food stylist Jill Van Cleave transformed a variety of fish and other foods into an elegant cover photograph; and copyeditor Leah Mayes thoroughly checked every line of copy.

Tor Kenward at Beringer Vineyards in Napa Valley, California, graciously contributed the valuable chapter on fish and wine.

Arn Arnam's first-class illustrations steal the show—again—and that's fine with me.

Respectful thank-yous to microwave experts Barbara Kafka and Thelma Pressman, who hold their own beaming lights in this quest to tame the microwave.

Information and advice are sincerely appreciated from *Chicago Tribune* colleagues JeanMarie Brownson, Bev Dillon, Susie Goldstein, Carol Haddix, and William Rice; Nancy Abrams of Chicago Fish House and the National Fish and Seafood Promotional Council, who helped me keep my facts straight; Antonia Allegra, director of culinary programs at Beringer Vineyards, who generously offered advice and the hospitality of her Napa home; Barry Conan, San Francisco tuna man; Gil Jaeger, Dodge Cove Maine Farm, Newcastle, Maine; George Koutsogiorgas, Greek Islands, Chicago; John Rowley, Fish Works!, Seattle; Millard Schmitt, Wheaton, Illinois, scaleman; and tastemaker and invaluable supporter, Gisela Riess, Mystic, Connecticut.

Also, assistance is appreciated from the Alaska Department of Fish and Game; Catfish Institute; Bob Rubin, Chicago Fish House; Tony Strocchia, Dominick's Finer Foods, Chicago; Jane Morimoto, Evans Food Group; Hawaii Seafood Promotion Committee; International Microwave Power Institute, Clifton, Virginia; Jewel Food, Chicago; Randy Hamilton, Monterey Bay Aquarium; Felicia Gressette, *Miami Herald*; Emily Holt and Wendy O'Dea, National Fisheries Institute; Pick Fisheries; Maureen Clancy, San Diego Union; Seafood Marketing Council; Supreme Lobster and Seafood Co.; the United States Department of Agriculture; and Dr. Steven Otwell, University of Florida.

Of the many people who helped and encouraged me with this book, I'd like to thank my mother, Sophie Riess; my energetic sous chefs, Jennifer Hill and Susie Kiel; testers and tasters Virginia Partain, Anna and Dave Sanderson, and the whole Martin clan; indispensable Elizabeth Laubhan, who keeps our household semiorganized; Warren Riess and the gang in Maine; Janie Tennison; and two guys with a thumbs-up attitude toward life: Al Borcover and Larry Townsend.

For making me think I was a great fisherman, a warm thank-you to my father, Herbert Riess, who can hook a bloodworm and shuck oysters better than anyone.

And a very special thanks to my husband, Tom, and our children, Jeff and Ashley, who kept our family humming through a thousand nights of fish—again.

INTRODUCTION

I am on a mission. And I invite—no, challenge—you to come along.

As this book goes into print, more people in this country own microwave ovens than dishwashers. That's a fact. And more people use those ovens to reheat than to cook.

That's a shame.

We need to beware of "microwave" becoming synonymous with "mediocre." You *can* cook in a microwave oven, and with very fine results. But you have to learn how to operate the machine, and you have to choose what a microwave oven cooks best.

In my first book, *Glorious Vegetables in the Microwave,* I chose vegetables, one of the food categories that the microwave oven cooks best, and presented chapters on fifty separate varieties, from artichokes and jicama through zucchini.

With encouragement from my publisher, colleagues, and readers who are hungry for "microwave recipes that work," I next concentrated on sauces in *Sumptuous Sauces in the Microwave.*

Now I turn to fish.

Fish in the microwave is, well, glorious. The microwave oven's method of fast, moist cooking is ideal for fragile fish fillets and even whole fish. Fish come out tender and juicy, ready to eat right off the plate, if you wish.

Because food doesn't stick to the plate when you cook in the microwave, you don't have to add butter or margarine to the fish dishes—a noteworthy advantage for those trying to cut back on fats.

Fishy smells—a major hurdle that trips otherwise eager cooks—are minimal in the microwave oven. The fish cooks so fast that the good aromas hardly have time to seep out the oven vents. Unpleasant smells from fish bits and oils burning in butter just don't happen if you're cooking fast and with little fat in the microwave. And the cooking equipment goes right into the dishwasher.

Once you've had some easy successes with fish in the microwave, you are likely to find yourself eating fish more often.

This is wonderful.

A wealth of medical evidence points to fish as the food of the future. Americans need to cut down on fats, particularly saturated fats found in meat products. Low-fat fish answer the need for more healthful protein, and even high-fat fish are touted as a source of Omega-3 fatty acids, believed useful in preventing heart disease.

To encourage you to try a variety of fish, I have included fifty chapters covering fifty different species. They run from popular and familiar shrimp, salmon, orange roughy, and trout to more unusual abalone, eel, octopus, mahimahi, and shark.

Browse through the chapters even if you are determined to never cook, say, amberjack. You may become tempted by Amberjack with Tomato-Dill Sauce and try the topping on your usual flounder, instead. Or you may decide to substitute trout for walleye in the Walleye-and-Walnut Salad.

As you try new fish and like them, use the substitute chart in this book to lead you to similar fish. But then do read the chapter covering that new fish.

All fish are not created equal. Orange roughy and oreo dory look like similar white fillets, but orange roughy has a finer texture. Bargain-priced Greenland turbot isn't turbot at all. Those slices of beautiful, orange-colored opah are doing just what they are supposed to do when they cook and turn from orange to pink to beige.

And all fish don't cook the same in the microwave. Conventional cooking has its "Canadian rule" which calls for 10 minutes per inch, at its thickest point. The rule for microwave cooking is by weight: approximately 4 minutes per pound of fish.

But I have found exceptions.

Very light-textured fillets, such as sole or flounder, cook faster, often 3 minutes per pound, because microwaves more easily penetrate light-textured foods. Dense bluefish cooks slower, about 5 minutes per pound. Very thick fillets are difficult to cook evenly because the outer edges will be overcooked before the centers are done; such fillets are best sliced in half.

Although I find that most fish are best cooked on high power in the microwave, I have also found exceptions. Abalone, octopus, and squid need to be cooked on medium or medium-low power to remain tender.

Clams can be opened successfully in the microwave oven. Oysters can not.

Whole crab and whole Maine lobster are a disaster in the microwave oven. Cook them by conventional methods. But use the microwave to heat precooked crabs and to cook spiny lobster tails—on medium power.

Crayfish can be prepared in the microwave, but only 1 pound at a time and only until a maroon-red—not "lobster" red—or they will be overcooked.

These tips, and more, are included in the introductory material found in Part I and in individual fish recipe chapters.

Glorious Fish in the Microwave is not a diet book. There is room in my life, and in this book, for mahimahi with unctuous bearnaise, whole catfish with butter-pecan sauce, and salmon Benedict with orange hollandaise.

However, I've taken care to include a wealth of healthful recipes.

Portions are small because this is the way I eat: small portions of fish, meat, or chicken, with larger portions of vegetables, grains, and fruit.

And so this book remains a personal book, one that reflects my tastes and my own favorites. There are no recipes here for breaded fish in the microwave, because I haven't yet found such a recipe that satisfies me.

Nutrition, speed, ease, variety, great taste—these are serious reasons to start cooking fish in the microwave.

But in truth, I also had a lot of fun writing this book. *Glorious Fish in the Microwave* is more than a collection of recipes. It is:

- Conquering octopus in the microwave with a friendly Greek restaurateur leading the way.
- Speeding away in a cab with the first opah to land in Chicago in ten days, and most likely the only one that month destined for a microwave oven.
- Urging a houseful of New Englanders in the woods of Maine to cook their lobsters in the microwave, then admitting that it wasn't such a good idea.
- Watching fresh tuna arrive in the early morning fog at Fisherman's Wharf, San Francisco, and learning how to judge a very fine catch.
- Playing—gently—with black abalone at the Monterey Bay Aquarium.
- Walking the wharfs along the Connecticut coastline, pining after the bluefish that got away.

NOTE: *The first recipe in each of the fifty fish chapters typically includes little, if any, added fat. Instead, I work with herbs, spices, mustards, and vegetables for added interest. Look for the* ❤ *symbol that marks these no-added-fat recipes.*

Also, I arranged each of the fifty fish chapters with the easiest recipes at the beginning of each chapter. The recipes within each chapter then become increasingly more time-consuming or require more unusual ingredients.

IN THE MICROWAVE

PART I
THE BASICS

THE MICROWAVE

HOW A MICROWAVE WORKS

Microwaves are short radio waves. The waves themselves are not hot; that is, they do not give off heat like charcoal in a grill or like an electric coil that heats air in a conventional oven.

Instead, microwaves pass through many materials, such as glass, ceramic, paper, and most plastic, without causing heat. That is why you can cook food in a glass bowl in a microwave oven and still find the bowl cool enough to handle.

However, microwaves are absorbed by water, sugar, starches, and fats. Microwaves excite water molecules, and when the molecules move, the friction causes heat, just as rubbing your hands together causes heat.

The magnetron tube in a microwave oven works like a broadcasting station, sending out the waves. The waves travel in a straight line, bouncing off metal walls and any fans designed to move the waves within a microwave oven. It is important that you never operate your microwave oven when it is empty, or the microwaves could damage the magnetron tube.

Microwaves penetrate about ⅓ inch to 1½ inches into foods, depending on the density of the food. This outer inch of food heats up, and the heat transfers to cook the rest of the food.

Some foods, such as a medium-sized fish fillet, cook perfectly in the microwave oven with little fuss. Other dishes need to be stirred or rearranged so that the microwaves can reach uncooked portions. Like other foods in the microwave oven, fish fillets, steaks, and chunks cook more evenly if they are the same size.

COOKING POWER AND TIMES

Every microwave oven has an output wattage, which is the amount of microwave energy the machine has for cooking. Ovens vary from about 400 to 720 watts, and the larger ovens typically have the highest power.

Low-wattage ovens (400–500 watts) take from a few seconds to a few minutes longer to cook food than high-wattage ovens (600–700 watts). Recipes in this cookbook include a range of times so that they can be used by both low-wattage and high-wattage ovens. However, cooking times are approximate because microwave ovens—even those with the same wattage output—vary depending on the manufacturer.

Deluxe microwave ovens often feature automatic systems that sense the moisture given off by the food so that a computer can calculate when the food is finished cooking. However, I find that the computer too often is set to overcook the foods for my taste. I prefer to select the cooking times myself.

When you follow a recipe from this cookbook for the first time, try the shorter cooking time, then check the food to see if you need more time. After preparing a few recipes, you should find a consistent pattern that suits your machine and taste.

Common power settings are not yet standardized. As a guide, however, "high" means 100 percent power, or full power; "medium-high" is 70 percent power; "medium" is 50 percent power, or half power; "defrost" is 30 percent power; and "warm" is 10 percent power.

Fish generally is cooked on high power. I find that this keeps the flesh juicy. (You should, however, be sure to check individual recipes for exceptions.)

EQUIPMENT

Microwave cookware gets more practical and beautiful each year. But your cupboards probably already contain enough equipment to get you started.

Do not use metal pans, gold- or silver-rimmed plates, or utensils with screws or metal handles. Microwaves will be reflected off the metals and may damage the oven. Delicate glassware and china are not recommended.

Glass, ceramic, and plastic bowls and dishes are best. Microwaves pass through these materials. To test whether a favorite plate or bowl is microwave-proof, put it in the microwave oven next to a glass measure filled with a cup of cool water. MICROWAVE on high power for 1 minute. If the water is warm but the plate you are testing feels cool to the touch, the plate is fine for the microwave oven. If it feels slightly warm, you could use it for reheating foods but not for long cooking. If the dish feels hot, do not use it in the microwave oven.

Even if dishes are suitable for the microwave oven, heat may transfer from the cooked food and make the container too hot to handle. Use oven mitts when removing dishes from the microwave oven.

Just as with conventional cooking, recipes work best if you use cooking equipment of the recommended size. If a bowl is too large, the food will spread out and may cook unevenly. If a bowl is too small, certain foods such as sauces may overflow. In general, foods cook best in the microwave oven in bowls that are just large enough to hold them; that is, in bowls that are not too large.

To make it easier to use this cookbook, the recipes are written so that you don't need to use browning dishes, temperature probes, or other special-use accessories.

Most of the dishes in this book can be made if you have microwave-proof dinner plates and serving plates, 1-quart and 2½-quart covered casseroles, a 3-quart bowl, 2-cup and 4-cup measures, and plastic or wooden spoons.

COVERING TECHNIQUES

Covering holds in heat and moisture, helping foods cook faster and more evenly in the microwave oven. When a recipe in this cookbook says "cover," use a tight-fitting lid or plastic wrap. If using plastic wrap, fold back at least one corner to create a vent; this helps prevent the wrap from splitting and also makes it possible to stir food without removing the wrap.

When cooking fish, I find it best to make two vents, preferably between fillets, so that the fish itself remains mostly covered. This allows some heat to escape yet keeps the fish moist and tender.

Some recipes call for other coverings. Waxed paper is used when you want to prevent splattering and promote even cooking but don't want to trap in moisture. Paper towels are used for a similar purpose, and they also absorb moisture.

Take care when removing covers. Open casseroles and remove plastic wrap by lifting the far corner. This allows hot steam to escape and avoids burns.

Foil wrap may be used in the microwave oven to protect parts of the fish from overcooking. Keep the pieces of foil smooth and at least 1 inch from the sides of the oven.

COOKING IN THE MICROWAVE

A microwave oven saves you time, allows you to cook with less water and fat than conventional methods for more nutritious results, creates easier cleanup, and doesn't heat the house in summer.

But you can't just push buttons and walk away.

Feel the food as it cooks; use your fingers or a fork to test for doneness and stir or rearrange as necessary. Ingredients straight from the refrigerator will need more time to cook than those at room temperature. A thin fish fillet may need less time than a thick one. A densely textured fillet may need more time than a finely textured fillet of the same size. Recipe times can serve only as a guide.

And taste as you cook. The intensity of herbs and spices varies, and you may need to adjust the seasoning. If you are using canned ingredients such as chicken or beef broth, taste before adding salt.

WHAT A MICROWAVE OVEN CAN'T DO

While a microwave oven is ideal for many dishes, it doesn't replace all conventional cooking methods.

Large amounts of water take longer to boil in the microwave than on the stove, so use your stove to cook a pot of pasta. A cup of uncooked rice is a toss-up; it takes about the same amount of time, so use whichever appliance is more convenient at the moment.

Besides the dangers of the high heat and of handling hot oil, deep frying takes too long in the microwave. Ditto for a large turkey. Soft- or hard-boiled eggs are best left to the stove, too; steam builds up inside the shells and causes the eggs to explode into a sticky mess in the microwave.

FISH AND SEAFOOD

WAYS FISH COME TO MARKET

- Whole: completely intact, as it came from the water; 45 percent edible.

- Drawn: with only innards removed; 50 percent edible.

- Dressed or pan-dressed: gutted, with scales, head, tail, and fins removed; 67 percent edible.

- Split: dressed, then cut lengthwise down the middle, with backbone removed; 100 percent edible, except for small pin bones.

- Steaks: dressed, then cut crosswise into ¾- to 1-inch steaks; 90 percent edible, or 100 percent if no bones.

- Fillets: the sides of the fish, cut away from the backbone, with or without the skin; 100 percent edible, except for small pin bones.

SELECTING FISH AND SEAFOOD

Walking into a fish store or the fish department of the grocery store is quite a different experience from just a few years ago. In addition to familiar sole, swordfish, and shrimp, you are likely to find mounds of shiny black mussels, deep-red-streaked shark steaks, whole catfish, and delicate opah steaks.

However, while the varieties may be new, the ways to select fresh fish remain the same.

First, find out when your fish department gets its delivery of fresh fish, and plan to shop those days. An extra day in the refrigerator—whether it be at your home or at the store—can make a significant difference in the quality of a fish.

Then, be flexible when you shop. Although some varieties such as trout, catfish, and crayfish are being raised successfully, most fish are still caught by line or net. Supplies of fish just don't arrive as regularly as crates of carrots. Be prepared to buy the best-looking fish featured that day.

Whole Fish

To shop for fish you need to use your eyes—and nose. A fresh whole fish should have bulging, not sunken, eyes. Also, with the exception of walleye pike, which has naturally cloudy eyes, the eyes should have no signs of yellow or brown discoloration. The body of the fish should look taut and feel firm when touched. Fish quickly develop a surface bacteria which has a mild odor. However, after rinsed under cold water, the fish should smell clean and fresh, without fishy or ammonia odors.

Steaks and Fillets

Fresh fish steaks or fillets have a natural, moist brightness. Fish that have been frozen will look duller but likely still are fine to eat. Avoid those with yellowed or browned edges, signs of refreezing or otherwise poor handling. Ask your fish dealer to hold up the fillets or steaks so that you can smell them. Like whole fish, the cut fish should smell clean and fresh. Indeed, very fresh fillets will smell more like a cut cucumber than fish.

Frozen and Canned

Very fresh fish are ideal, but frozen and canned products are more than convenient. These commercially prepared products can be more nutritious than fresh fish that has been stored too long at the store or in your refrigerator. Some fish, such as true Dover sole, are almost always found frozen because of the high cost of transporting the fresh fish from England or France. And if you want a particular fish out of season, you will have to settle for frozen. Buy the freshest fish when you can, and supplement with good quality frozen or canned products.

When buying frozen fish, avoid packages stacked above the load line in display cases. Check that the package is neat and flat, with no torn wrappings, ice, or drips indicating that the product was thawed and refrozen. Although the fish may still be healthful, the texture and taste will suffer from refreezing.

There is a place on our shelves—and in this cookbook—for canned fish, too. A can of tuna makes a fine lunch, salmon elevates a plain potato to an entree, and a can of minced clams inspires the topping for a fine pasta dinner.

CLEANING FISH

If you buy only fish fillets and steaks, there is no cleaning involved, except perhaps for a few pin bones and a willful fish scale or two. And even with whole fish, you have the option of letting the fishmonger handle the whole chore.

However, even if you intend never in your lifetime to clean a whole fish, it is a good idea to be able to recognize a job well done.

Most fish need to be gutted immediately, so this job is often done right on a fishing boat. If it wasn't, however, to gut the fish use a knife to slit the belly from the anus forward to the head. Use your hand to remove the innards, and scrape away the blood from along the spine. Do not wash in fresh water because this will speed the breakdown of the flesh. Wrap the fish in a moisture-holding material such as newspaper or seaweed, and keep it chilled. Don't do anything more until you are ready to prepare the fish.

For the final cleaning, first scale the fish. Lay the fish on its side on newspaper, and use one hand to hold the fish by its tail. Take a scaler, or the blunt side of a knife, and scrape from tail to head to remove the scales. Turn the fish over and repeat. This is a pretty messy job, with wayward scales flying here and there, and is best done outdoors.

Next, remove the fins. These may include a dorsal fin running along the top of the fish, pectoral fins at either side, a pelvic fin along the front bottom, and an anal fin farther back. To remove a fin, take a sharp knife and make a ¼- to ½-inch V-shaped wedge on either side of the fin, and lift out the fin.

Now, do a more thorough job of cleaning the cavity. Use your hand to carefully remove the roe, if any, from triangular-shaped compartments on either side of the cavity. The elastic-textured, white- to orange-colored roe can be saved for eating.

Scrape away any leftover blood and innards, and rinse the fish, inside and out, under cold running water. To help the fish stay fresher during storage, dip it into a pot of salted water. Pat it dry with paper towels.

Heads or Tails

Cooking a whole fish with its head and tail intact makes a more dramatic presentation, gives you less waste and a little more fish to eat, and is easier, I think, than carving up the uncooked fish.

However, there are two good reasons to remove the head: you are squeamish, or the whole fish won't fit in the microwave.

To remove the head, use a large, sharp knife to slice through the flesh just behind the gills. If the fish is small, you can continue to cut right through the spine to sever the head. If the fish is large, cut behind both gills, then place the fish on the edge of a table and snap off the head.

The truly initiated can continue to probe for two delicacies: fish cheeks and tongues. The tender, bite-sized cheeks are located in the head near the gills, about where a fish would have ears. The tongue, of course, is in the mouth. Cut out the tongue and cheeks, and cook them as you would scallops. The cheeks also can be removed after the whole fish is cooked.

To remove the tail, use a sharp knife to simply slice through the tail, just where the flesh begins.

FILLETING A FISH

You can fillet a fish either before or after cooking, and both times have their advantages. If you cook the fish first, the flesh becomes easier to remove, and you will have more fish to eat and less waste. If you fillet before cooking, you don't have to bother with cleaning and cooking the whole fish.

To fillet a whole, uncooked fish, first decide if you are going to skin the fillets. If not, you must first scale the fish.

After scaling, or if you are going to skin the fillets, lay the fish on its side. Use a filleting knife—thin, narrow, and flexible—to make a cut just behind the gill covers, until the knife just touches the backbone. Turn the knife, and cut and scrape along the bone to separate the flesh into one boneless fillet. Turn the fish over and fillet the other side.

You may want to keep the skin on more delicate fish to help the fillet stay together while cooking. For more sturdy fish, place the fillet skin-side down on a cutting board, and grab the tail with one hand. With your other hand, hold a knife flat between the skin and flesh, and cut and scrape away from the tail to remove the skin.

See specific chapters for details on how to clean catfish, clams, crayfish, eel, mussels, octopus, oysters, shrimp, and squid.

STORING FISH AND SEAFOOD

The best way to keep fish fresh is to get it into the refrigerator as soon as possible. If you are going to eat the fish that day (which is ideal), unwrap the fish, rinse it under cold water, pat it dry with paper towels, and rewrap it in plastic wrap. Place the package in the back of the refrigerator where the temperature should be as close as possible to 32° Fahrenheit.

If you need to keep the fish overnight or for an extra day, rinse it and pat it dry, then place it on a cake rack with a plate or shallow baking pan underneath to catch any liquids. To keep the fish at a constant temperature and prevent dehydration, throw a layer of crushed ice into the baking pan, but be sure that the ice doesn't touch the fish. Cover both fish and pan tightly with plastic wrap or foil. After 24 hours, repeat the whole cleaning process, rinsing the fish, cake rack, and pan, and adding new ice.

Store live oysters, clams, mussels, and lobsters in the refrigerator wrapped in damp material, such as seaweed or paper towels or newspapers. They are living creatures, so do not store them directly on ice or in airtight containers. And do not store them in fresh water, which will kill them.

Store shucked oysters and clams in the coldest part of the refrigerator in the container in which you purchased them. Surround the container with ice if possible.

FREEZING AND DEFROSTING FISH

If you are not going to use a fish within a couple days of bringing it home, it is best to freeze it. Rinse the fish under cold water, pat it dry with paper towels, and wrap it tightly in plastic wrap. Wrap it again in foil wrap, and freeze it.

It is best to let fish thaw in the refrigerator overnight. However, you can use the microwave to help you get started.

To partially defrost fish, place it on a rack in a dish (a bacon rack is ideal) and cover it with the plastic wrap. For 1 or more pounds of fish, MICROWAVE on defrost or medium-low for about 3 minutes, turning the fish over and separating the fillets. Let the fish stand for 3 minutes between defrosting sessions. For smaller fillets, make the cooking and resting sessions about 15 seconds each.

Do not let the fish get warm to the touch, or you will start to cook the fish. Stop sessions when you can bend the still ice-cold fish, and let the fish finish defrosting in the refrigerator.

Do not thaw fish at room temperature. This damages the texture and flavor and may cause spoilage.

Do not refreeze fish. Although the fish may still be healthful enough to eat, the taste and texture suffer.

Defrost fish completely before cooking in the microwave oven.

HOW LONG TO COOK FISH

Cooking time varies by the weight, shape, and thickness of the fish. As a rule, fish takes about 4 minutes per pound in a 600- to 700-watt microwave oven. However, thick fish steaks and whole fish take slightly longer; thin fillets like perch and delicate shrimp take less. Read about the various cuts and see specific fish chapters.

HOW DO YOU TELL WHEN FISH IS DONE?

This has to be the most-often asked question about fish cooked in the microwave—or cooked by any method, for that matter.

The first rule is to forget the old rule about cooking fish until it flakes. When fish flakes, it is overcooked.

A perfectly cooked piece of fish will break when cut with a fork but will still be moist.

Test for doneness just before the recipe's lowest suggested cooking time. Use a fork to gently probe the fish in its thickest portion, preferably near the largest bone. When almost all of the flesh is opaque, the fish should be removed from the oven and set on the counter for a few minutes. The center or thickest portion will finish cooking on the counter.

When checking fish for doneness, don't be misled by the wet-looking fat on some fish, such as salmon. The fat will remain very moist even after the rest of the flesh is cooked.

Some fish make it easy to eyeball doneness by color. Opah turns from orange to pink, then to beige as it completes cooking. Crayfish turn a maroon-red. Check each specific fish chapter.

HOW TO COOK FILLETS

Fillets are flat portions of fish from either side of the backbone and typically have only small pin bones. They are no-fuss, easy to portion, and easy to cook—thus very popular with busy cooks.

Cook fillets tightly covered with plastic wrap, vented, on high power. With high power, the fish loses very little juice (about half as much as when cooked on medium power), resulting in a moist, tender fillet.

Place fillets skin-side down to prevent small fillets such as perch from curling. Slashing the skin across the width of the fillet also helps. If a fillet has a thin end, tuck it under for more even cooking. Arrange the thicker part of the fillet along the outside of the plate.

Thicker fillets will take a little more time per pound to cook than the thinner ones.

Servings:
- ¼ to ⅓ pound per person

Timing Guidelines:
- Thin fillets, to ½ inch: 3–5 minutes per pound
- Thick fillets, ¾ to 1 inch: 5–6 minutes per pound

HOW TO COOK STEAKS

Steaks are cut across the fish, which on narrow fish makes flat, U-shaped pieces. Steaks from large fish may be square or rectangular.

Cook fish steaks tightly covered with plastic wrap, vented, on high power. With high power, the fish steaks retain more natural juices than when cooked at lower power.

Arrange steaks on plate with the base of the U-shape to the outside. Rearrange midway through cooking, if necessary.

Thicker steaks will take a little more time per pound to cook than the thinner ones.

It's tricky to cook a very thick fillet or steak evenly in the microwave. If the steak is quite thick, I slice it in half horizontally. If the steaks are cooking and the edges are almost done while the center is almost raw, cut the steak in half, expose the undercooked portion to the outside, and continue cooking. Better yet, start out with four evenly sized, ¼-pound servings, and they will cook up perfectly.

Servings:
- ¼ to ⅓ pound per person

Timing Guidelines:
- Thin steaks, to ½ inch: 4–5 minutes per pound
- Thick steaks, ¾ to 1 inch: 5–6 minutes per pound

HOW TO COOK WHOLE FISH

Whole fish—head and tail intact—are fun to bring home and are exciting to serve. The only limitation will be the inside dimensions of your microwave oven.

If the whole fish is too large for your microwave oven, cut off the head and discard it, or save it for soup. Still too large? Cut off the tail. Otherwise, I like to keep the head and tail intact. It makes a more dramatic presentation, and you don't waste as much fish.

When you buy a whole fish, ask that it be gutted and scaled. A few scales left on the fish are not a big problem; they will slip off easily with the skin when the fish is done cooking.

If the whole fish is intact, cover the head and tail loosely with foil wrap to keep them from overcooking. The thin tail portion will cook when heat from the rest of the fish transfers to the tail. Be sure to keep the foil smooth and at least 1 inch from the sides of the oven.

Cover whole fish with plastic wrap, turning back one or two corners to vent. The tight but vented covering gives evenly cooked, moist fish.

You can cook whole fish right on a microwave-proof serving plate. If the fish is larger than 2 pounds, it cooks more evenly if you turn the fish over after about 5 minutes while the fish is still firm and holds together well.

I've cooked whole fish both on high power and medium power, and I prefer the slightly juicier texture you get with high power. You do have to watch the fish, however, because it will overcook with just one extra minute in the microwave.

When testing for doneness, use a fork to probe the flesh right in the middle of the fillet portion. Stop cooking when the thickest portion is opaque when pulled apart gently with fork. Let stand, covered, 10 minutes.

If you have undercooked the fish, return it to the microwave oven, or fillet the fish and return the fillets to the microwave oven.

Stuffing won't add extra time if it is cooked first.

Carving a whole, cooked fish is very similar to filleting an uncooked one. With the fish on its side, use a knife to make a cut just behind the gill covers, until the knife just touches the backbone. Turn the knife and run along the bone to separate and lift out one boneless fillet. Starting from the tail, lift out the exposed backbone and head, leaving the second fillet on the platter.

Timing Guidelines (steamed, whole fish, with head and tail intact—fish with head removed will cook slightly faster—and 1–2 tablespoons lemon juice):

- ½-pound whole fish: 3½–4 minutes
- 1-pound whole fish: 4–6 minutes
- 2-pound whole fish: 8–12 minutes
- 3-pound whole fish: 15–18 minutes
- 4-pound whole fish: 18–20 minutes

TIPS FOR MICROWAVING FISH

Be sure to read your oven's manual for instructions on how to use your specific machine, and read the recipe through once before you start cooking. But here are some general tips:

- When you pull back the plastic wrap from a plate of fish to create vents, pick spots between the fillets so that the fish itself is still covered. This keeps the fish moist, while allowing room for air pressure to escape.
- Make two vents—not just one. I find that this keeps juices from boiling hard, so that the fish remains tender.
- If a fish steak is thick—more than 1½ inches—slice it in half horizontally to make two thinner fillets. This will help the fish cook more evenly in the microwave.
- Use fresh fish or defrost fish completely before cooking.
- Just like vegetables and fruits, fresh fish have peak seasons. Check in at your fish department regularly to keep up with the current catch.
- Keep an open mind about "new" fish. Deeper fishing and consumer demand for more fish means more quality choices in the fish department.
- Weigh fish to get a more precise cooking time.
- Do not overcook fish. Delicate fish is more tender and juicy when cooked until just opaque. If a recipe gives a range of cooking time, test after the shortest suggested time.
- Remember to allow for standing time. Fish will continue to cook for several minutes after you remove it from the microwave. Take this time into account when you judge for doneness.
- Salt most fish after cooking. Salt attracts microwaves and can cause uneven cooking if applied directly on fish before cooking. It doesn't matter as much if the salt is dissolved in enough cooking liquid or in a sauce.
- A larger mass of food takes longer to cook in the microwave. If you double a recipe, add one-half more time and check frequently for doneness.
- Thicker shapes take longer to cook than thin ones. Position thicker parts toward the outside of the dish where they will receive more microwave energy. Fold under any thin portions of fillets.
- Turn over large fish after about 5 minutes for more even cooking.

- For fillets, rotate a quarter- or half-turn midway through cooking for more even results.
- For soups and sauces, stir cooked, outside portions to the inside.
- Use small pieces of aluminum foil to shield areas that you don't want to cook or overcook, such as the head and thin tail end of a whole fish. This is also a good technique if you want to defrost only a few slices of bacon. Keep the foil smooth and at least 1 inch from the sides of the microwave.
- When you are cooking fish and vegetables together, arrange larger, slower-cooking vegetables, such as carrots and broccoli flowerets, on the outside of the dish for more even cooking. Faster-cooking vegetables, such as thin asparagus, mushrooms, bell peppers, scallions, and zucchini sticks, may be placed in the center.
- MICROWAVE vegetables until slightly limp and easy to pierce before putting on a skewer with fish for kabobs.
- Bones are easier to remove after fish fillets are cooked. Tweezers do a great job on the small bones.
- If an accompanying sauce takes more than a few minutes to make, make the sauce before you cook the fish, and keep it warm.
- Out of fresh lemon? Substitute fresh lime juice or orange juice.
- Reheat fish on medium or medium-low power.
- Use leftover fish to make a first-class sandwich or as the focal point of a salad.
- Many wooden spoons may be left right in the bowl when cooking in a microwave oven and will remain cool to the touch. However, I find that old wooden spoons that have darkened from age and oil do get quite hot. Experiment carefully.
- To remove fish smells from your microwave oven, place a cut lemon in a custard cup and MICROWAVE on high for 1 minute.
- Save fish heads and tails in a plastic bag in the freezer until you have enough to make homemade fish stock.
- Use white pepper, rather than black pepper, on light-colored fish to avoid unattractive speckles.
- Serve light-colored fish on dark plates for better presentation.

FISH SUBSTITUTES

The beauty of fish is that they are not created equal. It would be marvelous, indeed, if we could walk into a fish store and see an exotic, midnight-blue opah, a monochromatic striped bass, and a fresh flounder with both of its eyes on one side of its enormous, flat body. Seeing the whole fish lined up together, it would be much easier to appreciate the various species.

In reality, the best most people get to see in a fish store or grocery store is a neat display of clean, white fillets, thick steaks in various shades from grey to red, and perhaps some whole trout or red snapper.

No wonder some people believe that all fish taste the same.

Learning to appreciate fish is not unlike learning to appreciate wine. Like red wines and white wines, fish fall easily into categories of lean, moderately lean, and oily. But within those categories fish still differ. Meaty-textured monkfish, delicate and sweet flounder, and bland, flaky cod all qualify as very low-fat, white-colored fish fillets. But they taste and cook quite differently.

Use the following lists to help make substitutes when you are buying fish for a favorite recipe. But use them, too, to create recipes for a new fish. If you like oreo dory, you'll likely enjoy kingclip; if orange roughy is a family favorite, try flounder or sole; if you love salmon, you're a candidate to try char.

In picking the suggested substitutes, I considered texture, oil content, and taste. However, there is a difference between bluefish and mackerel, or between swordfish and tuna—and that's the beauty of fish.

Substitutes

Abalone: geoduck, whelk
Amberjack: mahimahi, shark, swordfish, tuna
Bluefish: mackerel, mullet, salmon
Buffalofish: carp, grouper, kingclip, snapper, whitefish
Catfish: porgy, striped bass, trout, sometimes char
Char: salmon, trout, sometimes catfish
Clams: mussels, sometimes oysters
Cod: haddock, halibut, flounder, grouper, pollack
Crab: sometimes lobster or shrimp
Crayfish: shrimp, lobster
Eel: mackerel (in soups)
Flounder: pompano, sole, turbot
Grouper: Atlantic cod, haddock, halibut, pollack, snapper, striped bass
Haddock: Atlantic cod, orange roughy, pollack, grouper
Halibut: mahimahi, shark, swordfish, tuna; for Greenland halibut: pollack, kingclip, oreo dory
Kingclip: oreo dory, pollack
Lobster: monkfish, sea scallops, sometimes crab and shrimp
Mackerel: bluefish, eel, mullet, sometimes ono
Mahimahi: halibut, ono, snapper, shark, swordfish, tuna
Monkfish: scallops, grouper, lobster tail
Mullet: bluefish, buffalofish, mackerel, sometimes eel
Mussels: clams, sometimes oysters
Octopus: chicken
Ono: mahimahi, swordfish, tuna, sometimes mackerel
Opah: mahimahi, swordfish, tuna
Orange roughy: flounder, haddock, pompano, sole, snapper
Oreo dory: kingclip
Oysters: sometimes clams and mussels
Pacific rockfish: red snapper, striped bass
Perch: catfish, cod, orange roughy, porgy, sole, snapper

Pike: cod, haddock, pollack
Pollack: cod, haddock, flounder, sole
Pompano: orange roughy, sole, turbot
Porgy: catfish, perch
Salmon: char, trout, whitefish
Scallops: oysters, mussels, shrimp
Shark: halibut, mahimahi, swordfish, tuna
Shrimp: crayfish, lobster
Smelt: anchovies, herring
Snails: sometimes clams
Snapper: grouper, pompano, striped bass
Sole: flounder, turbot
Squid: sometimes clams
Striped bass: grouper, snapper
Swordfish: halibut, mahimahi, ono, shark, tuna
Trout: char, salmon
Tuna: mahimahi, ono, shark, swordfish
Turbot: flounder, sole
Walleye: pike, trout
Whitefish: char, salmon, trout

FAT LEVEL

As you can see from the following lists, fish is a particularly fine source of low-fat protein. In fact, half of the species featured in this book fall into the very-low-fat category, with 2 percent or less fat by weight.

By comparison, the same amount of cooked chicken with no skin is 3.5 percent fat (a low-fat selection); sirloin steak, 8.5 percent fat (medium-fat); and ground beef, 18.5 percent fat (high-fat).

However, the amount of fat is only one consideration; another is the type of fat—saturated or unsaturated.

Much of the fat in meat products such as chicken and beef is saturated fat, which is believed to contribute to heart disease. Fish, even the high-fat species, have much less saturated fat. For example, about 41 percent of the fat in sirloin steak is saturated; only 17 percent of the fat in salmon is saturated.

And then, of course, many fish boast the Omega-3 fatty acids, Star-Trek-like heroes which are believed to actually lower the levels of saturated fats and thus help promote a healthy heart.

Continual research reveals new and often conflicting advice about fats as they relate to our health. But a pattern seems clear: substitute fish or chicken for some of the red meat that you used to eat, keep portions small (a total of 6 ounces of meat or fish a day), and enjoy a variety of fish, from very low-fat flounder to Omega-3-rich salmon, mackerel, and bluefin tuna.

Fat Level of Fish

Very Low-Fat (2 Percent or Less Fat)

Abalone
Clams
Cod
Crab (Alaska king)
Crayfish
Flounder
Grouper
Haddock

Kingclip
Lobster
Mahimahi
Monkfish
Octopus
Pacific rockfish
Perch
Pike
Pollack

Scallops
Shrimp
Snails
Snapper
Sole
Squid
Tuna (skipjack, yellowfin)
Walleye

Low-Fat (2.1–5.0 Percent Fat)

Bluefish
Catfish
Halibut
Mullet
Mussels

Ono
Oysters
Porgy
Salmon (pink)
Shark
Smelt

Striped bass
Swordfish
Trout
Tuna (Bluefin)
Turbot (European)

Medium-Fat (5.1–10.0 Percent Fat)

Amberjack
Buffalofish

Orange roughy
Pompano

Salmon (coho, sockeye)
Whitefish

High-Fat (10.1 Percent or More Fat)

Eel

Mackerel

Salmon (Chinook)

NUTRITIONAL CONTENT
Based on 100 Grams (3½ ounces) Raw Edible Portion

Species	Calories	Protein (Grams)	Fat (Grams)	Cholesterol (Milligrams)	Sodium (Milligrams)	Iron (Milligrams)
Abalone	105	17.10	0.76	85	301	3.19
Amberjack	157	20.07	7.89	47	86	1.16
Bluefish	124	20.04	4.24	59	60	0.48
Buffalofish	127	17.83	5.60	66	49	1.24
Catfish	116	18.18	4.26	58	63	0.97
Clams (11 small)	74	12.77	0.97	34	56	13.98
Cod (Atlantic)	82	17.81	0.67	43	54	0.38
Cod (Pacific)	82	17.90	0.63	37	71	0.26
Crab (Alaska king)	84	18.29	0.60	42	836	0.59
Crayfish	89	18.66	1.06	139	53	2.45
Eel	184	18.44	11.66	126	51	0.50
Flounder	91	18.84	1.19	48	81	0.36
Grouper	92	19.38	1.02	37	53	0.89
Haddock	87	18.91	0.72	57	68	1.05
Halibut	110	20.81	2.29	32	54	0.84
Kingclip	74	14.70	0.30	N/A	N/A	N/A
Lobster (Northern)	90	18.80	0.90	95	N/A	N/A
Lobster (Spiny)	112	20.60	1.51	70	177	1.22
Mackerel (Atlantic)	205	18.60	13.89	70	90	1.63
Mahimahi (dolphinfish)	85	18.50	0.70	73	88	1.13
Monkfish	76	14.48	1.52	25	18	0.32

Species	Calories	Protein (Grams)	Fat (Grams)	Cholesterol (Milligrams)	Sodium (Milligrams)	Iron (Milligrams)
Mullet	117	19.35	3.79	49	65	1.02
Mussels	86	11.90	2.24	28	286	3.95
Octopus	82	14.91	1.04	48	N/A	5.30
Ono	124	24.1	2.30	N/A	82	N/A
Orange Roughy	126	14.70	7.00	20	63	0.18
Oreo Dory	51	9.80	N/A	N/A	77	0.54
Oysters (Eastern: 7 medium)	69	7.06	2.47	55	112	6.70
Oysters (Pacific: 2 medium)	81	9.45	2.30	N/A	106	5.11
Pacific Rockfish	94	18.75	1.57	35	60	0.41
Perch (Atlantic)	94	18.62	1.63	42	75	0.92
Pike	88	19.26	0.69	39	39	0.55
Pollack	92	19.44	0.98	71	86	0.46
Pompano	164	18.48	9.47	50	65	0.60
Porgy (Scup)	105	18.88	2.73	N/A	42	0.53
Salmon (Chinook)	180	20.06	10.44	66	47	0.71
Salmon (Coho)	146	21.62	5.95	39	46	0.70
Salmon (Pink)	116	19.94	3.45	52	67	0.77
Salmon (Sockeye)	168	21.30	8.56	62	47	0.47
Scallops (6 large or 15 small)	88	16.78	0.76	33	161	0.29
Shark	130	20.98	4.51	51	79	0.84
Shrimp	106	20.31	1.73	152	148	2.41
Smelts	97	17.63	2.42	70	60	0.90

Species	Calories	Protein (Grams)	Fat (Grams)	Cholesterol (Milligrams)	Sodium (Milligrams)	Iron (Milligrams)
Snails	75	14.40	1.90	N/A	N/A	25.00
Snapper	100	20.51	1.34	37	64	0.18
Sole	91	18.84	1.19	48	81	0.36
Squid	92	15.58	1.38	233	44	0.68
Striped Bass	97	17.73	2.33	80	69	0.84
Swordfish	121	19.80	4.01	39	90	0.81
Trout (Rainbow)	118	20.55	3.36	57	27	1.90
Tuna (Bluefin)	144	23.33	4.90	38	39	1.02
Tuna (Skipjack)	103	22.00	1.01	47	37	1.25
Tuna (Yellowfin)	108	23.38	0.95	45	37	0.73
Turbot	95	16.05	2.95	N/A	150	N/A
Walleye	93	19.14	1.22	86	51	1.30
Whitefish	134	19.09	5.86	60	51	0.37

SOURCES: U.S. Department of Agriculture. *Composition of Foods: Finfish and Shellfish Product.* Washington, D.C.: *USDA Handbook No. 8-15*, rev. September 1987.

New Zealand Fishing Industry Board.

SAMPLE MENUS

Add healthy variety to your life with fish appetizers, soups, salads, and entrees. Here are some suggested menus to get you started. Starred (*) dishes are recipes in this book.

Halibut Kabob with Yellow Pepper Puree*
Couscous
Chopped Spinach
Fresh Oranges

Swordfish with Smashed Garlic*
Baby Squash
Baked Potato with Yogurt-Dill Topping
Raspberry Sherbet

Monterey Squid Chowder*
Spicy Shrimp Boil*
Corn on the Cob
Tossed Salad
Strawberry Shortcake

Whole Catfish with Butter-Pecan Sauce*
Wild Rice
Broccoli Spears
Lemon Pie

Cod and Broccoli Soup*
Baking Powder Biscuits
Tomato Salad
Sharp Cheddar Cheese with Apples

———

Crayfish Etouffée*
Rice
Okra Salad
Fresh Peaches

———

Pike and Pea Pods*
Almond Rice
Sliced Acorn Squash
Lemon Sherbet

———

Red Snapper and Tortilla-Lime Soup*
Cornbread
Flan

———

Scallops with Passion Fruit Sauce*
Fresh Asparagus Spears
Herbed Rice
Almond Cookies

———

Lemon-Crab Soup*
Sweet Sesame Shrimp Salad*
Crusty Rolls
Orange Sherbet

———

Fresh Bluefish Pâté*
French Bread
Lobster Tail and Grapefruit Salad*
Cappuccino and Cookies

———

Mackerel on Tangy Napa*
Poppy-Seed Noodles
Dilled Carrots
Warm Cinnamon-Applesauce

———

Vegetable Soup
Linguine with Cherrystones*
Red and Green Grapes

———

Orange-Orange Roughy*
Spinach Noodles
Yellow Wax Beans
Oatmeal Cookies

———

Pompano in Parchment*
Broiled Tomato Halves
New Potatoes
Fresh Strawberries

———

Whole Porgy with Fennel Seeds*
Braised Celery
Baby Carrots
Granny Smith Apples

———

Opah with Warm Raspberry Vinaigrette*
Fresh Asparagus Spears
Thin Egg Noodles
Lemon Sorbet

———

Eel in Green Sauce*
Boiled Potatoes
Sliced Tomatoes
Wine-Soaked Cherries

———

Bouillabaisse*
French Bread
Artichoke Salad
Camembert Cheese with Pears

———

Wisconsin Fish Boil*
Boiled Potatoes
Cole Slaw
Cherry Pie

WINE AND FISH

BY TOR KENWARD

Long before the advent of the microwave, wine was an indispensable part of the world's epicurean fast-food habit. Centuries before Noah planted his first vineyard, men cultivated the vine to make wine, a wine perhaps unfit for today's table but one which performed a valuable service in the life of early Western man. Poets and men of letters praised wine as the beverage which turned a simple meal into a feast. A handful of bread and cheese taken with a cup of wine still may be man's most noble fast-food combination, no matter what miracles may be wrought in a microwave oven.

The teaming of wine and food, a daily ritual for people in most northern Mediterranean countries, remains a mystery to others. But rest assured that pairing wine and food is very, very simple.

Choosing a good wine for a meal is as easy as determining the amount of salt and pepper for a dish, because each wine has its own identity or flavor. A chef who learns the fundamental structure of a wine and the basic flavor elements will hold the secret ingredient to transform a simple fish entree into a classic dish.

Let's start with Chardonnay and Cabernet Sauvignon, two grape varieties with uniquely different flavor spectrums. Chardonnay tends to be a full-bodied white wine, Cabernet Sauvignon a full-bodied red wine. The flavors of a wine truly reflect its vineyards, soil, and climate, as well as how the vineyard manager chooses to maintain the flavor and how a winemaker decides to style or make his wine.

Tor Kenward, Beringer Vineyards vice president and winery spokesman, is author of *Vintage California*.

The flavor of a Chardonnay may remind a taster of pineapple, mango, green apple, or a variety of flower associations. One taster's pineapple may be another's mango, but we can finally arrive at some consensus, as shown in the flavor association summaries at the end of this chapter. As you read the associations, think of each one as a subtle nuance or flavor you can add to a dish. And think structure.

Wine has a basic structure built on acids, alcohol, esters, tannins, and sugar. As beverages go, wine is on the acidic, low-pH scale. Milk is high pH, or less acidic; natural fruit juice is more like wine but, like soda, is too sweet to complement most fine cuisine.

Wine, more than any other beverage, can cleanse the palate, or the sensitive areas around the mouth that perceive taste. In this way, wine adds great new fascination to any meal, for while the palate is cleansed and refreshed by the gentle acids or tannins, the esters or trace flavor elements add character to the dish.

The moderate alcohol level in a wine helps carry the esters to the nose, and voilà, a meal acquires a vibrant new spice. Like alcohol, tannins add body to a wine and, like acid, cut and cleanse the fats or oils in food. Tannins are best described as those elements in a hearty breakfast tea that dry out the roof of your mouth and create a puckering sensation. Tannins are most commonly perceived in red wines.

As you go about choosing wines that go with fish, don't be hampered by the red meat/red wine and white meat/white wine mentality. Think of the structure of the dish, then select the wine.

For example, red wine can be a wise choice for more oily, dense-fleshed fish such as salmon or tuna because the light tannins cut and cleanse the fats in these oilier fish. Delicate white wines such as Fume Blanc or dry Chenin Blanc might go very well with lighter, leaner fish such as sole and trout. Some fish dishes are superb with lighter red wines, such as a lightly chilled Beaujolais or a room-temperature Pinot Noir. However, a very tannic Cabernet Sauvignon may have too much tannin and body for any fish.

I prefer medium- to full-bodied white wines with rich shellfish such as abalone, crab, scallops, and lobster when these are cooked simply or with basic butter or cream sauce. The wine's natural acids cut the fat and oil, its subtle flavors mingle with the flavor of the fish, and the whole effect can be magical if neither the dish nor the wine overwhelms the other. Chardonnay in most of its California guises (and the more expensive French versions) is typically full-bodied and can make cold-water, higher-fat fish like monkfish and salmon sing. Sometimes shellfish such as crab displays a slight sweetness that goes well with a Riesling or Chenin Blanc that is neither totally dry nor too sweet.

I cannot overemphasize how important it is to know a little more about a wine than its variety and price. Ask your wine merchant about its body (light to full), structure (acidic to flabby, or out of balance), basic flavors, and sugar level.

Fuller-flavored dishes need fuller-flavored wines. Oilier fish demand wines with good acids and medium to full body. Light fish match up better with more delicate wines. Butter or cream sauces require a balanced wine, crisp with sufficient acid.

The array of Chardonnays on the market is considerable. Take some of the time that you save by using the microwave oven and ask your wine merchant about the wines. And wisely let this varietal guide to wine and food lead the way.

VARIETAL GUIDE TO WINE AND FOOD PAIRINGS
Chardonnay

The white grape of Burgundy France, and now planted in virtually every wine-producing country (Chablis, Meursault, Montrachet, Pouilly-Fuisse). Also one of the cornerstone grapes of fine champagnes and California sparkling wines. Medium to full body. Best with medium- or fuller-flavored dishes.

Flavor associations: pineapple and other tropical fruits, green apple, vanilla (usually from oak aging).

Sauvignon Blanc/Fume Blanc

These are the same in California and range in style and flavor from herbal and flowery to fruit or melon associations. In France, they are the base of white Graves and some Loire Valley wines. Light to full body. Because of its pronounced flavors, best with medium- to full-bodied fish dishes. They can handle garlic and herbs well.

Flavor associations: bell pepper, freshly mown grass, gooseberry, melon. (*Note:* Often blended with semillon, which gives a fruity, fig association.)

White Riesling/Johannisberg Riesling

These are the same and are usually styled to retain a touch of the grape's natural sugar. Very sweet versions abound, and sugars in these dessert versions should be on the label. Light to medium body. Fruity to floral flavors can offset sharp spices in dishes (up to a point). Fine partners with sweet shellfish such as crab.

Flavor associations: a wide variety of fruits as well as honey, honeysuckle, and jasmine. (*Note:* Gewürztraminer can be used in place of many Rieslings, but flavors are often spicier, reminiscent of litchi nuts, lanolin, or "off-dry." Chenin Blanc with light, fruity character is also possible here.)

Cabernet Sauvignon

The king of red wines is usually too big and too tannic for most fish dishes. But lighter, well-aged, older versions can make an exciting match. Try these with heavier-flavored—but not too spicy—fish dishes with tomato sauces, or denser fish barbecued over hard woods and/or coals. Medium to full body.

Flavor associations: Cassis, wild berries, green olives, mint.

Pinot Noir

The great red of Burgundy, France. Look for lighter- to medium-bodied versions to stand up to oilier, denser fish dishes. Can hold its own with eel, bluefish, mackerel, tuna, and salmon. Light to full body.

Flavor association: cherries, wild berries, to herbal "beet root" tones. (*Note:* A slightly chilled Gamay Beaujolais or Gamay may be an excellent substitute or an even better choice if you are worried that the Pinot Noir is too rich or tannic for the dish.)

PART II
THE RECIPES

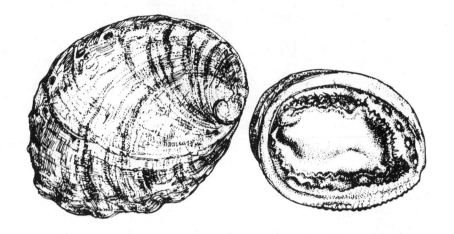

ABALONE

In the touch pools of the Monterey Bay Aquarium, Monterey, California, abalone sit motionless and pretty much ignored as tourists grab for beautiful starfish or colorful seaweed to inspect. Abalone, a big marine snail, just isn't that exciting to look at—from the outside.

Its black, green, or deep-reddish shell is very hard and thick, making it difficult prey for species such as octopus or sea otters who love what lies inside the hard shell What lies in an iridescent pink-and-blue shell, often used as a source of mother-of-pearl, is snowy white, firm, low-fat, mild-tasting meat cherished particularly by the Chinese and Japanese. Indeed, it is at Chinese and Japanese restaurants that most Americans have their first contact with abalone.

Natural predators and overfishing have threatened the supply of abalone along parts of the West Coast, so harvesting is government regulated. The abalone you see on the menu or order from your fish department likely will have come frozen from Mexico or Japan, where supplies are more plentiful.

Fresh abalone meat is quite tough and needs to be tenderized by pounding. Frozen abalone typically comes cut into steaks and tenderized. If not, cut and pound as directed in Abalone with Lemon Juice in this chapter.

Do not overcook abalone, or the meat will be tough. I find that high power toughens abalone in the microwave, so I recommend medium-low power for more tender results.

⌒❤ ABALONE WITH LEMON JUICE

If you haven't prepared abalone before, cut off a little piece of the raw meat and eat it. It will taste pretty bland and will be chewy but not tough. Light cooking will bring out a delicate flavor and make the meat more tender—though still firm. Overcooking will make it tough. Feel and taste as you cook for best results. Serve with a favorite sauce, such as teriyaki, or plain in a salad.

Preparation time: 10 minutes
Microwave time: 3–3½ minutes
Servings: 4–6

1 pound abalone
1 tablespoon fresh lemon juice

1. Frozen abalone typically comes cut into ¼-inch-thick steaks and tenderized. If not, slice across the muscle to cut into thin steaks. Pound with a veal pounder or the blunt side of a cleaver until tender but not shredded. Cut into ¾-inch strips.
2. Mix abalone and lemon juice in 2½-quart casserole. Cover with plastic, vented. MICROWAVE (medium-low) 3–3½ minutes until tender, stirring twice. Let stand 2 minutes. Drain.

TIP: To cook ½ pound of abalone, follow Step 1, put abalone on dinner plate, and drizzle with 1 tablespoon fresh lemon juice. Cover with plastic wrap, vented. MICROWAVE (medium-low) 2–2½ minutes until tender, stirring twice. Let stand 2 minutes. Drain.

ABALONE IN GINGER AND GARLIC SAUCE

Abalone marinates briefly then cooks in a delicious Oriental sauce. The recipe serves two as an entree, or four as a side dish.

Preparation time: 10 minutes
Microwave time: 3–4½ minutes
Servings: 2–4

½ **pound abalone**
½ **teaspoon minced garlic**
½ **teaspoon minced fresh ginger**
1 **tablespoon soy sauce**
1 **tablespoon dry white wine**
⅛ **teaspoon sesame oil**
1 **teaspoon cornstarch dissolved in 1 tablespoon water**
1 **green onion, white and first 2 inches of green, sliced**

1. If abalone is not already cut and tenderized, slice across the muscle to cut into thin steaks. Pound with a veal pounder or the blunt side of a cleaver until tender but not shredded. Cut into ¾-inch strips.
2. Put abalone, garlic, ginger, soy sauce, wine, and sesame oil in 1-quart casserole. Let sit 5 minutes to marinate.
3. Cover with plastic, vented. MICROWAVE (medium-low) 2–2½ minutes until tender, stirring twice. Use a slotted spoon to remove abalone to another plate. Stir cornstarch mixture into remaining marinade. MICROWAVE (high), uncovered, 1–2 minutes until juices thicken. Mix abalone and thickened juices. Top with onions.

WARM ABALONE AND ARTICHOKE SALAD

There are two pleasant surprises when you serve this salad: the snowy white abalone, and the fresh taste of the tiny frozen peas that are only defrosted, not cooked.

Preparation time: 10 minutes
Microwave time: 2–2½ minutes
Servings: 4

½ **pound abalone**
2 **tablespoons fresh lemon juice**
1 **tablespoon cider vinegar**
1 **teaspoon Dijon mustard**
¼ **teaspoon salt**
Dash of freshly ground black pepper
¼ **cup vegetable oil**
1 **9-ounce package frozen artichoke hearts, defrosted and drained**
¼ **cup frozen small peas, rinsed to defrost**

1. If abalone is not already cut and tenderized, slice across the muscle to cut into thin steaks. Pound with a veal pounder or the blunt side of a cleaver until tender but not shredded. Cut into ¾-inch strips.
2. Put abalone on dinner plate and drizzle with 1 tablespoon lemon juice. Cover with plastic wrap, vented. MICROWAVE (medium-low) 2–2½ minutes until tender, stirring twice. Let stand 2 minutes. Drain.
3. In a small bowl, whisk remaining lemon juice, vinegar, mustard, salt, and pepper. Whisk in oil.
4. Toss abalone in half of the mustard dressing. Arrange abalone and artichokes on salad plates. Drizzle with remaining dressing. Scatter peas into salad.

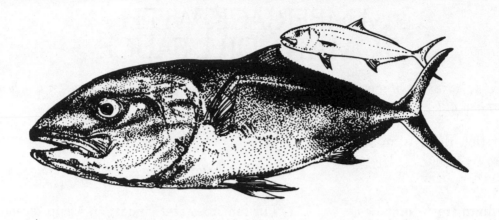

A M B E R J A C K

Amberjack is a new fish to many people, a name that appears on upscale restaurant menus and amid the mind-boggling selection of larger fish stores. If you see it, buy it. If you don't see it, order it. It's well worth your attention.

Amberjack is one of many tropical and subtropical fish called jacks that are eaten regularly in the Caribbean, South America, and Africa. A brownish fish with golden tones and an amber-colored band from head to tail, amberjack is caught in the Western Atlantic from Massachusetts to Brazil and from the west coast of Africa to the Mediterranean.

The flesh on its thick fillets is mostly pink, edging into deep red, reminiscent of free-roaming range veal. The scales are fine, but the fish has a thick and tenacious skin. Use a knife to cut the skin off, or leave it on the fish and pull it off after the fish has been cooked. The best feature of amberjack is that when it cooks up, its texture and taste are similar to fresh tuna—a very nice treat.

Because amberjack tends to run large, you likely will deal only with fillets or steaks, and pretty hefty ones, at that. I find that these thick (1½-inch) amberjack steaks need one more minute per pound than an equal amount of thin fillets from smaller fish. Count on about 5–6 minutes per pound for thick amberjack steaks; or, for better cooking control, cut extra-thick steaks in half horizontally.

❧ AMBERJACK WITH TOMATO-DILL SAUCE

There is no added fat in this simple presentation, just fresh fish, fresh tomatoes, a touch of vinegar, and dill.

Preparation time: 10 minutes
Microwave time: 9–11 minutes
Servings: 4

2 medium fresh tomatoes, peeled, seeded, and chopped, *or* 2–4 canned, drained and chopped
1 teaspoon white wine vinegar
1 teaspoon fresh dill *or* ¼ teaspoon dried
⅛ teaspoon salt
⅛ teaspoon freshly ground black pepper
1 pound amberjack steaks
1 tablespoon fresh lemon juice

1. Put tomatoes and vinegar in 4-cup measure. MICROWAVE (high), uncovered, 4–5 minutes until tomatoes thicken. Stir in dill, salt, and pepper. Keep warm.
2. Place amberjack on a plate. Drizzle with lemon juice. Cover with plastic wrap, vented. MICROWAVE (high) 4–5 minutes until center of steak is almost opaque when tested with a fork. Let stand 3 minutes to finish cooking. Drain. Remove skin. Top fish with tomato-dill sauce to serve.

TIP: To peel a fresh tomato, use a paring knife to cut out the stem. Make an X on that same bottom side. Plunge the tomato into rapidly boiling water for 20–30 seconds, then rinse under cold water. Use fingers to pull the skin off the tomato.

BUTTERCRUMB AMBERJACK

Yes, it's rich with butter—that's why it tastes so good.

Preparation time: 5 minutes
Microwave time: 7–9 minutes
Servings: 4

1 pound amberjack steaks
1 tablespoon and 1 teaspoon
fresh lemon juice
½ cup (1 stick) butter
½ cup fine, dry bread crumbs

1. Place amberjack on a plate. Drizzle with 1 tablespoon lemon juice. Cover with plastic wrap, vented. MICROWAVE (high) 4–5 minutes until center of fish is almost opaque when tested with a fork. Let stand 3 minutes to finish cooking. Drain. Remove skin.
2. Put butter in 2-cup measure. MICROWAVE (high), uncovered, 2–3 minutes to melt. Stir in bread crumbs and remaining lemon juice. Spoon over fish.

AMBERJACK CHUNKS WITH ANCHOVY SAUCE

An assertive anchovy sauce matches well with a full-flavored fish such as amberjack, and the chunks are a clever way to stretch a pound of fish to feed five people. Serve with fresh green beans and sliced garden tomatoes.

Preparation time: 10 minutes
Microwave time: 4–5 minutes
Servings: 4

1 **pound amberjack fillets, skinned and cut into 1½- by 1-inch chunks**
3 **tablespoons fresh lemon juice**
3 **anchovy fillets, chopped coarse**
1 **teaspoon minced garlic**
⅛ **teaspoon salt**
⅛ **teaspoon freshly ground black pepper**
4 **tablespoons olive oil**
2 **tablespoons minced fresh parsley**

1. Arrange amberjack around the edge of a plate. Drizzle with 1 tablespoon lemon juice. Cover with plastic wrap, vented. MICROWAVE (high) 3–4 minutes until centers of chunks are almost opaque when tested with a fork. Drain.
2. Put anchovies and garlic in 2-cup measure. Use fork to mash. (Mixture will be lumpy, but will smooth out after it has cooked.) Stir in remaining lemon juice, salt, and pepper. MICROWAVE (high), uncovered, 1–1½ minutes. Whisk in oil and parsley until smooth. Transfer fish to a serving plate, if desired. Drizzle with anchovy sauce.

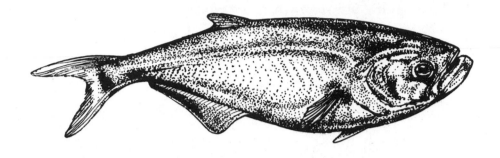

BLUEFISH

I have never caught a blue.

Every possible weekend, when the tides off the Connecticut coast were right, the sun was promising, and the bluefish were running, my father would stoke up the boat. "We're going to catch a blue," was the last phrase he uttered as we headed out the door. "Have the warm butter ready."

Like the fishermen who pursue them, bluefish run in packs, voraciously eating the smaller fish they pass. A too-polite distance from the professional boats, we caught the fresh air, gossip, and eager flounders when the rest of the boats were hauling in bluefish. But I never caught a blue.

Fortunately, the rest of the world has great luck with the silvery-blue fish, which are caught in the Atlantic Ocean from the New England coast down to Florida, as well as on the eastern coast of South America, the western coast of Africa, and around Australia. Averaging 3–6 pounds each, the young blues are commonly called *snappers*, and the larger adults, *choppers*.

Bluefish is a dark-fleshed fish that lightens when cooked, is rich with oils, and has an assertive ocean taste and soft texture. Some cooks cut away its darkest, stronger-tasting flesh, but since I like the taste, I keep it in.

Bluefish is particularly delicious when paired with a tangy mustard, as in the following Bluefish with Honey-Mustard Sauce, or with zesty capers, as in Bluefish with Caper Veloute. Because of its soft, oily texture, it makes a particularly fine Fresh Bluefish Pâté.

I find that dense bluefish fillets need a little more time than most other fillets to cook in the microwave oven. For a 600- to 700-watt machine, count on about 5 minutes per pound, instead of the usual 4 minutes.

Ah, and if you do catch a bluefish, gut it immediately and scale it while it's wet. That's sound advice from the fish store where we would sometimes drop in after fishing.

⌒♥ BLUEFISH WITH HONEY-MUSTARD SAUCE

Rich, oily bluefish needs no extra cooking fat, just this sweet and tangy mustard topping.

Preparation time: 5 minutes
Microwave time: 5–6 minutes
Servings: 4

2 tablespoons Dijon mustard
2 tablespoons fresh lemon juice
1 tablespoon honey
⅛ teaspoon freshly ground black pepper
1 pound bluefish fillets

1. In a small bowl, whisk together mustard, lemon juice, honey, and pepper.
2. Arrange bluefish skin-side down on a plate with thickest portions to the outside and any thinner ends turned under, if necessary. Spread with mustard mixture. Cover with plastic wrap, vented. MICROWAVE (high) 5–6 minutes until thickest portion is just opaque when tested with a fork. Let stand 5 minutes. Drain juices.

BLUEFISH WITH CAPER VELOUTE

Capers, the pelletlike buds of the caper bush, add a distinctive, pungent taste to this bluefish dish. Be sure to taste the sauce before adding salt because the pickled capers already will have been soaked in vinegar and salt. The recipe makes a generous amount of sauce. To cut it in half, see the Tip below.

Preparation time: 10 minutes
Microwave time: 13–18 minutes
Servings: 4

2 tablespoons butter
2 tablespoons flour
1 cup chicken stock or broth
½ cup whipping cream
2 tablespoons drained, coarsely chopped capers
¼ teaspoon salt, or to taste
⅛ teaspoon freshly ground white pepper
1 pound bluefish fillets
1 tablespoon fresh lemon juice

1. Put butter in 4-cup measure. MICROWAVE (high), uncovered, 2–3 minutes, until the butter melts and is very hot. Thoroughly whisk in flour. MICROWAVE (high), uncovered, 2–3 minutes until the mixture bubbles furiously.
2. Thoroughly whisk in broth and cream. MICROWAVE (high), uncovered, 2–3 minutes until bubbles that start at the edge of the sauce fill in and completely cover the top of the sauce. Thoroughly whisk.
3. MICROWAVE (high), uncovered, 2–3 minutes until sauce thickens enough to coat a spoon. Thoroughly whisk in capers. Taste. Add suggested salt and pepper, or to taste. Keep sauce warm.
4. Arrange bluefish skin-side down on a plate with thickest portions to the outside and any thinner ends turned under, if necessary. Drizzle with lemon juice. Cover with plastic wrap, vented. MICROWAVE (high) 5–6 minutes until thickest portion is just opaque when tested with a fork. Let stand 5 minutes. Drain. Serve fish drizzled with Caper Veloute.

TIP: To make half the sauce, use half of each sauce ingredient and subtract about 1 minute from each of the sauce cooking times in Steps 1, 2, and 3.

⌇❤ FRESH BLUEFISH PATE

Bluefish has a naturally soft and oily texture that makes it ideal for pâté. To keep this on the healthful side, there are no enriching egg yolks, cream, or butter in this pâté. Note that the first three steps of the recipe can be done a day ahead. Serve the pâté as an appetizer with plain bagel or pita chips. For menu suggestions see page 23.

Preparation time: 15 minutes
Microwave time: 7–10 minutes
Chilling time: 2 hours or overnight
Yield: 3 cups

2 pounds bluefish fillets
2 tablespoons fresh lemon juice
3 large garlic cloves
1 small onion
2 tablespoons fresh thyme *or* 1½ teaspoon dried
3 tablespoons minced fresh chives
3 tablespoons chopped fresh parsley
1 teaspoon salt
¾ teaspoon freshly ground black pepper

1. Cut bluefish into 5–6-ounce pieces and arrange skin-side down in a circular fashion on a large plate with thickest portions to the outside and any thinner ends turned under, if necessary. Drizzle with lemon juice. Cover with plastic wrap, vented.
2. MICROWAVE (high) 7–10 minutes until thickest portion is just opaque when tested with a fork, rotating plate and rearranging fish as necessary. Let stand 5 minutes. Drain.
3. Skin fish and remove any small bones. Cover and chill in refrigerator at least 1 hour or overnight. Cut into 2-inch chunks.
4. Peel garlic and onion, drop into food processor, and process until minced. Add fish, thyme, chives, parsley, salt, and pepper. Process until smooth, stopping several times to scrape down sides of container. Cover and refrigerate mixture at least 2 hours or up to 3 days. Let soften to spreadable before serving.

TIP: *To make half the recipe, use 1 pound of bluefish fillets, cover, and MICROWAVE (high) 5–6 minutes. Cut the remaining ingredients in half.*

TIP: *For a smoother, slightly glistening finish, add 3 tablespoons softened butter to the cooked fish in the food processor in Step 3.*

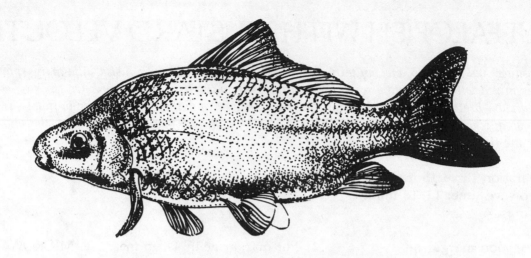

BUFFALOFISH

Buffalofish is an eye-catcher in the fish department display case, a large, dark-brown or bluish specimen with comical, protruding lips that make it look like it has been sucking its thumb all day. Indeed, buffalofish is a member of the sucker family and does use those lips to suck up algae, plants, and small crustaceans for dinner.

Buffalofish are freshwater fish, and their quality depends on the waters where they are caught: buffalofish from deep, cold rivers and lakes will have a superior, firm, sweet meat, whereas those from shallow, muddy waters will reflect that muddy taste.

Even the best of buffalofish are strong-tasting. So, like salmon, you don't want to use their heads and bones for fish stock. Buffalofish also have a lot of bones, particularly in the rib area, and because of its good-sized head, the yield from a buffalofish is fairly low for fish, about 25 percent.

Probably because of its strong taste and numerous bones, many people shy away from buffalofish. Happily for those who like buffalofish, this keeps the price of this big fish quite low.

BUFFALOFISH WITH MUSTARD VELOUTE

This sauce has a smooth, creamy texture—but no cream. It starts with just a little margarine that is mixed with flour into a roux. Natural juices from the fish, plus some extra stock or bottled clam broth, then are cooked until the sauce reduces and thickens. Because buffalofish cooks so quickly in the microwave, I like to start the sauce, cook the fish, then finish the sauce while the fish is standing.

Preparation time: 15 minutes
Microwave time: 13–18 minutes
Servings: 4

1 teaspoon margarine
1 teaspoon flour
½ cup fish stock, bottled clam broth, or chicken broth
1 pound buffalofish fillets
⅛ teaspoon salt
⅛ teaspoon freshly ground black pepper
1 teaspoon Dijon mustard or other smooth, brown mustard

1. Put margarine in 4-cup measure. MICROWAVE (high), uncovered, 1–2 minutes until margarine melts and is very hot. Whisk in flour. MICROWAVE (high), uncovered, 1–2 minutes until mixture bubbles. Whisk in stock. MICROWAVE (high), uncovered, 5–6 minutes until sauce is thick and reduced by half, stirring once when sauce begins to bubble. Set aside.

2. Place buffalofish on a plate, skin-side down with thickest portions to the outside. Cover with plastic wrap, vented at one corner. MICROWAVE (high) 4–5 minutes until thickest part of fish is almost opaque when tested with a fork, rearranging fish once. Drain fish but reserve ¼ cup of liquid; pour into measure with sauce. Let fish stand, covered, 5 minutes to finish cooking. Remove skin.

3. Return measure to microwave oven. MICROWAVE (high), uncovered, 2–3 minutes until sauce is thick. Taste for saltiness. Whisk in salt, if desired, pepper, and mustard. Drizzle sauce over fish.

⌒♥ SWEET-AND-SOUR BUFFALOFISH SALAD

Cooked, chilled buffalofish fillets are served with nibs of corn and sweet red pepper in a sweet-and-sour sauce.

Preparation time: 15 minutes
Microwave time: 5–7 minutes
Chilling time: 3 hours or overnight
Servings: 4–6

1 pound buffalofish fillets, skin intact
1 tablespoon fresh lemon juice
1 tablespoon cornstarch dissolved in 2 tablespoons water
⅓ cup cider vinegar
1 tablespoon soy sauce
¼ cup apricot jam
2 tablespoons ketchup
2 tablespoons brown sugar
1 teaspoon grated lemon zest
½ cup cooked corn, drained and chilled
⅓ cup minced sweet red pepper

1. Put buffalofish skin-side down on a plate with thickest portions to the outside. Drizzle with lemon juice. Cover with plastic wrap, vented at one corner. MICROWAVE (high) 4–5 minutes until thickest part of fish is almost opaque when tested with a fork, rearranging fish once. Let fish stand, covered, 5 minutes to finish cooking. Drain. Remove skin. Chill in refrigerator 3 hours or overnight.

2. Put cornstarch mixture in 4-cup measure, and stir in vinegar, soy sauce, jam, ketchup, brown sugar, and lemon zest. MICROWAVE (high), uncovered, 1–2 minutes until thick.

3. To serve, arrange chilled fish on plates. Sprinkle corn and pepper over fish and drizzle with warm sweet-and-sour dressing.

TIP: *Instead of apricot jam try peach or an orange marmalade.*

⌇❤ WHOLE BUFFALOFISH WITH BARBECUE SAUCE

This tangy sauce works well with strong-tasting fish such as buffalofish. The fish is brushed well with the sauce, then left to marinate for an hour before cooking. Extra sauce is served on the side.

Preparation time: 10 minutes
Marinating time: 1 hour
Microwave time: 9–11 minutes
Servings: 4

**1 2–3-pound buffalofish,
     cleaned and scaled**
¼ cup ketchup
1 tablespoon honey
1 tablespoon wine vinegar
1 teaspoon prepared horseradish
1 tablespoon fresh lemon juice
¼ teaspoon Worcestershire sauce
**⅛ teaspoon hot sauce, such as
     Tabasco**

1. Rinse buffalofish well and set on a large platter or in 3-quart flat casserole.
2. Mix the rest of the ingredients in a small bowl. Use half the sauce to brush the fish well, inside and out. Reserve remaining sauce. Cover fish, and marinate 1 hour in the refrigerator.
3. Wrap the fish head and tail smoothly with foil. Cover whole fish and platter with plastic wrap, vented at one corner. MICROWAVE (high) 4–5 minutes until fish starts to cook at the edges but is still firm. Carefully turn fish over, keeping foil on.
4. MICROWAVE (high) 5–6 minutes or until thickest portion of fish is almost opaque when tested with a fork; remove foil for last 2 minutes, if necessary. Let fish stand on counter for 5 minutes to finish cooking. Pour off juices. Reheat extra sauce to serve on the side.

TIP: When using foil in the microwave, be sure to keep it smooth and at least 1 inch from the sides of the microwave.

HOT MARINATED BUFFALOFISH WITH PEPPERS

I find that thick, strong-tasting fish such as buffalofish benefit from a brief, hot marinade before cooking in the microwave.

Preparation time: 20 minutes
Marinating time: 5 minutes
Microwave time: 16–21 minutes
Servings: 4

1 **2–3-pound buffalofish, cleaned and scaled**
½ **teaspoon salt**
⅛ **teaspoon freshly ground black pepper**
1 **medium onion, sliced thin**
1 **cup thinly sliced green bell pepper**
1 **cup thinly sliced sweet red pepper**
1 **teaspoon minced garlic**
2 **tablespoons olive oil**
1 **medium tomato, chopped**
2 **teaspoons chopped fresh thyme *or* ½ teaspoon dried**
2 **bay leaves, crumbled**
¼ **cup wine vinegar**

1. Rinse buffalofish well. Sprinkle with salt and pepper. Set aside.
2. Put onion, green and red pepper, garlic, and olive oil in 3-quart flat casserole large enough to hold the fish. Cover. MICROWAVE (high) 2–3 minutes to soften slightly. Stir in tomato, thyme, bay leaves, and vinegar. Cover. MICROWAVE (high) 2–3 minutes until vegetables are soft.
3. Place fish in casserole. Spoon warm tomato mixture into cavity and over the fish. Let stand 5 minutes to marinate.
4. Scrape most of tomato mixture off the fish and reserve. Cover head and tail smoothly with foil. Cover casserole with plastic wrap, vented at one corner. MICROWAVE (high) 4–5 minutes until fish starts to cook at the edges but is still firm. Carefully turn fish over, keeping foil on.
5. MICROWAVE (high) 5–6 minutes or until thickest portion of fish is almost opaque when tested with a fork: remove foil for last 2 minutes, if necessary. Let fish stand on counter for 5 minutes to finish cooking.
6. Drain fish and pour juices into 4-cup measure. MICROWAVE (high), uncovered, 3–4 minutes to thicken. Stir in tomato mixture, and serve over fish.

TIP: *Keep foil smooth and at least 1 inch from the sides of the microwave.*

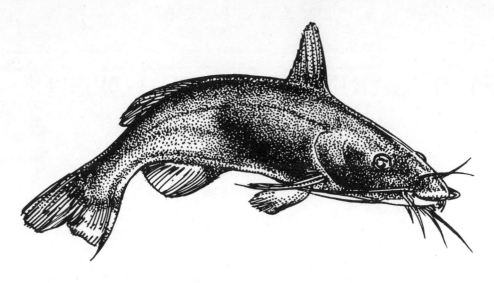

CATFISH

It was with great humiliation that I caught my first catfish. My dad, a junior-high-school friend, and I were off for a weekend in New Hampshire, supposedly angling for trout. But all I reeled in were catfish—easy river prey. The humiliation ended, however, when the owner of the local bed-and-breakfast fried up my catch for breakfast. This wonderful fish, scorned for its lack of excitement on the reel, has been a favorite on my table ever since.

Getting fresh catfish is much easier today. It is one of the first fish to be successfully farmed and is a major business in the South, particularly in Mississippi. There in the flatlands between the Mississippi River and the hill country, more than 500 million catfish live in man-made ponds.

Unlike wild, bottom-feeding catfish, farm-raised catfish are top-fed soybean and corn pellets, which give these fish an especially mild, sweet flavor.

Because of professional farming, fresh catfish is one of the few freshwater fish that is available virtually year-round. And the abundance keeps the price moderate and stable. A traditional fish on Southern tables, catfish now has become one of the more popular fish featured in Northern restaurants and supermarkets.

One disadvantage of getting catfish so easily in the supermarkets is that you rarely get to see catfish heads, which are fascinating. The whiskers, or feelers, which a catfish uses to find food as it feeds at night, indeed make the fish look like a primordial cat—or a marred billboard lady or precursor to the Clark Gable mustache.

One advantage of farmed and prepped catfish is that you don't have to deal with the skin. The black-speckled skin of a catfish is thick and strong, much like that of eel, and very hard to remove.

If you are faced with a fresh, whole catfish, the safest way to skin it is to start with a large nail, which you drive halfway into a large board. Use a knife to cut through the skin of the catfish, just behind each pectoral fin, and all around the "neck" of the fish. Force the head onto the nail to keep the fish in place. Use pliers to yank the skin off the fish.

Once you get this far, there is one reward: catfish have a simple skeletal structure and very few bones. About half of a whole catfish is edible meat, a high proportion for fish.

If you purchase catfish fillets, you will find that they are medium-thick—thicker than sole, but not as thick as monkfish. Instead of the usual 4 minutes per pound, these thicker fillets often require 5 or 6 minutes per pound to cook through.

The most popular way to serve catfish certainly is fried—which I don't recommend in the microwave. But its firm texture and sweet, rich flavor make catfish very versatile, from the simple combination with leek and lemon to a pairing with orange-spiked sweet potatoes.

⌒♥ CATFISH WITH LEEK AND LEMON

No extra fat: just catfish fillets, drizzled with plenty of lemon juice and topped with thinly sliced leek. Very easy. Very good.

Preparation time: 5 minutes
Microwave time: 4–8 minutes
Servings: 4

1 leek
1 pound catfish fillets, skinned
2 tablespoons fresh lemon juice
⅛ teaspoon freshly ground black pepper

1. Trim off root end of leek. Slice in half lengthwise, and wash well under running water. Separate tender, green inner section; cut into 3-inch julienne strips and set aside. Save thicker, white outer stalk for other uses, such as soups or flavoring (see Tip below).
2. Arrange catfish on a plate with thickest sides to the outside. Drizzle with lemon juice; sprinkle with pepper. Arrange julienned leek on top of fish. Cover with plastic wrap, vented at one corner. MICROWAVE (high) 4–8 minutes until thickest portion is just opaque when tested with a fork, rearranging once. Let stand 5 minutes to finish cooking. Drain and serve.

TIP: Use outer layers of leeks to flavor a side dish of fat-free potatoes. Quarter 3 or 4 unpeeled, red potatoes and add to 2½-quart casserole with 2 tablespoons water and the leek, chopped. Cover. MICROWAVE (high) 9–11 minutes until just tender, stirring after 3 minutes. Drain. Sprinkle with freshly ground black pepper and a tablespoon of grated lemon zest.

CATFISH AND RED CABBAGE SALAD

This pretty fall salad entree is sweetened with a honey dressing that marries well with catfish. You need only ¾ pound of catfish to make four attractive salad servings, so the recipe is ideal for a leftover fillet or two.

Preparation time: 20 minutes
Microwave time: 4–8 minutes
Servings: 4

DRESSING
1 teaspoon minced garlic
3 tablespoons white wine vinegar
⅛ teaspoon red pepper flakes
⅛ teaspoon dried oregano
¼ teaspoon salt
⅛ teaspoon freshly ground black pepper
½ cup vegetable oil
¼ cup honey

SALAD
¾ pound catfish fillets, skinned
1 tablespoon fresh lemon juice
2 cups shredded red cabbage
2 Red Delicious apples, cored, sliced thin
½ cup chopped walnuts

1. To make the dressing, put garlic, vinegar, red pepper, oregano, salt, and black pepper in 4-cup measure. MICROWAVE (high), uncovered, 1–2 minutes to soften garlic and dried spices. Whisk in oil and honey. (The dressing can be made up to a week ahead and stored, covered, in the refrigerator.)

2. To make the salad, arrange catfish on a plate with thickest sides to the outside. Drizzle with lemon juice. Cover with plastic wrap, vented at one corner. MICROWAVE (high) 3–6 minutes until thickest portion is just opaque when tested with a fork, rearranging once. Let stand 5 minutes to finish cooking. Drain fish. (Fish may be prepared ahead.) Cut fish into bite-sized chunks.

3. To serve, arrange cabbage on a plate as base for the salad. Top with fanned apple slices and fish. Sprinkle with nuts. Drizzle dressing over fish, then over the rest of the salad.

TIP: If the salad is to be served with just-cooked, slightly warm catfish, have the rest of the salad ingredients at room temperature. If using previously cooked fish for a cold salad, use crisp-cold apples and cabbage.

WHOLE CATFISH WITH BUTTER-PECAN SAUCE

A whole catfish purchased in a fish department usually comes without the head and already skinned. And be thankful for that—skinning a catfish is a tricky job! (See chapter introduction for instructions on how to skin a catfish.)

The remaining whole catfish is cooked up quite plainly here, with just a little lemon juice, then served with butter-soaked pecans. Note that the whole fish is turned over after only 3 minutes while still quite raw, so the fish doesn't flake and fall apart in the process. For menu suggestions see page 22.

Preparation time: 10 minutes
Microwave time: 10–13 minutes
Servings: 4

1 2-pound whole catfish, cleaned and skinned
1 tablespoon fresh lemon juice
4 tablespoons butter
¼ cup chopped pecans

1. Put catfish in a casserole or on a large plate. Drizzle with lemon juice. Wrap tail loosely with smooth foil to keep from overcooking. Cover casserole or plate with plastic wrap, vented at one corner.

2. MICROWAVE (high) 3–4 minutes until fish starts to cook but is still firm. Turn fish over. MICROWAVE (high) 5–6 minutes until flesh near the bone is almost opaque when tested with a fork. Let stand on counter 5 minutes to finish cooking. Drain.

3. Meanwhile, put butter in 1-cup measure. MICROWAVE (high), uncovered, 1–2 minutes to melt. Line a sieve with cheesecloth, and pour the butter through the cheesecloth and into another 1-cup measure or other small container; repeat if necessary. (Instead you can use a large spoon to carefully remove the foam from top of the melted butter after allowing the butter to settle for 3 minutes.) Stir in pecans. MICROWAVE (high) 1 minute to heat through. Serve butter-pecan sauce on the side or over the fish.

TIP: When using foil in the microwave, keep the foil smooth and at least 1 inch from the sides of the microwave.

TIP: Step 3 calls for clarifying the butter; that is, melting and straining it to remove the foamy white milk solids. This leaves a clear, oily liquid known as clarified butter. It looks neater than just melted butter and can be heated to a higher temperature than whole butter without burning.

TIP: The clarified butter can be stored in the refrigerator for several months.

CATFISH WITH ORANGE-SPIKED SWEET POTATOES

It may seem an unusual combination, but naturally sweet catfish works very well with sweet potatoes in this easy one-plate entree for two.

Preparation time: 10 minutes
Microwave time: 7–12 minutes
Servings: 2

1 large sweet potato
2 tablespoons fresh orange juice
1 8-ounce catfish fillet, skinned and cut in half
1 tablespoon orange marmalade
1 tablespoon butter
Thin slices peeled fresh orange, for garnish

1. Peel sweet potato and cut into ½-inch-wide french-fry-like strips. Arrange in single layer on a plate. Sprinkle with orange juice. Cover. MICROWAVE (high) 3–4 minutes until potato starts to soften, rearranging once.
2. Arrange catfish on top of potato. Spread with marmalade. Cover with plastic wrap, vented at one corner. MICROWAVE (high) 3–6 minutes until thickest portion of fish is just opaque when tested with a fork, rearranging once. Let stand 5 minutes to finish cooking.
3. Pour juices from plate into 1-cup measure. Stir in butter. If sauce is too cold to melt butter, MICROWAVE (high), uncovered, 30 seconds to heat. Pour sauce over fish. Garnish with orange slices.

TIP: Sweet potatoes taste best when they are cooked until soft—no al dente here! If the fish has finished cooking but the sweet potato needs an extra minute or two, first remove the cooked fish, then continue cooking the sweet potato.

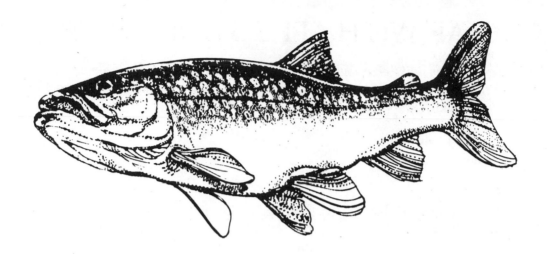

CHAR

A close relative of trout, char is a lovely white- to red-fleshed fish that cooks and tastes like salmon—but generally costs less.

The lower price is not an indication of quality, because a fine, rich char easily rivals salmon as a dinner fish. However, char isn't as well known among shoppers, and fish stores often have trouble selling this fine fish.

The most commonly available variety of char is Arctic char, found in the coastal regions of the Alaskan Peninsula and the Bering Strait, and the arctic regions of Canada, Greenland, Iceland, Norway, and Siberia. Arctic char in these areas are anadromous; that is, they migrate from sea to a river to spawn.

Char also is found in landlocked lakes in Maine, Canada, and Europe, but these freshwater versions are smaller and considered less desirable eating than the sea-swimming char.

Treat char fillets and steaks as you would salmon in the microwave.

CHAR WITH APPLES AND CIDER

The rich flavors of salmonlike char and cider blend nicely with slices of fresh apple. This dish has no added fat but would taste good with a tablespoon of butter or margarine stirred into the juices at the last minute.

Preparation time: 10 minutes
Microwave time: 4–8 minutes
Servings: 4

1 Granny Smith apple, peeled, cored and cut into ½-inch slices
1 tablespoon fresh lemon juice
1 pound char fillets
¼ cup cider

1. Arrange apple slices flat on a dinner plate or pie plate. Drizzle with ½ tablespoon lemon juice. Arrange char on top of apple slices, with thickest portions to the outside. Drizzle with remaining lemon juice. Pour cider over the fish. Cover with plastic wrap, vented.
2. MICROWAVE (high) 4–8 minutes until thickest portion of fish is almost opaque when tested with a fork. Let stand 2 minutes on counter. Spoon juices over fish and apples.

CHAR WITH LEMON-ALMOND RICE

Rich-flavored char is cooked with only a touch of lemon, then paired with almond-spiked rice.

Preparation time: 10 minutes
Microwave time: 21–28 minutes
Servings: 4

1 cup uncooked long-grain white rice
2 cups chicken stock or broth
¼ teaspoon almond extract
4 tablespoons fresh lemon juice
⅓ cup finely sliced almonds
1 pound char fillets
2 tablespoons chopped fresh chives

1. Put rice, chicken broth, almond extract, and 3 tablespoons lemon juice in 2½-quart casserole. Cover. MICROWAVE (high) 5–7 minutes to boiling, then MICROWAVE (medium) 5–7 minutes.
2. Stir in almonds. Cover tightly. MICROWAVE (medium) 7–9 minutes until liquid is absorbed. Let rice mixture stand on counter 5 minutes to finish cooking.
3. Put char on a plate with thickest portions to the outside. Drizzle with remaining lemon juice. Cover with plastic wrap, vented. MICROWAVE (high) 4–5 minutes until thickest portion is just opaque when tested with a fork. Let stand 2 minutes to finish cooking. Drain.
4. Gently mix rice mixture. Flake fish over rice and sprinkle with chives.

TIP: I like the almonds still a bit crunchy in this dish. For softer nuts, add them earlier, just after the liquids boil.

CHAR AND BLACK BEAN SALAD

Light-colored char and black beans contrast well in this colorful salad entree.

Preparation time: 15 minutes
Microwave time: 7–9 minutes
Servings: 6–8

1 pound char fillets
1 tablespoon fresh lemon juice
2 15-ounce-cans black beans
4 slices uncooked bacon
3 tablespoons olive oil
2 tablespoons cider vinegar
¼ teaspoon salt
**⅛ teaspoon freshly ground black
   pepper**
1 large tomato, diced
**2 green onions, white and first
   2 inches of green, sliced**
2 tablespoons minced fresh dill

1. Put char on a plate with thickest portions to the outside. Drizzle with lemon juice. Cover with plastic wrap, vented. MICROWAVE (high) 4–5 minutes until thickest portion is just opaque when tested with a fork. Let stand 2 minutes to finish cooking. Drain. Let cool slightly, and flake.
2. Rinse and drain beans. Set aside.
3. Put bacon on four paper towels and lift onto a plate. Put another paper towel on top of bacon. MICROWAVE (high) 3–4 minutes until crisp. Crumble and set aside.
4. Whisk olive oil, vinegar, salt, and pepper in 3-quart casserole. Gently mix in fish, beans, bacon, tomato, onion, and dill. Serve at slightly warm or room temperature.

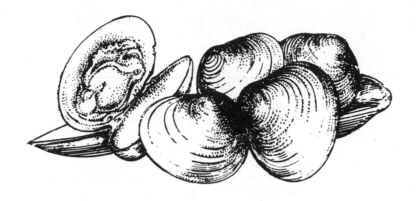

CLAMS

Fresh clams are the true essence of the ocean—briny, sweet, tender morsels, wonderful either raw or cooked. Even as a child I loved them, served raw on the half shell and sitting in crushed ice, or steamed and served with lots of butter and napkins.

Clams are found along both coasts but are identified particularly with the East Coast. They come in two main forms: soft-shelled clams, also called *steamers*, and hard-shelled clams. There is also a 4- to 8-inch-long, narrow clam called the *razor clam*, but it is seldom marketed.

Soft-shelled is a misnomer, for the shells of such clams are not soft, but thin and brittle. These clams are usually eaten cooked, and most typically steamed or fried.

The common hard-shelled clams are all the same species, the quahog (pronounced CO-hog), but they are called different names according to size. Smallest of the hard-shelled clams, the three- to four-year-old ones are called *Littleneck clams*, named after Little Neck Bay, Long Island. As they grow larger, five-year-old clams are called *Cherrystone* clams, named after Cherrystone Creek, Virginia. Any larger, 3 inches or more in diameter, and the clams are called simply *quahogs*, tough critters assigned to chowders.

Another subspecies of hard-shelled clams is the mahogany clam, with reddish-brown shells and a light, smoky taste. Mahogany clams are only recently being harvested from deep ocean waters and are a special treat if you can get them.

Hard-shelled clams can be eaten either raw or cooked, and tend to get tough when overcooked.

The microwave can be a real aid to those who have trouble opening raw, hard-shelled clams. The raw clams can be placed in the microwave, hinged sides to the outside, and in 1–3 minutes a half dozen clams will open just wide enough to let you finish the job. If you watch them carefully, the clams will still be uncooked and can be chilled quickly to serve on the half shell. (This trick doesn't work with oysters on-the-half-shell because they take so long to open in the microwave that they cook inside.) It's not the best way to open clams, however, for they lose that truly fresh brightness; but if you haven't got the skills of a clam shucker, it's a reasonable second choice.

In this chapter you will find Clam Basics, a microwave method for wonderfully messy steamers with dipping butter, and two versions of clams with pasta, one using fresh clams and one with canned.

In trying to figure where to place the recipe for Bouillabaisse, our traditional Christmas Eve dinner, with a variety of fish and shellfish, I decided it belonged with the clams. You can substitute mackerel for eel, or cod for haddock, but the taste of fresh clams is hard to duplicate.

CLAM BASICS

To test for freshness, touch live clams. Hard-shelled clams should close their shells, and soft-shelled clams should pull back their necks when touched. Discard any that don't. Store clams in the refrigerator, wrapped in damp material such as seaweed, damp paper towels, or newspaper.

Hard-shelled clams should be scrubbed. Soft-shelled clams, which can contain sand, should be soaked for an hour in salted water (⅓ cup salt to 1 gallon water). However, I find that this is not necessary if you rinse the clams well under running water before cooking, then carefully drain the cooking broth to leave the grit behind, and swish the steamed clams in broth before eating them.

Cook clams on a plate deep enough to hold the cooking juices; a dozen clams gives off about ½ cup of natural juices. Arrange clams along the outside of the plate, overlapping if necessary, with hinged sides to the outside. No added liquid is needed, although a little wine or other liquid may be added as flavoring. Cover the plate tightly with plastic wrap. Cook on high power.

If you are using the microwave to open clams that are to be eaten raw, remove clams as soon as the shells start to part, even if this means standing by the microwave and removing the clams one or two at a time. Once the clams open wide, they will be cooked.

Similarly, if you are steaming clams, remove clams just as they open wide, even if this means pulling them out one or two at a time. (Take care: the shells will be hot.) Tender steamed clams get tough if cooked even 10 seconds too long.

Timing Guidelines:

- **Soft-shelled (Steamers)**
  To steam:
      ½ pound (12 clams): 2–3 minutes
      1 pound (24 clams): 3–3½ minutes
- **Littlenecks**
  To open:
      6 clams: 1–2 minutes
      12 clams: 2–3 minutes
  To steam:
      6 clams: 2–3 minutes
      12 clams: 3–4 minutes
- **Cherrystones**
  To open:
      6 clams: 2–3 minutes
      12 clams: 3–3½ minutes
  To steam:
      6 clams: 3–4 minutes
      12 clams: 5–7 minutes

CLAM BROTH

Sweet, aromatic clam broth is a wonderful by-product from cooking fresh clams. Follow the cooking instructions and time guidelines in Clam Basics in this chapter to cook the clams. A dozen Cherrystone clams yields ½ cup clam broth.

STEAMERS IN NATURAL BROTH WITH DIPPING BUTTER

Steamers are a favorite in our family, a wonderful—and messy—way to dig in and start dinner.

Serve steamed clams in a large bowl with a small bowl or mug of the clam broth, a small cup of clarified butter (included in the recipe), and a lemon wedge for each person. Diners may squirt the lemon juice into their butter, if they desire.

To eat the cooked steamers, snap open clams, gently detach the meat, and use fingernails to scrape and pull off the black covering from the clam neck. Holding the clam by its neck, swish it in the clam broth to clean off any dirt, dip it in the butter, and pop it all into your mouth. Chew. Swallow.

For the finale, we like to drink the dipping broth, enhanced with just a touch of salt and pepper.

Preparation time: 2 minutes
Microwave time: 4–6 minutes
Servings: 2–3

1 pound fresh soft-shelled clams (steamers)
½ cup (1 stick) butter
Lemon wedges
Salt
Pepper

1. Rinse clams under running water. Discard any that are gapping or badly cracked. Put clams and ¼ cup water in 3-quart casserole. (The water isn't necessary for cooking, but it creates more broth for dipping.) Cover with plastic wrap, vented.
2. MICROWAVE (high) 3–4 minutes until liquid boils and clams open slightly. Remove clams just as they open wide, even if this means pulling them out one or two at a time. (Take care: the shells will be hot.) Do not overcook. Strain broth and divide into a bowl or mug for each person.
3. Put butter in 2-cup measure. MICROWAVE (high), uncovered, 1–2 minutes to melt. Line a sieve with cheesecloth, and pour the butter through the cheesecloth and into another container. Repeat if necessary, to rid butter of its white, foamy milk solids. (Instead you can

use a large spoon to carefully remove the foam from the melted butter after allowing it to settle for 3 minutes.) Pour clear, or clarified, butter into a cup for each person. This clarified butter looks neater than just melted butter and can be heated to a higher temperature without burning.

TIP: Clarified butter can be stored in the refrigerator for several months.

TIP: To make this a low-fat dish, eliminate the butter and dip the clams only in their broth. My husband, Tom, prefers his clams this way: natural and light.

LINGUINE WITH CHERRYSTONES

This version of clams with pasta uses fresh, whole Cherrystone clams and a light wine-and-clam broth that lets you enjoy the fresh clam taste. If you have all the ingredients chopped and ready on the counter, you can make the clams and broth in the microwave in the time it takes to cook the linguine conventionally on the stove. If you get interrupted, toss the cooked linguine with a little vegetable oil, cover, and reheat later—in the microwave. For menu suggestions see page 23.

Preparation time: 15 minutes
Microwave time: 7–12 minutes
Servings: 4

2 tablespoons butter
2 teaspoons minced garlic
¼ cup minced onion
¼ cup dry white wine
1 teaspoon chopped fresh basil
   or **¼ teaspoon dried**
⅛ teaspooon red pepper flakes
⅛ teaspoon freshly ground black pepper
1 bay leaf, broken in half
8 Cherrystone clams, scrubbed clean
1 pound linguine, cooked, drained, and hot
¼ cup chopped fresh parsley

1. Put butter, garlic, and onion in 2½-quart casserole. Cover tightly. MICROWAVE (high) 2–3 minutes to melt butter and soften vegetables. Stir in wine, basil, red pepper, black pepper, and bay leaf. Cover tightly. MICROWAVE (high) 2–3 minutes until mixture just starts to boil.
2. Arrange clams around edge of a dish, hinged side to the outside. Cover with plastic wrap, vented. MICROWAVE (high) 3–6 minutes until clams just open wide, even if this means pulling them out one or two at a time.
3. Remove clams, pouring juices into casserole mixture as you remove them. Reserve four clams. Remove meat from the remaining four clams; chop coarse and add to the wine mixture in the casserole. Remove bay leaf halves. Reheat if necessary.
4. Pour clam and wine mixture over the linguine, and toss well. Garnish platter with the four reserved whole clams. Sprinkle with parsley.

FETTUCINE WITH WHITE CLAM SAUCE

With a bit of attention and herbs and spices, canned clams turn into a very tasty sauce for pasta. This version is chock-full of clams plus the heady flavors of garlic, hot pepper, and lemon. I like to add a cup of peas for color. There is no need to cook the frozen peas—just rinse them under the faucet, and let them drain and defrost while you make dinner.

Preparation time: 15 minutes
Microwave time: 5–8 minutes
Servings: 4

3 tablespoons olive oil
½ cup minced onion
2 teaspoons minced garlic
1 tablespoon minced hot pepper
½ cup dry white wine
3 tablespoons minced fresh
  basil *or* 1 teaspoon dried
1 teaspoon chopped fresh
  oregano *or* ¼ teaspoon dried
⅓ cup fresh lemon juice
2 10-ounce cans minced clams,
  drained
3 tablespoons chopped fresh
  parsley
1 teaspoon salt
¼ teaspoon freshly ground black
  pepper
1 pound linguine, cooked,
  drained, and hot
1 cup fozen tiny peas, rinsed to
  thaw
½ cup freshly grated Parmesan,
  if desired

1. Put olive oil, onion, garlic, and hot pepper in 2-quart casserole. Cover tightly. MICROWAVE (high) 2–3 minutes until vegetables are soft.
2. Stir in wine, basil, oregano, and lemon juice. Cover tightly. MICROWAVE (high) 2–3 minutes until simmering.
3. Stir in clams. Cover tightly. MICROWAVE (high) 1–2 minutes to heat through. Stir in parsley, salt, and black pepper.
4. Toss linguine with clam sauce and peas. Sprinkle with Parmesan, if desired.

TIP: Before mincing the hot pepper, discard the seeds and trim away the pithy core. The veins or core and the adjacent seeds contain the most heat and can be an unpleasant surprise in the sauce.

TIP: Choose a good quality wine for this sauce—one you would be pleased to drink with dinner. The half-cup is a substantial amount and will greatly affect the flavor of the sauce.

BOUILLABAISSE

Bouillabaisse is the traditional Christmas Eve dinner in our home, served with crusty bread, a light salad, and a dry, German white wine. Basically a fish soup, bouillabaisse starts with a homemade fish stock, which is time-consuming to make but well worth the effort. All the little details, such as the orange zest and saffron, do make a difference in taste, so don't be tempted to cut corners.

Ideally, the soup should boast a variety of fish: firm fish, such as halibut, monkfish, perch, and eel; and flaky fish, such as flounder, orange roughy, and sole.

Although shellfish typically are not used in the bouillabaisse of Southern France, I also like to throw in a handful of shrimp, a couple of squiggly squid, and fresh mussels or clams. The mussels or clams are dramatic-looking, and as they cook they add that final fresh seafood flavor to the broth.

Note that the fish that require the most cooking time are added first, and quick-cooking seafood such as shrimp are added at the very end. (Perch is an odd one: it is a firm-fleshed fish, but it cooks up so quickly that I add it with the fast-cooking, flaky fish.)

The recipe is lengthy, but most of the work can be done ahead of time. The fish stock may be made up to two days in advance and kept, covered, in the refrigerator. The fish can be cut up in the morning. Before you start cooking, it is helpful to have all your fish cut and lined up on the counter in cooking order. The final cooking takes only about 15 minutes.

For menu suggestions see page 24.

Preparation time: 30 minutes
Microwave time: 44–53 minutes
Servings: 4

STOCK
  1 leek, washed and chopped
  1 small onion, chopped
  2 tablespoons olive oil
  2 cloves garlic, minced
  **1 pound ripe tomatoes,
     chopped, *or* 1 pound canned
     tomatoes, drained and
     chopped**
3½ cups water
  ½ cup dry white wine
  ¼ cup chopped fresh parsley
  1 2-inch piece orange zest
  1 bay leaf, crushed

1. Put leek, onion, and olive oil in 3-quart casserole. Cover. MICROWAVE (high) 3–4 minutes to soften and develop flavor, stirring after 1 minute. Stir in garlic. MICROWAVE (high) 1 minute to soften.

2. Stir in the rest of the ingredients for the stock. Cover. MICROWAVE (high) 18–20 minutes until boiling, stirring after 10 minutes to rearrange bones. MICROWAVE (medium) 10–12 minutes to develop flavor. Strain, pressing out juices. Taste, and add salt if needed.

3. Return finished stock to casserole. Cover. MICROWAVE (high) 3–4 minutes or until

1 teaspoon fresh thyme *or* ¼
   teaspoon dried
⅛ teaspoon dried fennel seeds
2 pinches saffron strands
½ teaspoon salt
⅛ teaspoon freshly ground
   black pepper
2 pounds fish bones and heads,
   washed

BOUILLABAISSE

2 pounds firm fish fillets, cut
   into 1-inch pieces (pick from
   two or three varieties, such
   as eel, halibut, and
   monkfish)
8 whole clams or mussels,
   scrubbed
1 pound flaky fish fillets, cut
   into 2-inch pieces (pick from
   two or three varieties, such
   as flounder, orange roughy,
   and sole, or perch)
2 squid, cleaned, sliced into
   rings
12 medium-sized raw shrimp,
   peeled and deveined
4 rounds of hard-toasted
   French bread
¼ cup minced fresh parsley

boiling. Lift cover and carefully stir in the cut-up, firm-fleshed fish. Cover. MICROWAVE (high) 3–4 minutes or until stock is almost boiling.

4. If using hard-shelled clams, add them next. Cover. MICROWAVE (high) 1 minute.

5. Stir in cut-up, flaky fish. Cover. MICROWAVE (high) 2–3 minutes until almost boiling.

6. Stir in squid. If using mussels or soft-shelled clams, add them now. Cover. MICROWAVE (high) 1 minute. Stir in shrimp. Cover. MICROWAVE (high) 2–3 minutes or until stock boils, clams or mussels have opened, and shrimp have just turned pink. If shrimp are ready but clams haven't opened yet, lift out clams and put on a shallow plate. Cover. MICROWAVE (high) 20–30 seconds or until clams open. Pour juices back into soup.

7. Use a slotted spoon to lift out fish and arrange on a platter or in individual large soup bowls. Pour broth into a large soup tureen. Add bread rounds to tureen. Allow guests to serve fish from platter, then ladle broth and a round of bread into each bowl. Garnish with parsley.

TIP: For a good-tasting stock, use the heads, bones, tails, and skin of the fish, rinsing well to remove all blood. Light-flavored fish make the best-tasting stock. Avoid using salmon, sturgeon, buffalofish, and other strong-tasting fish.

TIP: If you don't have enough fish bones for the stock, use bottled clam broth and omit the added salt.

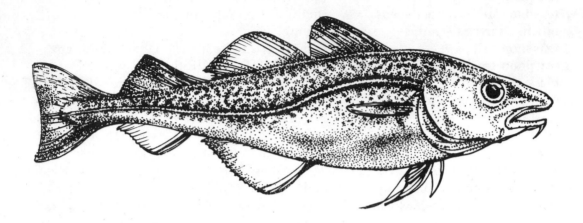

C O D

Humble cod are like ordinary carrots: abundant, inexpensive, healthful, and underrated.

One of the first major industries in colonial New England, cod sustained the souls and stomachs of coastal pioneers who made frugal use of the large fish. Like the mighty buffalo, no part of the cod went to waste, from the white flesh to the cheeks, tongue, roe, and even the liver, the source of medicinal cod liver oil.

Cod are members of the Gadidae family, saltwater fish that thrive in cold ocean waters. The most commonly eaten species are Atlantic cod, hake, haddock, and pollack. The last two species are so common that they are given their own chapters in this book.

Most of the Atlantic cod that come to market are 2½–10 pounds each; the smaller cod (and haddock), 1½–2½ pounds, are known as scrod. Cod is sold fresh in steaks or fillets, frozen in convenient 10-ounce or 1-pound packages, or precooked into sticks and frozen.

Purists needn't scoff at the fresh-frozen cod. The quality is excellent, and the price is typically one or two dollars less per pound than fresh or defrosted mild white fish fillets sold behind a fish counter.

The only drawback I have found with these frozen packages is that you can't depend on the size of the fillets. Once you defrost the package, sometimes you find one large, thick fillet; sometimes two medium-sized fillets and a couple of little pieces. For more even cooking results in the microwave, you will want to put the larger fillets toward the outside of the dish and the smaller bits in the center.

Some packages of frozen cod have directions that call for cooking a pound of defrosted cod on high power for 5–8 minutes. I find that this is too much cooking time. When using a 600- to 700-watt microwave oven, cook cod for 4 minutes per pound—until the center of the fish is almost opaque when tested with a fork. Then let the cod stand on the counter a few minutes to finish cooking.

Cod tends to break into large, firm flakes once cooked, so it's a good idea to plan a dish where the flakes are wanted. Because the flakes do remain firm, cod is particularly suited to soups.

✄❤ COD WITH FRESH TOMATO

When the ingredients are fresh, a simple dish like this can become a repeated favorite.

Preparation time: 10 minutes
Microwave time: 8–10 minutes
Servings: 4

2 medium tomatoes, peeled, seeded, and chopped, or 2–4 canned tomatoes, drained and chopped
1 teaspoon minced garlic
2 teaspoons minced fresh basil or ½ teaspoon dried
⅛ teaspoon salt
⅛ teaspoon freshly ground black pepper
Dash cayenne pepper
1 pound cod fillets
1 tablespoon fresh lemon juice

1. Put tomatoes and garlic in 4-cup measure. MICROWAVE (high), uncovered, 4–5 minutes until tomatoes thicken. Stir in basil, salt, pepper, and cayenne. Keep warm.
2. Arrange cod on a plate with thickest portions to the outside and any small fish scraps in the center. Drizzle with lemon juice. Cover with plastic wrap, vented. MICROWAVE (high) 4–5 minutes until thickest portion of cod is almost opaque when tested with a fork. Let stand 3 minutes. Drain. Top with fresh tomato mixture to serve.

COD SMOTHERED IN MUSHROOMS

This is a very easy-to-like dish, in which natural juices from the mushrooms and cod are thickened with a little butter and flour and touched with thyme.

Preparation time: 10 minutes
Microwave time: 13–17 minutes
Servings: 4

½ **pound fresh, whole mushrooms**
1 **tablespoon butter**
1 **tablespoon flour**
1 **teaspoon fresh thyme** *or* ¼ **teaspoon dried**
¼ **teaspoon salt**
⅛ **teaspoon freshly ground black pepper**
1 **pound cod fillets**
1 **tablespoon fresh lemon juice**
2 **tablespoons chopped fresh parsley**

1. Wipe mushrooms clean; slice and put in 9-inch pie plate. Put butter on top. Cover. MICROWAVE (high) 5–6 minutes until mushrooms are tender, stirring once. Blend in flour. MICROWAVE (high), uncovered, 2–3 minutes to slightly thicken. Stir in thyme, salt, and pepper.
2. Arrange cod on top of mushrooms, with thickest portions to the outside and any small fish scraps in the center. Drizzle with lemon juice. Cover with plastic wrap, vented. MICROWAVE (high) 4–5 minutes until thickest portion of fish is almost opaque when tested with a fork. Let stand 3 minutes.
3. Lift fish onto a serving plate. Stir mushroom mixture, and MICROWAVE (high), uncovered, 2–3 minutes until thick and hot. Pour mushroom mixture over fish. Sprinkle with parsley.

COD AND BROCCOLI SOUP

Broccoli is given a 2-minute head start in this light soup before the cod is added so that the two are perfectly cooked at the same time. For menu suggestions see page 23.

Preparation time: 10 minutes
Microwave time: 13–18 minutes
Servings: 4

2 tablespoons butter
¼ cup minced onion
2 tablespoons flour
2 cups fish or chicken stock
2 cups chopped broccoli flowerets
½ cup milk
⅛ teaspoon cayenne pepper
½ teaspoon salt
¼ teaspoon freshly ground black pepper
1 pound cod fillets, cut into 1-inch chunks

1. Put butter and onion in 2½-quart casserole. MICROWAVE (high), uncovered, 2–3 minutes until onion is soft. Blend in flour. MICROWAVE (high), uncovered, 1–2 minutes to cook flour.
2. Stir in stock. Cover. MICROWAVE (high) 4–5 minutes until it boils and slightly thickens. Stir well.
3. Stir in broccoli, milk, cayenne, salt, and pepper. Cover. MICROWAVE (high) 2–3 minutes until broccoli starts to soften.
4. Stir in cod. Cover. MICROWAVE (high) 4–5 minutes until centers of fish pieces are just opaque. Let stand 3 minutes.

HOT GERMAN COD SALAD

Warm, sliced potatoes and chunks of cooked cod are tossed with a zesty bacon dressing. Serve with fresh broccoli.

Preparation time: 15 minutes
Microwave time: 19–23 minutes
Servings: 6

4 large yellow potatoes
1 pound cod fillets
1 tablespoon fresh lemon juice
4 strips uncooked bacon, diced
2 tablespoons minced shallots
2 tablespoons apple juice
3 tablespoons cider vinegar
1 teaspoon dry mustard
1 teaspoon salt
1 egg, well beaten
2 green onions, white portion and first 2 inches of green, sliced

1. Scrub potatoes and prick several times with fork. Put potatoes on corners of a paper towel. MICROWAVE (high) 10–12 minutes until potatoes are just soft, turning towel 180 degrees after 6 minutes. Let stand 3 minutes. Peel, cut in half lengthwise, and slice.
2. Arrange cod on a plate with thickest portions to the outside and any small fish scraps in the center. Drizzle with lemon juice. Cover vented with plastic wrap. MICROWAVE (high) 4–5 minutes until thickest portion of fish is almost opaque when tested with a fork. Let stand 3 minutes. Drain. Cut into 1½-inch chunks.
3. Put bacon and shallots in 4-cup measure. MICROWAVE (high), uncovered, 4–5 minutes until bacon is cooked. Stir in apple juice, vinegar, mustard, and salt. MICROWAVE (high) 1 minute to blend.
4. Beat a teaspoon of hot bacon marinade into egg. Beat egg into remaining hot marinade until well mixed. Arrange potatoes and fish on serving platter. Pour hot marinade over them. Gently mix. Sprinkle with green onions.

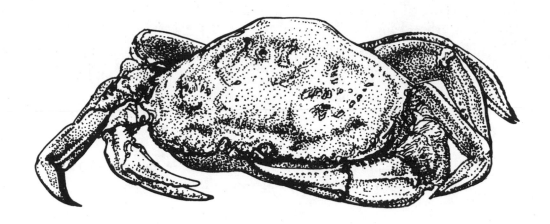

CRAB

Like shrimp and lobster, crab sets an immediate tone to dinner. A crab legs appetizer with rich maltaise sauce or a lighter lemon-crab soup says "party" with panache.

Nothing else looks like crab. Nothing else tastes like crab. Even the best surimi, the imitation crab made from white fish such as pollack, uses some real crab or crab juice for flavor.

American consumers can select from a wide variety of crab, including Alaska king from Alaska, Dungeness and snow from the Pacific Coast, dramatically colored stone crab from the Southern Atlantic, and blue crab from the Gulf and Atlantic Coasts.

And there may be additional varieties to enjoy. In 1962, a ship from the National Marine Fisheries Service scouring the waters of the Gulf of Mexico for unidentified species found a few buff-colored crabs and entered them on the scientific logs. Geryon fenneri, or *golden crab*, was declared a new species, and there is a budding effort in Florida to market these golden-meat crabs whose shells remain pale even after cooking.

Precooked crab legs such as Alaska king or snow crab can be successfully reheated in the microwave on medium power. However, the microwave is not the best way to cook fresh, whole crab. Like lobster, the tomalley of the crab gets overcooked in the microwave and turns to liquid, a messy and wasteful ordeal. It is better to cook whole crab conventionally on top of the stove.

When purchasing Alaska king or snow crab legs or cluster as an entree, allow 5 or 6 ounces per serving. To thaw, place frozen crab in a shallow pan, cover with plastic wrap, and let sit overnight in the refrigerator.

Frozen crabmeat also is available in 6-ounce packages. Most of the meat is from the legs and has plenty of pretty, salmon-pink color; the natural juices—which should be saved to use in other dishes—give a good, strong crab flavor.

Canned crab typically comes in 6-ounce cans, packed in water. The least expensive canned crab typically found in supermarkets is called fancy white and is made of tiny shreds of white meat only; it costs about one-third the price of frozen crab. It doesn't look as pretty as the frozen variety and lacks the intense crab flavor, but it is fine for mixing into a thick sauce. Premium white canned crab tastes the same as fancy white crab, but it has larger pieces; it is about one-third more expensive than fancy white.

In many dishes you can interchange the source of crab or use less-expensive canned crab and garnish with more attractive fresh or frozen pieces.

✿ LEMON-CRAB SOUP

Expensive crab is stretched in this lovely, light soup that is both good-tasting and healthful. Pink-colored fresh or frozen crabmeat looks prettier in this dish than canned white crabmeat. For menu suggestions see page 23.

Preparation time: 10 minutes
Microwave time: 19–23 minutes
Servings: 4

1 teaspoon minced garlic
2 green onions, white and first
2 inches of green, chopped
4 cups chicken stock or broth
¼ cup uncooked rice
2 tablespoons fresh lemon juice
6 ounces crab meat, preferably
fresh or frozen
⅛ teaspoon ground white pepper

1. Mix garlic, onions, and 2 tablespoons chicken stock in 2½-quart casserole. Cover. MICROWAVE (high) 1–2 minutes to soften.
2. Stir in rice, lemon juice, and 2 cups chicken stock. Cover. MICROWAVE (high) 5 minutes to boil, then MICROWAVE (medium) 10–12 minutes until rice is tender.
3. Stir in remaining stock and the crab and pepper. Cover tightly. MICROWAVE (high) 3–4 minutes until heated through.

TIP: You can save time if you have a cup of leftover cooked rice. Skip Step 2, stir in remaining ingredients, cover, and MICROWAVE (high) until heated through.

TIP: For a more attractive soup, note that white pepper is used rather than black.

CRAB LEGS MALTAISE

Precooked crab legs need only to be heated to bring out their flavor. For a tasty sauce, a rich maltaise—a variation of hollandaise with a touch of orange.

Preparation time: 5 minutes
Microwave time: 4–5 minutes
Servings: 4

1½ **pounds precooked crab legs in shell, split or cracked**
½ **cup (1 stick) unsalted butter**
3 **large egg yolks**
1½ **tablespoons fresh lemon juice**
2 **tablespoons fresh orange juice**
1 **tablespoon grated orange zest**

1. Put crab on a plate. Do not cover. MICROWAVE (medium) 3–4 minutes until thoroughly heated.
2. For the sauce, put butter in 4-cup measure. MICROWAVE (high), uncovered, 20 seconds to soften, but do not melt. (Butter straight from the refrigerator may need up to a minute.)
3. In a small bowl, mix egg yolks and lemon juice. Add to butter. MICROWAVE (high), uncovered, 1 minute, whipping with whisk every 15 seconds. Sauce should be smooth and thick. Stir in orange juice and zest. Serve sauce on the side for dipping.

CRAB AND ARTICHOKE DIP

A quick appetizer is minutes away if you have a can of crabmeat and a can of artichoke hearts to add to refrigerator staples. Because the crab is mixed into a thick sauce, an inexpensive can of small crab pieces works just fine. This dip is best warm, so cook just before serving. Serve with pita crisps or crackers.

Preparation time: 10 minutes
Microwave time: 5–6 minutes
Yield: 3 cups of dip

½ **cup sour cream**
½ **cup mayonnaise**
10 **drops hot sauce such as Tabasco**
1 **6-ounce can crabmeat, drained**
1 **14-ounce can artichoke hearts, drained and chopped**
½ **cup grated Parmesan**

Combine sour cream, mayonnaise, and hot sauce in 1-quart casserole. Stir in remaining ingredients. Cover with waxed paper. MICROWAVE (medium) 5–6 minutes until heated through but not boiling, stirring after 3 minutes.

CRAB- AND SHRIMP-TOPPED POTATOES

If you keep potatoes, cheese, and a box of frozen crab and shrimp on hand, it's easy to turn out these satisfying seafood- and cheese-stuffed baked potatoes. Serve two halves for each person.

Preparation time: 30 minutes
Microwave time: 13–16 minutes
Servings: 4

4 large baking potatoes
¼ cup (½ stick) butter
½ cup milk, or as needed
1 tablespoon chopped fresh dill
   ***or* 1 teaspoon dried**
¼ teaspoon salt
¼ teaspoon freshly ground
   black pepper
½ cup grated Parmesan
1½ cups shredded cheddar
   cheese
6 ounces frozen crab and
   shrimp meat, defrosted
2 green onions, white and first
   2 inches of green, chopped

1. Scrub potatoes well. Prick tops with fork. Put potatoes on corners of paper towel. MICROWAVE (high) 10–12 minutes until potatoes are just soft when squeezed, turning towel 180 degrees after 6 minutes. Let stand 3 minutes.
2. Cut potatoes in half horizontally. Scoop out centers, leaving a ½-inch thick shell. Mash the scooped-out potato. Mix in the butter, milk, dill, salt, pepper, Parmesan, and 1 cup of the cheddar. Mix until the cheeses and butter have melted and mixture is fluffy. Stir in the crab and shrimp, reserving a few attractive pieces for garnish. Spoon mixture into potato shells.
3. MICROWAVE (high), uncovered, 3–4 minutes to heat through. Sprinkle with reserved cheddar and the onions. Garnish with reserved crab and shrimp. Serve immediately.

TIP: *The amount of milk is approximate and will depend on the size and variety of potato. Add enough milk until the potatoes progress from sticky to fluffy but not mushy. You want a little less milk than you would for mashed potatoes, so that the filling mounds well.*

TIP: *Note that the cheese topping is not cooked. This keeps the cheese from getting overcooked and tough. Instead, the grated cheese is added at the end and simply melts over the hot potato.*

TIP: *If you substitute other cheese to mix with the mashed potatoes, be sure to select a colorful cheese for the topping.*

CREAMY CRAB AND MUSHROOMS

This versatile dish can be served over rice for a quick family meal or dressed up for guests by serving it in individual ramekins or scallop shells. The dish goes under the broiler for a minute to brown.

Preparation time: 15 minutes
Microwave time: 16–21 minutes
Broiling time: 1 minute
Servings: 4

2 cups (about 4 ounces) sliced fresh mushrooms
2 tablespoons butter
2 tablespoons flour
½ cup chicken stock or broth
½ cup milk
2 tablespoons dry white wine or sherry
6 ounces crab meat, preferably fresh or defrosted
1 teaspoon fresh thyme *or* ¼ teaspoon dried
¼ teaspoon salt
⅛ teaspoon freshly ground black pepper
Dash of cayenne pepper
¼ cup grated Parmesan
2 tablespoons minced fresh parsley

1. Put mushrooms and butter in 1-quart microwave- and oven-proof casserole. Cover. MICROWAVE (high) 3–4 minutes until soft, stirring after 2 minutes. Stir in flour until well mixed.
2. MICROWAVE (high), uncovered, 2–3 minutes until bubbly. Stir in stock and milk. MICROWAVE (high), uncovered, 10–12 minutes until bubbly and thick, stirring twice.
3. Stir in wine, crab, thyme, salt, pepper, and cayenne. MICROWAVE (high), uncovered, 1–2 minutes to heat through. If desired, transfer mixture to individual ramekins or scallop shells. Sprinkle with Parmesan. Put casserole or ramekins under broiler for 1 minute to brown the top. Sprinkle with parsley.

TIP: There is no cream in this recipe. The smooth, thick sauce is a veloute, an upscale white sauce, cooked extra long until it reduces to a creamlike texture. You can reduce fat even more by substituting margarine for the butter and skim milk for whole milk.

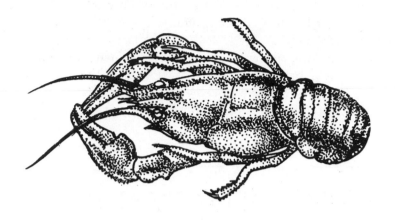

CRAYFISH

Crayfish are freshwater crustaceans that look like miniature lobsters but are milder tasting than either lobster or shrimp. Also called crawfish, crawdads, or mudbugs, there are about 300 species of these tiny creatures—plus an 8-pound Tasmanian version!—found around the world.

In the United States, 3- to 5-inch crayfish thrive in rivers and shallow lakes of the South and Pacific Coast, but particularly in Louisiana, where they are snapped up in nets, caught in baited traps, or just grabbed by hand. Currently there is so much demand that crayfish are being farmed in the South.

Like lobster, crayfish are cooked live, then shelled. Most people eat only the tailmeat, but real aficionados like to pick at the body and head as well, seeking the orange-yellow-colored "fat," or liver, which tastes like lobster tomalley.

The microwave oven will help you cook the crayfish faster, but picking out the meat is still laborious. Count on about five pounds of crayfish to yield a pound of shelled meat—and try to count on friends to help with the chore.

Spring is high season for fresh crayfish. If you're out of season—or out of time to cook and shell the crayfish—check your fish store for cooked and shelled crayfish at about twice the price of live, whole ones. Cooked medium-sized shrimp can be substituted in the following recipes.

CRAYFISH BASICS

Crayfish are soaked in salted water for 15 minutes before cooking to help cleanse them. The soaking water is discarded.

Although you can cook crayfish in the microwave without any water, they taste better when cooked with salt, and you need a cup of water to dissolve and spread the salt.

For the most even cooking, cook only 1 pound of crayfish at a time in the microwave. While the next batch is cooking, you will need the time to shell the already-cooked crayfish anyway.

Crayfish are done cooking in the microwave oven when they turn a deep brownish-red, with perhaps bright red claw tips. If you let the whole crayfish get as red as a cooked lobster, it will be overcooked and tough eating. If one or two of the batch are slow to cook, remove the cooked crayfish and return the rest to the microwave oven.

✑ STEAMED CRAYFISH

You get more even cooking results if you cook only 1 pound of crayfish at a time in the microwave. This will yield about 3 ounces of shelled meat (about one serving). If you need to cook several batches for a recipe, you can be busy shelling the already-cooked crayfish as the next batch cooks.

Preparation time: 20 minutes
Soaking time: 15 minutes
Microwave time: 6–8 minutes
Yield: 3 ounces tailmeat (about one serving)

1 tablespoon and 1 teaspoon salt
1 cup water
1 pound live crayfish

1. Fill sink or a shallow pan with cold water to cover crayfish and add 1 tablespoon salt. Let crayfish soak 15 minutes. Drain, and rinse well.
2. Put 1 cup water and remaining salt in 3-quart casserole. Cover. MICROWAVE (high) 2–3 minutes until boiling. Add crayfish. Cover. MICROWAVE (high) 4–5 minutes until the shells turn brownish-red and the very tips of the claws turn bright red. Drain.
3. When the crayfish are cool enough to handle, twist off the tails and use fingernail or a small spoon to remove the orange-yellow-colored "fat" from the body. Save the "fat" in a separate little bowl for another use. Save heads to make soups or sauces. Use fingers to crack tail shells and remove meat. Remove and discard any veins. Eat the cooked tailmeat as is, or use in any of the following recipes.

CRAYFISH WITH ORANGE VELOUTE

This mild, creamy sauce moistens but doesn't overpower crayfish. Use any leftover sauce to flavor a rice side dish.

Preparation time: 10 minutes
Microwave time: 8–12 minutes
Servings: 4–6

2 tablespoons butter
2 tablespoons flour
1 cup chicken stock or broth
½ cup whipping cream
2 teaspoons grated orange zest
2 tablespoons fresh orange juice
1 teaspoon fresh lemon juice
¼ teaspoon salt
⅛ teaspoon ground white pepper
1 pound cooked, shelled crayfish meat

1. Put butter in 4-cup measure. MICROWAVE (high), uncovered, 2–3 minutes until butter melts and is very hot. Whisk in flour. MICROWAVE (high), uncovered, 2–3 minutes until the mixture bubbles furiously.
2. Thoroughly whisk in broth and cream. MICROWAVE (high), uncovered, 2–3 minutes until bubbles that start at the edges of the sauce fill in and completely cover the top of the sauce. Whisk thoroughly.
3. MICROWAVE (high) 2–3 minutes until sauce thickens enough to coat a spoon. Thoroughly whisk in orange zest, orange juice, and lemon juice. Add salt and pepper, or to taste. Serve crayfish warm drizzled with sauce.

TIP: *For a lower-calorie version, omit cream and increase broth to 1½ cups. Add an extra 7–8 minutes to cooking time in the last step to reduce broth to a creamy texture. Be sure to taste before adding salt, because the reduction will intensify the saltiness of the broth.*

CRAYFISH AND ASPARAGUS SALAD

This light salad can be served chilled or warm.

Preparation time: 10 minutes
Microwave time: 4–6 minutes
Servings: 4

1 **pound fresh asparagus stems**
¼ **cup water**
½ **pound cooked, shelled crayfish meat, chilled (*See* Steamed Crayfish)**
1 **tablespoon white wine vinegar**
1 **teaspoon fresh lemon juice**
1 **teaspoon Dijon mustard**
½ **teaspoon finely minced garlic**
1 **teaspoon fresh tarragon *or* ¼ teaspoon dried**
⅛ **teaspoon salt**
⅛ **teaspoon freshly ground black pepper**
3 **tablespoons vegetable oil**
2 **green onions, white and first 2 inches of green, sliced**

1. Lightly peel asparagus stems and cut into 2-inch diagonal slices. Put asparagus and water in 1-quart casserole. Cover. MICROWAVE (high) 4–6 minutes until just tender. Drain. Chill in refrigerator for an hour. Just before serving, arrange crayfish and asparagus on a serving platter.
2. In a small bowl, whisk vinegar, lemon juice, mustard, garlic, tarragon, salt, and pepper. Whisk in oil. Drizzle over asparagus and crayfish, toss lightly. Sprinkle with green onions.

CRAYFISH ETOUFFEE

In Louisiana country, étouffée *means smothered, and in this dish cooked crayfish is smothered in a mound of Louisiana-style vegetables. For menu suggestions see page 23.*

Preparation time: 15 minutes
Microwave time: 24–34 minutes
Servings: 4

2 tablespoons butter
2 tablespoons flour
2 teaspoons minced garlic
½ cup chopped green bell pepper
¼ cup chopped celery
¼ cup chopped onion
½ teaspoon fresh basil
½ teaspoon salt
½ teaspoon freshly ground black pepper
¼ teaspoon cayenne pepper
2 cups fish stock *or* 1 cup clam juice and 1 cup chicken broth
1 pound cooked, shelled crayfish meat (*See* Steamed Crayfish)
4 cups hot cooked rice
4 green onions, white and first 2 inches of green, sliced

1. Put butter in 2½-quart casserole. MICROWAVE (high), uncovered, 1–2 minutes until melted and hot. Whisk in flour. MICROWAVE (high), uncovered, 5–6 minutes until rich brown.
2. Stir in garlic. Cover. MICROWAVE (high) 1–2 minutes to soften garlic. Stir in bell pepper, celery, onion, basil, salt, black pepper, and cayenne. Cover. MICROWAVE (high) 4–5 minutes until tender.
3. Stir in fish stock. Cover. MICROWAVE (high) 3–4 minutes until boiling. MICROWAVE (high), uncovered, 10–15 minutes to thicken. Stir in crayfish. Serve over rice, and sprinkle with green onions.

TIP: For Shrimp Etouffée, shell and devein raw shrimp, chop rough, and add at end to cooked étouffée mixture. Cover. MICROWAVE (high) 2–3 minutes until shrimp just turn pink.

CRAYFISH-STUFFED MIRLITON

Mirliton is the Louisiana name for chayote, a pear-shaped gourd also favored in Mexico and South America. Here, the mild-tasting, firm-textured vegetable is cooked, scooped out, and stuffed with cooked crayfish for an attractive appetizer or luncheon plate.

Preparation time: 15 minutes
Microwave time: 11 minutes
Servings: 4

2 medium chayotes
2 tablespoons water
3 tablespoons butter
1 teaspoon minced garlic
2 green onions, white and first 2 inches of green, sliced
2 cups fresh croutons (*see* Tip at end of this recipe)
1 tablespoon chopped fresh pimento
2 teaspoons fresh thyme *or* ½ teaspoon dried
2 teaspoons chopped fresh basil *or* ½ teaspoon dried
⅛ teaspoon cayenne pepper
¼ teaspoon salt
¼ teaspoon freshly ground black pepper
½ pound cooked, shelled crayfish meat, all but 12 chopped

1. Cut chayotes in half lengthwise. Put on a plate with necks pointing inward. Add water to plate. Cover with plastic wrap, vented. MICROWAVE (high) 6–9 minutes until skin is just tender, rotating once. Let stand, covered, 5 minutes.
2. Remove almond-shaped seed and eat it or reserve for other use. Discard white, pithy center. Scoop out chayote pulp, leaving ¼-inch shell. Set shells upside down to drain. Dice pulp. Reserve.
3. Put butter, garlic, and green onion in 1-quart casserole. MICROWAVE (high) 2 minutes, stirring once. Add chayote pulp and rest of ingredients except for the 12 whole crayfish tails. Mix gently.
4. Spoon mixture into chayote shells. Top with reserved crayfish.

TIP: To make croutons, put 2 tablespoons butter in 8" × 8" × 2" dish. MICROWAVE (high), uncovered, 30 seconds to melt. Stir in 2 teaspoons snipped parsley. Mix in 2 cups of ½-inch-cubed French bread. MICROWAVE (high), uncovered, 3–5 minutes, stirring every minute. Let cool.

TIP: To reheat, place stuffed mirlitons or chayotes on plate and cover with plastic wrap, vented. MICROWAVE (medium) 3–4 minutes or until warm.

TIP: The chayote seed has a wonderful nut-like taste, which deepens when the seed is briefly cooked.

EEL

This is a hard creature to sell. An octopus from the deep and a toothy shark are matinee idols compared to the lowly, slippery, slithery eel, always the villain, never destined to be the hero of a Walt Disney flick. Of course, this might make it easier to accept an eel as dinner—providing the kids don't catch a glimpse of the thing on the counter.

Actually, it's not a bad idea to present a dish such as Eel in Green Sauce without title and without ceremony. Just let your guests or family enjoy the meal and ask questions later.

Eel is a fine-tasting, high-fat creature, with a full-bodied, nutty flavor and meaty texture. It works well with beer, particularly in the following recipe using ale and black bread, and it also lends body to soup such as bouillabaisse or a simple leek broth.

On the downside, eel has a lot of bones. And, as with catfish, it is very difficult to peel its tough, deep green to black skin. To peel an eel in the traditional manner, you tie a cord around its "neck," hang the eel from a nail on the wall, use a knife to make a circular incision around and just under the neck, then use pliers to pull and yank the skin off. Frankly, I find it easier to peel the eel after it has been cooked.

Eel needs to be cooked on medium power in the microwave to keep it from getting tough. When it's done, the meat is tender, and the skin and bones slip away quite easily. This is the method I use for recipes in this chapter.

Eel are born at sea but are generally caught in fresh water. They are particularly prized in Scandinavia, Belgium, and Germany. A good time to find fresh eel is just before Christmas, when eel is a traditional part of European feasts.

ᗡ❤ EEL WITH ALE AND BLACK BREAD

In this old German recipe, eel is cooked in ale with black bread, then the liquid is strained to create a lovely, caramel-colored broth.

Preparation time: 10 minutes
Microwave time: 10–12 minutes
Servings: 4

1⅓ cups (12-fluid-ounce bottle)
   dark ale
¼ cup dry white wine
¼ medium onion, chopped
   rough
2 whole cloves
1 bay leaf, crushed
3 slices black bread, crumbled
1 teaspoon fresh lemon juice
1 small eel, cleaned and cut
   into 3-inch pieces
1 tablespoon minced fresh
   parsley

1. Put all ingredients except the eel and parsley in 2½-quart casserole. Cover. MICROWAVE (high) 3–4 minutes until almost boiling.
2. Add eel. Cover. MICROWAVE (medium) 7–8 minutes until eel is tender. Let stand, covered, 20 minutes on the counter to further tenderize eel.
3. Lift out eel. Use paring knife to remove skin. Remove bones, and arrange remaining fillets on serving plate. Strain broth over eel. Top with parsley.

⌒♥ EEL AND LEEK BROTH

An easy way to introduce eel is with a simple soup that gets its special character from eel and leek.

Preparation time: 20 minutes
Microwave time: 31–36 minutes
Servings: 4

1 leek
2 celery ribs with fresh yellow leaves, chopped
2 medium-sized carrots, chopped
¼ cup chopped fresh parsley
1 bay leaf, crushed
1 teaspoon fresh thyme *or* ¼ teaspoon dried
6 peppercorns
¼ teaspoon salt
½ cup dry white wine
3½ cups water
1 small eel, cleaned and cut into 3-inch pieces

1. Trim off root end of leek. Slice in half lengthwise and wash well under running water. Separate tender, green inner section; julienne, and set aside. Roughly chop thicker, white outer stalk section.
2. Put thicker, white section of leek, celery, and carrots in 3-quart casserole. Cover. MICROWAVE (high) 4–5 minutes to soften, stirring after 1 minute.
3. Stir in rest of ingredients, except for reserved julienned leeks. Cover tightly. MICROWAVE (high) 18–20 minutes until boiling, stirring after 10 minutes to rearrange eel. MICROWAVE (medium) 7–8 minutes until eel is tender.
4. Remove eel; skin, debone, and set aside.
5. Strain broth and return to casserole. Add reserved julienned leeks. Cover. MICROWAVE (high) 2–3 minutes until leeks are tender. Add eel.

EEL IN GREEN SAUCE

"At the first sign of spring, Berliners would go to the suburbs to look for a garden restaurant," *says German-born Gisela Riess. "When they got there, they would sit outside and order eel in a* *green sauce." We thumbed through some old German cookbooks to help create this microwave* *version of eel in green sauce. Serve with boiled potatoes.*

For menu suggestions see page 24.

Preparation time: 15 minutes
Microwave time: 18–21 minutes
Servings: 4

2 tablespoons minced onion
2 tablespoons butter
1 small eel, cleaned and cut into
3-inch pieces
2 tablespoons flour
½ cup dry white wine
½ cup fish stock or clam broth
¼ cup minced fresh parsley
¼ cup chopped fresh spinach
1 tablespoon chopped fresh
chervil
1 tablespoon chopped fresh
chives
4 tablespoons sour cream
Salt and pepper to taste

1. Put onion and butter in 2½-quart, round casserole. MICROWAVE (high), uncovered, 2 minutes to soften, stirring once.
2. Arrange eel pieces around sides of casserole. Cover. MICROWAVE (medium) 7–8 minutes until eel is tender and almost flakes when tested with fork. Remove eel; peel and debone. Set fillets aside and keep warm.
3. Blend flour into butter mixture. MICROWAVE (high), uncovered, 2 minutes until bubbly and hot.
4. Stir in wine and stock. MICROWAVE (high), uncovered, 6–7 minutes until thick and hot, stirring twice.
5. Stir in parsley and spinach. MICROWAVE (high) 1–2 minutes to wilt parsley and spinach. Stir in chervil, chives, and sour cream, and salt and pepper to taste. To serve, pour sauce over eel.

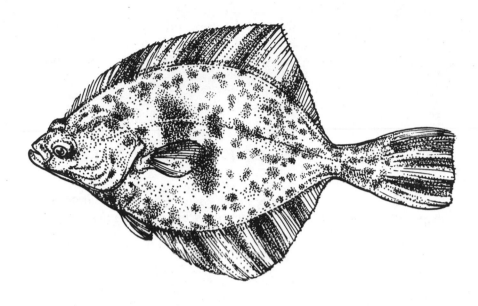

FLOUNDER

Catching flounder is no big deal off the New England coast where I grew up: pull the boat into a sandy cove, drop anchor, drop lines—and the flounder bite.

As a game fish, flounder garners little respect. But in the kitchen, the flatfish is welcome indeed. While not as delicate in flavor or texture as true Dover sole, the better varieties of flounder are sweet and mild, with a fine, tender texture. In fact, much of the "sole" sold in this country is actually flounder.

Flounder includes about 200 species of flatfish found in the Pacific and on both sides of the Atlantic Ocean, typically weighing in at 1–5 pounds but including the huge, 600- to 700-pound halibut—which gets a separate chapter in this book.

Flounder is a fascinating-looking creature because as it grows and adjusts to life at the bottom of the ocean, its body twists. One of its eyes shifts over so that the roundish flatfish has two eyes on its upper side.

Winter flounder, also called lemon sole, is a very abundant variety, especially along the Eastern Coast from Newfoundland to Chesapeake Bay. Winter flounder is small, about 1–2 pounds, with thin, fragile fillets.

American plaice, or dab, is a slightly larger flounder, about 1–3 pounds, found on both sides of the Atlantic. Summer flounder, or fluke, is larger still, about 3–5 pounds, and is caught from Maine to South Carolina.

Of the Pacific flounder, petrale is considered among the best. Arrowtooth flounder, caught in the North Pacific and off the coast of the USSR, and starry flounder are softer flounders of lesser quality.

　　Because most flounder fillets are relatively thin and light in texture, I find that they need slightly less time than other fish fillets to cook in the microwave oven. For a 600- to 700-watt microwave oven, count on only 3–4 minutes per pound.

✌♥ FLOUNDER WITH LEMON-THYME

Lemon-thyme is a lovely herb that is becoming increasingly easier to find in groceries and garden supply shops. When sprinkled on flounder with a little lemon juice, there is no need for added fat.

Preparation time: 2 minutes
Microwave time: 3–5 minutes
Servings: 4

1 pound flounder fillets
2 tablespoons lemon juice
2 tablespoons fresh lemon-
　thyme

Arrange flounder on a plate, with thickest portions to the outside and thin ends tucked under, if necessary. Drizzle with lemon juice. Sprinkle with lemon-thyme. Cover with plastic wrap, vented. MICROWAVE (high) 3–5 minutes until thickest portion is just opaque when tested with a fork. Let stand 5 minutes. Drain.

FLOUNDER ROLLS WITH SHALLOT BUTTER

When it's just two for dinner, try this fast and simple flounder, a favorite of Herbert and Gisela Riess of Mystic, Connecticut.

Preparation time: 5 minutes
Microwave time: 4–6 minutes
Servings: 2

2 teaspoons minced shallots
2 tablespoons butter or margarine
1 tablespoon fresh lemon juice
2 flounder fillets, about ⅓ pound each

1. Put shallots and butter in 1-cup measure. MICROWAVE (high), uncovered, 1–2 minutes until shallots are tender. Stir in lemon juice.
2. Roll flounder, starting with thinnest ends of fillets. Space rolls along edge of plate. Spoon shallot butter over fillets. Cover with plastic wrap, vented at one corner. MICROWAVE (high) 3–4 minutes. Spoon extra juices and butter over rolls. Let stand for 5 minutes.

MULTI-LETTUCE FLOUNDER SALAD

A multitude of colors—red, dark green, crisp white, and bright yellow—create an attractive backdrop for fresh flounder fillets.

Preparation time: 20 minutes
Microwave time: 3–5 minutes
Servings: 4

 8 **leaves red leaf lettuce**
12 **leaves fresh spinach**
 1 **head Belgian endive**
 1 **yellow bell pepper**
 1 **pound flounder fillets**
 1 **tablespoon fresh lemon juice**
 2 **tablespoons white wine vinegar**
 1 **teaspoon Dijon mustard**
 6 **tablespoons olive oil**
 ¼ **teaspoon salt**
 ⅛ **teaspoon freshly ground black pepper**
 2 **tablespoons fresh oregano *or* ½ teaspoon dried**

1. Wash and pat dry leaf lettuce and spinach. Separate endive leaves; wash and pat dry. Core, stem, and seed bell pepper; cut into thin julienne strips. Cover salad ingredients in airtight container or plastic wrap, and chill in refrigerator.

2. Arrange flounder on a plate with thickest portions to the outside and thin ends tucked under, if necessary. Drizzle with lemon juice. Cover with plastic wrap, vented. MICROWAVE (high) 3–4 minutes until thickest portion is just opaque when tested with a fork. Let stand 5 minutes. Drain. Cut fish into bite-sized pieces, and serve fish warm in salad or chill in refrigerator for at least an hour.

3. To make dressing, whisk vinegar, mustard, oil, salt, pepper, and half the oregano in 4-cup measure or small bowl.

4. Toss leafy salad ingredients and pepper with most of the salad dressing. Arrange on individual serving plates and place fish on top. Drizzle with remaining dressing and sprinkle with remaining oregano.

FLOUNDER AND BEURRE BLANC WITH HERBS

Beurre blanc is a simple, but rich, butter sauce that doesn't detract from the understated fine taste of a good flounder.

Preparation time: 10 minutes
Microwave time: 6–8 minutes
Servings: 4

1 pound flounder fillets
1 tablespoon fresh lemon juice
2 tablespoons dry white wine
2 tablespoons white vinegar
1 teaspoon fresh tarragon *or* **¼ teaspoon dried**
2 teaspoons minced shallots
8 tablespoons (1 stick) butter, diced, room temperature
Dash of salt

1. Arrange flounder on a plate with thickest portions to the outside and thin ends turned under, if necessary. Drizzle with lemon juice. Cover with plastic wrap, vented. MICROWAVE (high) 3–4 minutes until thickest portion is almost opaque when tested with a fork. Let stand 5 minutes. Drain.
2. Put wine, vinegar, tarragon, and shallots in 4-cup measure. MICROWAVE (high) 3–4 minutes until liquid is reduced to about 1 tablespoon.
3. Add butter gradually while whisking. Sauce should be creamy and foamy. Stir in salt. Drizzle beurre blanc over flounder, and serve remaining sauce on the side.

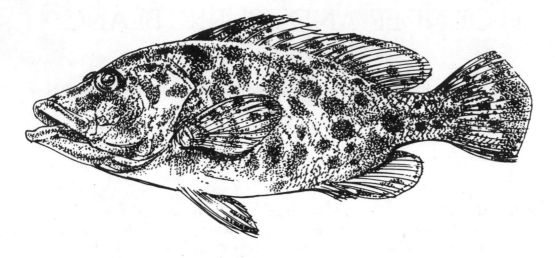

GROUPER

Grouper, a member of the sea bass family, is a beautiful-looking fish. Roundish and with big liquid eyes, common varieties include the pink-toned Red Grouper or the grayish Yellowmouth Grouper, which has yellow markings near its jaw.

Caught particularly in the warm Atlantic Ocean, off the coast of Florida, and in the Gulf of Mexico from Florida to Texas, colorful grouper is a bit of a chameleon, changing colors in the water to protect itself. When cooked, grouper has a very pleasant, sweet, nutty flavor that makes it a favorite with diners.

It also fits well in the microwave. Because of its roundish shape, a 4-pound whole grouper can fit in a 4-quart casserole that would be too short for trout or other narrow fish of the same weight. And most groupers are fairly small, about 2–3 pounds.

The skin on the white-fleshed grouper is quite thick and tough when uncooked, but it is removed easily after cooking.

GROUPER WITH ROASTED RED PEPPER AND CUCUMBER

There is no added fat here, but plenty of flavor from roasted sweet bell pepper. If you don't want to bother roasting the pepper, see the alternatives given in the Tips at the end of the recipe.

Preparation time: 10 minutes
Microwave time: 6–8 minutes
Servings: 4

½ **cup peeled, seeded, diced cucumber**
1 **red bell pepper, roasted, peeled, and diced**
⅛ **teaspoon salt**
⅛ **teaspoon freshly ground black pepper**
2 **tablespoons fresh lemon juice**
1 **pound grouper fillets**

1. Put cucumber in 4-cup measure. Cover with plastic wrap, vented. MICROWAVE (high) 2–3 minutes until tender. Stir in red pepper, salt, black pepper, and 1 tablespoon lemon juice. Set aside.

2. Arrange grouper on a plate with thickest portions to the outside. Drizzle with remaining lemon juice. Cover with plastic wrap, vented. MICROWAVE (high) 4–5 minutes until thickest portion is almost opaque when tested with a fork. Let stand 5 minutes. Drain. Top with warm pepper mixture.

TIP: *To roast a red pepper, put pepper under the broiler or hold with tongs directly over a gas flame, turning until skin is charred on all sides. Put pepper into paper bag, and close for 5 minutes. Remove from bag and peel skin under running water. Remove and discard core and seeds.*

TIP: *If you don't want to roast a fresh pepper, cook the cucumber, and stir in strips of canned roasted red pepper.*

TIP: *If you don't want the smoky flavor of roasted pepper, cook ½ cup of diced raw pepper with the cucumber for 2–3 minutes, and finish Step 1. The mixture will have a pleasant crunch because the pepper is not peeled.*

GROUPER WITH BUTTERY CRUMBS

Simple, buttery bread crumbs are a classic topping for fine-tasting fish such as grouper.

Preparation time: 10 minutes
Microwave time: 8–11 minutes
Servings: 4

1 pound grouper fillets
1 tablespoon and 1 teaspoon
**   fresh lemon juice**
6 tablespoons butter
3 tablespoons fine, dry bread
**   crumbs**

1. Arrange grouper on a plate with thickest portions to the outside. Drizzle with 1 tablespoon lemon juice. Cover with plastic wrap, vented at one corner. MICROWAVE (high) 4–5 minutes until thickest portion is almost opaque when tested with a fork. Let stand 5 minutes to finish cooking. Drain.
2. Put butter in 2-cup measure. MICROWAVE (high), uncovered, 2–3 minutes until butter is melted and hot. Stir in remaining lemon juice and bread crumbs. MICROWAVE (high), uncovered, 2–3 minutes until crumbs are moist and golden. Spoon buttery bread crumbs over fish.

GROUPER WITH BLACK OLIVE AND TOMATO TOPPING

Glossy black olives and summer-ripe tomatoes make a dramatic-looking sauce atop grouper fillets.

Preparation time: 10 minutes
Microwave time: 9–12 minutes
Servings: 4

1 tablespoon olive oil
2 tablespoons minced onion
1 teaspoon minced garlic
2 tablespoons dry white wine
2 medium tomatoes, peeled, seeded, and chopped
¼ cup pitted, chopped black olives
Dash red pepper flakes
1 pound grouper fillets
1 tablespoon fresh lemon juice

1. To make the sauce, put olive oil, onion, and garlic in 4-cup measure. MICROWAVE (high), uncovered, 1–2 minutes to soften. Stir in wine, tomato, olives, and pepper. MICROWAVE (high), uncovered, 4–5 minutes to thicken, stirring twice. Keep sauce warm.

2. Arrange grouper on a plate with thickest portion to the outside. Drizzle with lemon juice. Cover with plastic wrap, vented at one corner. MICROWAVE (high) 4–5 minutes until thickest portion is almost opaque when tested with a fork. Let stand 5 minutes to finish cooking. Drain. Top with olive and tomato sauce.

❧ WHOLE GROUPER WITH LEEK AND GINGER

The whole leek is used in this recipe: the tender parts are chopped and stuffed inside the fish, and the tough stems steam under the grouper, giving extra flavor to the cooking juices. Because of its large head, there are fewer servings of grouper per pound than most other fish. A nice 4-pound grouper serves 4–6 people. If your whole fish is less than 4 pounds, check Fish and Seafood (see Index) for cooking time guidelines.

Preparation time: 10 minutes
Microwave time: 20–25 minutes
Servings: 4–6

1 leek
1 4–5-pound whole grouper, cleaned, scaled
2 tablespoons fresh lemon juice
2 quarter-size slices fresh ginger, minced

1. Cut off and discard root end of leek. Trim dark green portion; wash, and spread on base of 4-quart flat casserole. Slice white portion of leek in half lengthwise; wash well under running water, separating stalk sections to remove dirt. Chop; reserve.
2. Rinse grouper well. Place on top of dark green leek stalks. Drizzle lemon juice inside cavity and over fish; place chopped leek and ginger in cavity. Wrap head and tail loosely with smooth foil wrap to prevent these areas from overcooking. Cover casserole with plastic wrap, vented at one corner.
3. MICROWAVE (high) 20–25 minutes until thickest portion of fish near the spine is almost opaque when tested with a fork. Let fish stand 10 minutes on counter to finish cooking. Drain. Top fish with chopped leeks and some of the juices.

TIP: *When using foil in the microwave, keep the foil smooth and at least 1 inch from the sides of the microwave.*

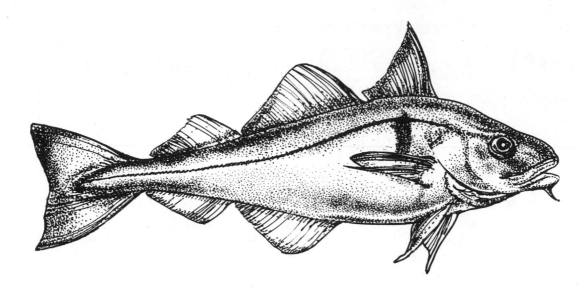

HADDOCK

A member of the cod family, haddock has firm, white flesh that is only somewhat softer than that of its larger and more popular cousin, Atlantic cod.

Haddock that comes to market is about 2–5 pounds, and the smallest haddock (as well as cod) is often sold as scrod. Haddock fillets are particularly suited to smoking. Indeed, smoked haddock, or *finnan haddie*, is a prized dish, which originated in Scotland.

Mild-tasting, fresh haddock fillets are very versatile, pairing well in the following recipes with tangy capers, salty olives and tomatoes, or even plantain with lime.

✺❤ HADDOCK WITH WINE AND CAPERS

No added fat here, just the taste of a good white wine, plus the tang of mustard and capers.

Preparation time: 5 minutes
Microwave time: 7–10 minutes
Servings: 4

¼ **cup dry white wine**
2 tablespoons fresh lemon juice
1 pound haddock fillets
1 teaspoon Dijon mustard
1 tablespoon capers, drained

1. Put wine in a dinner-sized plate that will hold the fish. MICROWAVE (high) 1–2 minutes to heat and slightly reduce wine. Stir in lemon juice. Turn haddock fillets several times in the mixture, and let stand 10 minutes to marinate.
2. Arrange haddock on plate skin-side down with thickest portions to the outside. Cover with plastic wrap, vented. MICROWAVE (high) 4–5 minutes until thickest portion is almost opaque when tested with a fork. Let stand 5 minutes to finish cooking.
3. Pour juices into 4-cup measure. MICROWAVE (high) 2–3 minutes to slightly reduce. Whisk in mustard. Stir in capers. Spoon sauce over fish.

HADDOCK WITH MEDITERRANEAN OLIVE SAUCE

Haddock is served with a generous amount of thick, olive-rich, homemade tomato sauce.

Preparation time: 20 minutes
Microwave time: 19–23 minutes
Servings: 4

1 tablespoon olive oil
½ cup minced onion
1 tablespoon minced garlic
½ cup dry white wine
1 cup peeled, seeded, chopped tomato
¼ cup chopped, pitted black olives
¼ cup chopped, pitted green olives
½ teaspoon capers, drained
½ cup bottled clam juice
¼ cup tomato paste
⅛ teaspoon red pepper flakes
1 pound haddock fillets
1 tablespoon fresh lemon juice

1. Put olive oil, onion, and garlic in 2-quart casserole. MICROWAVE (high), uncovered, 2–3 minutes to soften.
2. Stir in remaining ingredients except haddock and lemon juice. MICROWAVE (high), uncovered, 13–15 minutes to thicken, stirring twice.
3. Arrange fish on plate skin-side down with thickest portions to the outside. Drizzle with lemon juice. Cover with plastic wrap, vented. MICROWAVE (high) 4–5 minutes until thickest portion is almost opaque when tested with a fork. Let stand 5 minutes to finish cooking. Drain. Top with sauce.

TIP: Use extra sauce to top pasta or chicken.

⌣♥ HADDOCK WITH PLANTAIN AND LIME

Plantains, a close relative of the sweet banana, are a staple food of the tropics, where they are typically paired with fish and lime. This dish is very easy, because the plantain and haddock take the same amount of time to cook in the microwave. For added interest, we sprinkle a little fresh cilantro over both.

Preparation time: 5 minutes
Microwave time: 4–5 minutes
Servings: 4

1 black-ripe plantain
1 pound haddock fillets
2 tablespoons fresh lime juice
2 tablespoons minced fresh cilantro

1. Use knife, if necessary, to peel plantain. Slice in half lengthwise, then cut into four strips. Arrange cut-side down in single layer in center of a plate.
2. Arrange haddock around plantain, skin-side down and with thickest portions to the outside. Drizzle fish and plantain with lime juice. Cover with plastic wrap, vented. MICROWAVE (high) 4–5 minutes until plantain is yellow-orange and thickest part of fish is just opaque when tested with a fork. Let stand 5 minutes. Drain. Sprinkle with cilantro.

TIP: Don't let the color of the plantain fool you. The skin turns from green to yellow and finally to black before the plantain is fully ripe. (This takes about a week at room temperature.) Inside, the light yellow fruit remains firm and gets sweeter as the skin darkens. Once cooked, ripe plantain turns a light golden-orange and tastes much like a banana.

TIP: If the plantain and haddock won't fit on one plate, cook them separately. For the plantain, arrange cut-side down on a plate, drizzle with lime juice, and cover with plastic wrap, vented. MICROWAVE (high) 3–4 minutes until plantain is just tender and deepens to a yellow-orange color. Let stand 2 minutes. For the haddock, follow Step 2.

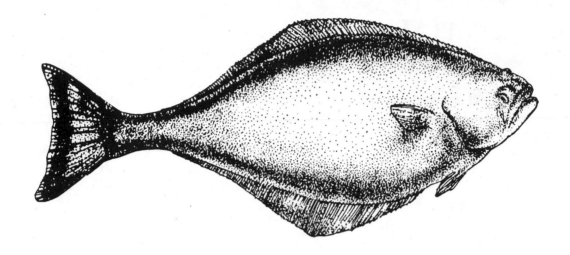

HALIBUT

Because of the wanton manner in which fish names are thrown about, halibut is a bit confusing to unravel. But let's give this a try. Halibut is a flatfish and, more specifically, one of four species of flounder. These flounder are the Atlantic, Pacific, California, and Greenland halibuts.

The first three halibuts are the largest of the flounders—the Atlantic edges up to 700 pounds—and its flesh is firm and dense, with a sweet, mild flavor; the meat is usually sold in steaks and tends to be relatively expensive. Greenland halibut—often marketed under the name turbot (a misnomer) or Greenland turbot—is flaky and stronger-tasting, decidedly inferior to the other halibuts; its meat is usually sold in fillets at bargain prices.

Although halibut is technically a flounder, it is given its own chapter in this book because the large halibut steaks cook up differently from the thin, delicate fillets of winter flounder. With their firm flesh, Atlantic, Pacific, or California halibut make a good kabob, as in the following Halibut Kabob with Yellow Pepper Puree. Again, because of their firm texture, they are excellent on the grill.

Greenland halibut (or turbot) can be a good buy—often the cheapest white fillet in the fish department—but it suffers quickly from poor handling. Most of this halibut comes to market frozen, so the fillets in the fish department have been thawed and are best used immediately. I find that if you refreeze Greenland halibut, it is more likely than other fish to develop a fishy smell and a yellowish freezer burn along the edges. The solution: don't refreeze this bargain fish, but serve it while still in good form with an assertive sauce as in Halibut with Brandied Mushrooms.

HALIBUT KABOB WITH YELLOW PEPPER PUREE

This is a beautiful and low-fat way to present fish such as sweet and firm-textured Atlantic, Pacific, or California halibut. Because it takes the longest to cook, the yellow bell pepper puree—simply cooked and pureed vegetables—is made first. The additional vegetables—mushrooms and red bell peppers—are given a 2-minute head start in the microwave, then attractively arranged with the halibut on wooden skewers. Because the halibut is cut into small chunks, it cooks faster than usual, just 3 minutes per pound in a 600- to 700-watt microwave oven. For menu suggestions see page 22.

Preparation time: 15 minutes
Microwave time: 15–19 minutes
Servings: 4

2 yellow bell peppers
1 medium red bell pepper
½ pound medium-sized mushrooms, wiped clean
1 pound halibut steaks
1 tablespoon fresh lemon juice

1. Stem, seed, and roughly chop yellow peppers; put in 2½-quart casserole. Cover. MICROWAVE (high) 10–12 minutes until very soft. Remove lid carefully. Let stand until cool enough to handle. Put peppers and cooking juices through a food mill or in a food processor, and process until smooth. Keep sauce warm.
2. Stem, seed, and cut red bell pepper into 1½-inch chunks. Put red pepper chunks and mushrooms in another 2½-quart casserole. Cover. MICROWAVE (high) 2–3 minutes to slightly soften vegetables. Drain.
3. Cut halibut into 1-inch chunks. Toss with lemon juice. Alternate fish, red pepper chunks, and mushrooms on four wooden skewers, leaving a little space between each item. Arrange skewers in the same direction on a dinner plate. Cover with plastic wrap, vented. MICROWAVE (high) 3–4 minutes until centers of the chunks are almost opaque, rotating and turning over the skewers every minute. Let stand 2 minutes. Spoon pepper puree on individual plates and place a halibut kabob on top.

TIP: The food mill will remove the skin and make the sauce smooth. The processor chops the skin as well, which makes the puree less smooth, but still quite nice for a quick sauce.

HALIBUT WITH BASIL AND BAY

Basil and crushed bay leaves are steeped in a little wine, which is then used to marinate the halibut before it is cooked in this no-added-fat entree.

Preparation time: 10 minutes
Microwave time: 5–6 minutes
Servings: 4

2 bay leaves, crushed
2 tablespoons chopped fresh basil *or* 2 teaspoons dried
⅛ teaspoon freshly ground black pepper
2 tablespoons dry white wine
2 tablespoons fresh lemon juice
1 pound halibut steaks

1. Mix bay leaves, basil, pepper, and wine in a plate large enough to hold the halibut. Cover. MICROWAVE (high) about 1 minute to heat. Stir in lemon juice. Turn halibut several times in mixture and let stand 10 minutes to marinate.
2. Arrange fish with thickest portions to the outside. Cover with plastic wrap, vented. MICROWAVE (high) 4–5 minutes until thickest portion is just opaque when tested with a fork. Let stand 5 minutes to finish cooking. Spoon juices over fish before serving.

❧ HALIBUT WITH BRANDIED MUSHROOMS

Halibut is cooked with a generous mixture of mushrooms and brandy, which is thickened with a little cornstarch to make a simple sauce. This recipe is particularly suitable for Greenland halibut fillets, which are often sold as turbot or Greenland turbot.

Preparation time: 10 minutes
Microwave time: 9–11 minutes
Servings: 4

½ **pound fresh mushrooms, roughly chopped**
¼ **cup good brandy, such as cognac**
¼ **teaspoon salt**
⅛ **teaspoon freshly ground black pepper**
1 **pound halibut fillets**
1 **teaspoon cornstarch, dissolved in 1 tablespoon water**

1. Put mushrooms, brandy, salt, and pepper in 2½-quart casserole. MICROWAVE (high), uncovered, 4–5 minutes until mushrooms are tender.
2. Arrange halibut on a plate with a lip (a 10-inch pie plate is good), with the thickest parts to the outside and any thin ends tucked under, if necessary. Pour mushroom mixture over fish. Cover with plastic wrap, vented. MICROWAVE (high) 4–5 minutes until thickest part of fish is almost opaque when tested with a fork. Let stand 5 minutes to finish cooking.
3. Drain juices into 1-cup measure (or into the mushroom casserole if you don't want to dirty another container). Stir in the dissolved cornstarch. MICROWAVE (high), uncovered, about 1 minute until sauce thickens. Pour sauce over mushrooms, gently mix together, then spoon over fish.

TIP: *Note that the mushrooms and brandy are cooked first. This gives the mushrooms time to soften and to absorb flavor from the brandy, and it also lets the alcohol from the brandy burn off so that the sauce doesn't taste rough.*

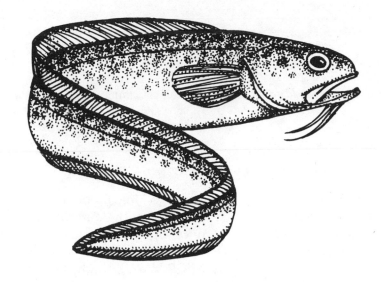

KINGCLIP

Relatively new on the market, kingclip is a mild-tasting fish caught in ocean waters near New Zealand and the southern coasts of Australia and South America.

You're not likely to see the whole fish for sale, but it is an odd-looking fish, somewhat eel-shaped with a long, tapering tail. The shape explains the thick, tapered fillets that you will see at the market.

Kingclip fillets are very white with a bland flavor and dense texture. It doesn't flake like cod, but it is not as dense as monkfish. It is more like oreo dory, which makes a good substitute.

Because its texture is naturally firm, take special care not to overcook kingclip, or the fish will become quite chewy.

✒ KINGCLIP WITH DIJON MUSTARD

Zesty mustard and chives add taste without fat to this simple fish dish.

Preparation time: 5 minutes
Microwave time: 4–5 minutes
Servings: 4

1 pound kingclip fillets
1 tablespoon fresh lemon juice
1 tablespoon Dijon mustard
1 tablespoon chopped fresh chives

1. Arrange kingclip on a plate with thickest portions to the outside. Drizzle with lemon juice. Spread mustard on top of fish. Sprinkle with chives. Cover with plastic wrap, vented.
2. MICROWAVE (high) 4–5 minutes until thickest portion is opaque when tested with a fork. Let stand 3–5 minutes to finish cooking. Drain.

KINGCLIP SALAD WITH ROSEMARY VINAIGRETTE

Mild-tasting kingclip benefits from the assertive aroma of fresh rosemary in this simple fish-and-tomato salad.

Preparation time: 15 minutes
Microwave time: 4–5 minutes
Servings: 4

SALAD
1 pound kingclip fillets
1 tablespoon fresh lemon juice
3 ripe tomatoes
1 head Bibb lettuce

ROSEMARY VINAIGRETTE
1 teaspoon minced shallot
¼ cup olive oil
2 tablespoons red wine vinegar
2 teaspoons chopped fresh rosemary *or* **½ teaspoon dried**
½ teaspoon Dijon mustard
⅛ teaspoon salt
Dash freshly ground black pepper

1. Arrange kingclip on a plate with thickest portions to the outside. Drizzle with lemon juice. Cover with plastic wrap, vented. MICROWAVE (high) 4–5 minutes until thickest portion is opaque when tested with a fork. Let stand 3–5 minutes to finish cooking. Drain. Let cool slightly. Cut into 1-inch chunks.
2. Wash and dry lettuce. Arrange leaves on serving plates. Wash tomatoes, and cut into ½-inch slices. Arrange on top of lettuce. Arrange kingclip on top of tomatoes.
3. To make vinaigrette, whisk all remaining ingredients in a small bowl. Drizzle over salad.

CURRIED KINGCLIP AND RICE

Curry- and cumin-spiced onions add an Indian flavor and attractive yellow color to both the kingclip and the rice.

Preparation time: 10 minutes
Microwave time: 24–30 minutes
Servings: 4

1 **cup chopped onion**	
1 **tablespoon butter**	
1 **tablespoon curry powder**	
1½ **teaspoons cumin seeds**	
1 **pound kingclip fillets**	
2 **cups chicken broth**	
1 **cup long-grained white rice, uncooked**	
2 **tablespoons minced fresh cilantro**	

1. Put onion and butter in 2½-quart casserole. Cover. MICROWAVE (high) 3–4 minutes to soften onions. Stir in curry powder and cumin. Cover tightly. MICROWAVE (high) 1–2 minutes to soften seeds.
2. Arrange kingclip on a dinner plate with thickest portions to the outside. Spread ⅓ of the onion mixture on top of fish. Set aside.
3. Add chicken broth and rice to remaining onion mixture. Cover. MICROWAVE (high) 5–6 minutes until boiling, then MICROWAVE (medium) 11–13 minutes until most of liquid is absorbed and rice is tender. Let stand, covered, 5 minutes.
4. While rice is cooling, cover fish with plastic wrap, vented. MICROWAVE (high) 4–5 minutes until thickest portion is just opaque when tested with a fork. Let stand 3–5 minutes to finish cooking. Drain. Place fish on top of rice; sprinkle with cilantro.

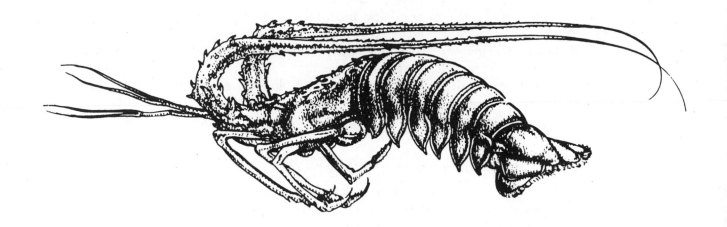

LOBSTER

Deep in the woods of coastal Maine, five convivial New Englanders—a nautical archaeologist, an oyster fisherman, an advertising writer, an ocean engineer, and a teacher—conspired on an unholy mission: find the way to cook live lobster in the microwave.

"Well, we had the first batch just plain on their backs," they reported by telephone to Chicago, "and it caused some, well, serious cleaning of the oven."

Thirty minutes later: "Okay, now we're doing headfirst into a shallow bowl, tail up over the side—they don't move much that way."

The phone didn't ring again for a while. Then, as the time between reports stretched out, the conversation switched to beer and the price of lobster at the local fisherman's co-op. The state of Maine, it seems, was not about to cast its vote for native whole lobster in the microwave.

And I don't vote for it either.

First of all, any time you eat whole lobster, you are faced with the psychology of killing it. The clear window of the microwave oven makes it difficult to pretend you don't know what's going on. Then, a whole lobster doesn't cook evenly; the claws are hard and dried out before the tail is done. And the final blow: cooking in the microwave ruins the tomalley.

I truly love Maine lobster, from the claws (my favorite) to the green liver, or tomalley. Unfortunately, when a whole lobster is cooked in the microwave, the tomalley turns to liquid and runs out, adversely affecting the flavor of the tailmeat on its way. Save your big lobster pot, and boil or steam your lobsters the old-fashioned way.

Lobster tail is another story, however. And another animal. Lobster tails that you buy frozen at the grocery store are not from the American lobster (*Homarus americanus*), found off the shores of Maine and the rest of New England. They are from the spiny lobster (*Panulirus argus*), a relative from warmer parts of the ocean around Florida, the Caribbean, and South America, and a very similar species around Africa, the Mediterranean, and Australia.

Spiny lobster have no substantial claws, but they do have a huge and meaty tail that is very similar to that of American lobster but has a coarser texture. Spiny lobster tails can be microwaved successfully, but they need to be defrosted first for best results.

LOBSTER TAIL BASICS

To defrost, put lobster tails on a roasting rack or inverted plate so that the lobster does not sit in water from melted ice as it defrosts. Arrange with thickest part of tails to outside. If there is a layer of thin paper frozen to the tail, just let it be; it will be easy to remove as the lobster defrosts.

Use your defrost cycle or low power to microwave the tail for about 6 minutes per pound, turning over once. Let stand 5 minutes after turning and before resuming defrosting, especially if the end of the tail starts to feel warm. Stop defrosting when you can bend all segments of the tail; ice crystals will still be on parts of the tail. Let stand 15–20 minutes to finish defrosting.

Use kitchen scissors to cut through the center of the backside; this makes the meat easier to remove and allows you to see when the meat is done cooking. Drizzle with lemon juice, if desired. Arrange on a plate with end of tail curled under and pointing to center of plate. Cover with plastic wrap, vented.

Cook lobster tails on medium power. They come out more tender and juicy than on high power. Lobster is done when meat is almost opaque. Let lobster tails stand, covered, 5 minutes to finish cooking.

Timing Guidelines:
- 1 12–14-ounce lobster tail: (medium power) 6–8 minutes
- 2 12–14-ounce lobster tails: (medium power) 12–14 minutes

⌒♥ ORIENTAL LOBSTER TAILS

This recipe adds extra flavor but no extra fat to lobster tails. Serve with lemon wedges.

Preparation time: 10 minutes
Microwave time: 13–15 minutes
Servings: 2–4

1 teaspoon minced fresh ginger
1 teaspoon minced garlic
2 tablespoons white wine
vinegar
2 tablespoons soy sauce
2 tablespoons fresh lemon juice
2 12–14-ounce lobster tails
Lemon wedges

1. Put ginger, garlic, vinegar, soy sauce, and lemon juice in 1-cup measure. MICROWAVE (high), uncovered, 30 seconds to 1 minute to heat.

2. Use kitchen scissors to cut through the center of each lobster tail's backside. Drizzle with ginger mixture. Arrange on a plate with ends of tails curled under and pointing to center of plate. Cover with plastic wrap, vented. MICROWAVE (medium) 12–14 minutes until meat is almost opaque when tested with a fork. Let lobster tails stand, covered, 5 minutes to finish cooking. Serve with lemon wedges.

LOBSTER TAILS WITH CLARIFIED BUTTER

This is the classic way to eat lobster: dipped in clarified butter. To clarify the butter, you melt it, then skim or strain it to remove the foamy white milk solids.

Preparation time: 10 minutes
Microwave time: 14–17 minutes
Servings: 2–4

2 12–14-ounce lobster tails
2 tablespoons fresh lemon juice
½ pound (2 sticks) butter
Lemon wedges

1. Use kitchen scissors to cut through the center of each lobster tail's backside. Drizzle with lemon juice. Arrange on a plate with ends of tails curled under and pointing to center of plate. Cover with plastic wrap, vented. MICROWAVE (medium) 12–14 minutes until meat is almost opaque when tested with a fork. Let lobster tails stand, covered, 5 minutes to finish cooking.
2. Put butter in 2-cup measure. MICROWAVE (high), uncovered, 2–3 minutes to melt. Line a sieve with cheesecloth, and pour the butter through the cheesecloth and into another container. Repeat if necessary to rid butter of its white, foamy milk solids. Serve lobster tails with a small cup of clarified butter for dipping, and lemon wedges.

TIP: Instead of using cheesecloth, you can use a large spoon to skim off and discard most of the foamy, white solids. Let the butter stand for 3 minutes on the counter to allow the rest of the milk solids to settle to the bottom. Skim or carefully pour the clear, or clarified, butter into a container. Discard the remaining white solids. Clarified butter looks neater than melted butter and can be heated to a higher temperature without burning.

TIP: Clarified butter can be stored in the refrigerator for several months.

LOBSTER TAIL MOUSSELINE

Lobster tails are cooked, then the meat is removed and served with mousseline sauce, which is a hollandaise sauce with whipped cream. The very rich sauce is a dietitian's nightmare—and absolutely delicious. Use it only if you promise to give up premium ice cream for a month!

Preparation time: 15 minutes
Microwave time: 13–15 minutes
Servings: 2–4

  2 **12- to 14-ounce lobster tails**
3½ **tablespoons fresh lemon juice**
  ½ **cup (1 stick) unsalted butter**
  3 **large egg yolks**
  ½ **cup whipped cream**

1. Use kitchen scissors to cut through the center of each lobster tail's backside. Drizzle with 2 tablespoons of the lemon juice. Arrange on a plate with ends of tails curled under and pointing to center of plate. Cover with plastic wrap, vented. MICROWAVE (medium) 12–14 minutes until meat is almost opaque when tested with a fork. Let lobster tails stand, covered, 5 minutes to finish cooking. When cool enough to handle, remove meat from tails. Cut into 1-inch slices.

2. Put butter in 4-cup measure. MICROWAVE (high) 20 seconds to soften but not melt. (Butter straight from the refrigerator may need up to a minute.)

3. In a small bowl, mix egg yolks and remaining 1½ tablespoons lemon juice. Add to butter. MICROWAVE (high) about 1 minute, whipping with whisk every 15 seconds. Sauce should be smooth and thick. Just before serving, gently fold whipped cream into sauce. Overlap lobster slices and spoon sauce down the center.

LOBSTER TAIL AND GRAPEFRUIT SALAD

Lobster and grapefruit have a natural affinity that is highlighted in this lobster-and-fruit salad with citrus dressing. It makes a beautiful summer luncheon plate.

Preparation time: 30 minutes
Microwave time: 12–14 minutes
Servings: 4

2 12- to 14-ounce lobster tails
2 tablespoons fresh lemon juice
2 pink grapefruit
1 medium cantaloupe
1 medium honeydew melon *or*
   ½ large
Curly red leaf lettuce
½ cup olive oil
1 teaspoon honey
2 teaspoons fresh lime juice
¼ teaspoon salt

1. Use kitchen scissors to cut through the center of each lobster tail's backside. Drizzle with lemon juice. Arrange on a plate with ends of tails curled under and pointing to center of plate. Cover with plastic wrap, vented. MICROWAVE (medium) 12–14 minutes until meat is almost opaque when tested with a fork. Let lobster tails stand, covered, 5 minutes to finish cooking. When cool enough to handle, remove meat from shells. Cover, and chill in the refrigerator for an hour.
2. Cut 1 grapefruit in half, and squeeze to obtain ¼ cup grapefruit juice for the dressing. Discard pulp and set aside juice.
3. Peel remaining grapefruit and separate into sections. Peel, seed, and cut cantaloupe and honeydew into half-moon slices. Cut chilled lobster tails into 1-inch slices. Line serving plates with lettuce, and arrange lobster and fruit on top.
4. To make dressing, whisk grapefruit juice, olive oil, honey, lime juice, and salt in 4-cup measure. Drizzle over salad.

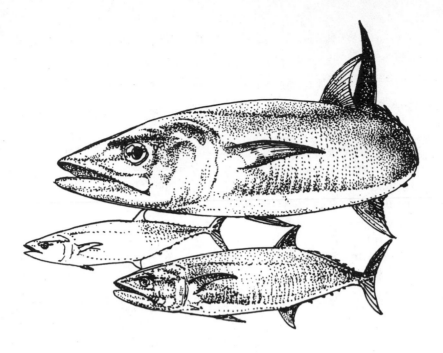

MACKEREL

Fresh mackerel is like fresh tuna: a deliciously oily, firm, darkish-fleshed fish that many people are reluctant to try for the first time—probably because it's oily, firm, and dark-colored. But once you try it, you'll open another wonderful world of dining pleasure.

That mackerel resembles tuna is no surprise because mackerel belongs to the Scombroidea family, which also includes the tunas.

Some of the more important varieties of mackerel are the Atlantic mackerel, king mackerel or kingfish, Spanish mackerel, and wahoo, known in Hawaii as *ono*, popular enough to merit its own chapter in this book.

In addition to being great-tasting, mackerel—such as a whole Atlantic mackerel—is a beautiful fish. The body of the iridescent blue-green fish is covered with a dark, almost snakelike print on its sleek back, and its streamlined, sporty-looking body flexes gracefully.

Mackerel is fatty compared to other fish, but the fat is polyunsaturated, high in Omega-3 fatty acids, which are believed to be beneficial in lowering blood cholesterol levels.

Mackerel is quite a bloody fish, so rinse it well before cooking. A whole, 1-pound mackerel makes a fine dinner for two or can be stretched to serve three if cut into 1-inch steaks.

MACKEREL ON TANGY NAPA

The assertive taste of mackerel works well with cabbage, especially if you add a little vinegar for extra tang. I like to use napa, or Chinese cabbage, for this dish. The cabbage cooks down to two neat portions. Two people can easily put away a 1-pound mackerel, but when cut into 1-inch steaks the mackerel can be stretched to serve three. For menu suggestions see page 23.

Preparation time: 5 minutes
Microwave time: 7–9 minutes
Servings: 2–3

**2 cups shredded cabbage,
   preferably napa**
1 tablespoon olive oil
1 tablespoon red wine vinegar
**1 1-pound mackerel, cut into
   1-inch steaks**
1 tablespoon fresh lemon juice

1. Mix cabbage, oil, and vinegar in 2½-quart flat casserole large enough to hold the mackerel. Cover. MICROWAVE (high) 3–4 minutes to soften cabbage.
2. Rinse fish well. Arrange steaks on top of cabbage; drizzle with lemon juice. Cover with plastic wrap, vented at one corner. MICROWAVE (high) 4–5 minutes until flesh nearest bones is almost opaque when tested with a fork. Let stand 2 minutes.

WHOLE MACKEREL WITH SPANISH OLIVE TOPPING

This thick, olive-rich topping can be made several days ahead and kept refrigerated. It pairs well with naturally oily mackerel.

Preparation time: 10 minutes
Microwave time: 10–13 minutes
Servings: 2

1 tablespoon olive oil
¼ cup minced onion
1 teaspoon minced garlic
2 tablespoons dry white wine
2 medium tomatoes, peeled, seeded, and chopped
¼ cup chopped, pitted green olives
Dash red pepper flakes
½ teaspoon capers
1 1-pound mackerel, whole, gutted, and cleaned
1 tablespoon lemon juice

1. To make the sauce, put olive oil, onion, and garlic in 4-cup measure. MICROWAVE (high), uncovered, 2–3 minutes to soften. Stir in wine, tomatoes, olives, and pepper. MICROWAVE (high), uncovered, 4–5 minutes to thicken, stirring twice. Stir in capers. Keep sauce warm.

2. Place mackerel in 2½-quart flat casserole. Drizzle with lemon juice. Wrap head and tail of fish loosely with foil wrap to prevent overcooking. Cover dish with plastic wrap, vented. MICROWAVE (high) 4–5 minutes until flesh closest to the bones is just opaque, turning fish over after 1½ minutes. Let stand, covered, 5 minutes. Drain and serve fish with topping.

TIP: When using foil in the microwave, keep foil smooth and at least 1 inch from the sides of the microwave.

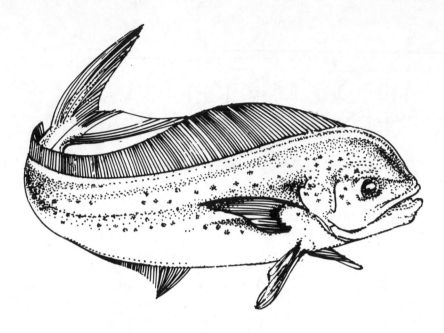

MAHIMAHI

Is mahimahi a dolphin? Yes—but no. Mahimahi is dolphin fish, a cold-blooded fish and member of the Coryphaena family, which swims at the bottom of the ocean. These fish are mistakenly linked to dolphin mammals such as Flipper, a bottle-nosed dolphin and member of the Delphinidae family.

With this issue behind you, you can prepare to enjoy one of the most popular tropical fish rightfully promoted by Hawaii. The beautiful, bright blue, green, and yellow fish is found in all tropical and subtropical seas, especially along the coasts of Hawaii and California, in the Gulf of Mexico, and in warm portions of the Atlantic.

A fairly large fish, generally from 5 to 40 pounds, mahimahi has firm flesh that is similar to fresh tuna but leaner. The firm texture makes mahimahi steaks easy to turn over while cooking without their breaking up.

There's romance to the name and image of Hawaii and mahimahi, so it's fun in the following recipes to pair mahimahi with a special rich béarnaise sauce or use it in an unusual, wild mushroom salad. Or, for a low-fat option, consider a tangy cucumber sauce.

⌒♥ MAHIMAHI WITH TANGY, LOW-FAT CUCUMBER SAUCE

Low-fat yogurt is the secret in this healthful cucumber sauce that marries well with tender mahimahi. Yogurt thins when heated, so serve the sauce at room temperature with just-cooked mahimahi, or store fish and sauce separately in the refrigerator and serve lightly chilled as a summer entree.

Preparation time: 10 minutes
Microwave time: 4–5 minutes
Servings: 4

½ **cup peeled, seeded, chopped cucumber**
½ **cup low-fat plain yogurt**
2 **tablespoons chopped fresh dill** *or* ½ **teaspoon dried**
2 **tablespoons chopped fresh parsley**
2 **green onions, white and first 2 inches of green, chopped**
1 **teaspoon grated lemon zest**
1 **pound mahimahi steaks**
1 **tablespoon fresh lemon juice**

1. Mix cucumber, yogurt, dill, parsley, onions, and lemon zest in a small bowl. Set aside.
2. Arrange mahimahi on a plate with thickest portions to the outside. Drizzle with lemon juice. Cover with plastic wrap, vented. MICROWAVE (high) 4–5 minutes until thickest portion is just opaque when tested with a fork, rearranging fish once. Let stand 5 minutes to finish cooking. Drain. Serve yogurt sauce on top of fish.

TIP: If the mahimahi steaks are quite thick, the fish may need an extra 1 or 2 minutes to cook. Check frequently—about every 20 seconds—to avoid overcooking.

TIP: Use any leftover sauce as a low-fat substitute for sour cream on baked potatoes.

MAHIMAHI WITH BEARNAISE

Tarragon-flavored béarnaise, classically served with beef tenderloin or steak, also works beautifully with firm-textured, juicy mahimahi. The sauce can be whipped up in the microwave in just 1 minute while the mahimahi stands to finish cooking.

Preparation time: 10 minutes
Microwave time: 5–6 minutes
Servings: 4

1 pound mahimahi steaks
2 tablespoons fresh lemon juice
½ cup (1 stick) unsalted butter
3 large egg yolks
2 tablespoons dry white wine
1 teaspoon minced shallots
2 tablespoons fresh tarragon *or*
1 teaspoon dried

1. Arrange mahimahi on a plate with thickest portions to the outside. Drizzle with 1 tablespoon lemon juice. Cover with plastic wrap, vented. MICROWAVE (high) 4–5 minutes until thickest portion is just opaque when tested with a fork, rearranging fish once. Let stand 5 minutes to finish cooking.
2. Put butter in 4-cup measure. MICROWAVE (high) 20 seconds to soften but not melt. (Butter straight from the refrigerator may need up to a minute.)
3. In a small bowl, mix remaining lemon juice, egg yolks, wine, shallots, and tarragon. Add to butter. MICROWAVE (high), uncovered, 1 minute, whipping with whisk every 15 seconds. Sauce is done when it is smooth and thick. Present fish with a tablespoon of béarnaise atop each serving and the rest of the sauce on the side.

TIP: If you make half the sauce, there will still be at least one tablespoon for each serving. Follow Steps 2 and 3, using 4 tablespoons butter, 1 egg yolk, 2 teaspoons fresh lemon juice, 1 tablespoon wine, ½ teaspoon minced shallots, and 2 teaspoons fresh tarragon or ¼ teaspoon dried. Cook in Step 3 for 40–50 seconds.

MAHIMAHI AND WILD MUSHROOM SALAD

Don't let the length of this recipe discourage you. The wild mushroom dressing can be made days ahead, and the mahimahi can be prepared up to one day ahead, then assembled with fresh salad ingredients for an elegant salad entree. Dried porcini mushrooms can be found in Italian or specialty food stores. Dried shiitake mushrooms, found in Oriental or specialty stores, may be substituted.

Preparation time: 30 minutes
Soaking time: 10 minutes
Microwave time: 8 minutes
Servings: 4

1 pound mahimahi steaks
1 tablespoon fresh lemon juice
4 tablespoons (½ ounce) dried porcini mushrooms
½ cup red wine vinegar
¼ cup diced sweet red pepper
1 small onion, sliced thin
½ cup olive oil, preferably extra virgin
1 tablespoon chopped fresh tarragon *or* ½ teaspoon dried
¼ teaspoon salt
⅛ teaspoon freshly ground black pepper
2 cups Bibb lettuce
1 cup lightly packed fresh watercress leaves and stems
1 cup thin strips Belgian endive
½ pound button mushrooms, sliced
4 ripe plum tomatoes, cubed

1. Arrange mahimahi on plate with thickest portions to the outside. Drizzle with lemon juice. Cover with plastic wrap, vented. MICROWAVE (high) 4–5 minutes until thickest portion is just opaque when tested with a fork, rearranging fish once. Let stand 5 minutes to finish cooking. Let fish cool slightly, then cut into 1½-inch cubes. (Fish may be made up to a day ahead and kept chilled in refrigerator.)

2. To make dressing, put dried mushrooms and vinegar in 1-cup measure. Cover with plastic wrap. MICROWAVE (high) about 1 minute to boiling. Let stand, covered, 10 minutes to soak.

3. Drain mushrooms through water-soaked cheesecloth or a coffee filter, reserving liquid. Rinse mushrooms briefly under cold water to remove grit. Trim and discard tough ends from mushrooms; chop mushrooms.

4. Put red pepper, onion, and olive oil in 4-cup measure. MICROWAVE (high) 1–2 minutes to soften. Add chopped mushrooms, reserved liquid, tarragon, salt, and pepper. Whisk well with fork. (Dressing can be made ahead and stored up to a week in the refrigerator.)

5. To assemble salad, arrange lettuce and watercress on serving plates. Top with mahimahi. Arrange Belgian endive, button mushrooms, and tomatoes on salads. Drizzle with wild mushroom dressing.

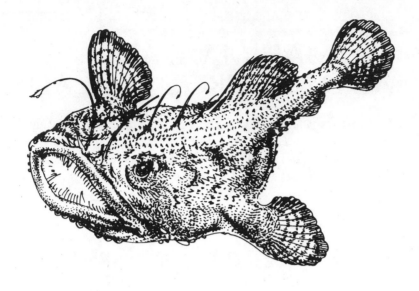

MONKFISH

Now here's a fish you don't want to judge by its cover. One of the most bizarre-looking fish that we eat, monkfish is also a culinary delight, a sweet, firm-textured fish that earns its title of "poor man's lobster."

Also known as angler, lotte, or goosefish, monkfish has a huge, wide head, tiny eyes, a wide mouth, and a wide, flat body ideal for skimming the bottom of the sea. When it wants to attract smaller fish, it erects or "angles" a small appendage on top of its head, and as the curious little fish venture near, the monkfish closes in on its prey.

Monkfish are caught along the Atlantic Coast, particularly in New England, and also in the Mediterranean. Usually the head is discarded, and the long, narrow tail is the only part marketed.

The texture of the monkfish is indeed somewhat similar to that of lobster—but to the firmer meat of an African lobster tail, not to that of succulent Maine lobster. The slightly similar taste comes from the monkfish's vast and upscale diet which includes flounder, ducks, crabs—and lobster.

Monkfish tail has a second skin or membrane which should be trimmed before cooking for better texture. The tail is thick and dense and tends to curl up when cooked. For this reason, I prefer to cut it into medallions, so that it cooks more evenly.

⌒♥ GARLIC-RUBBED MONKFISH

A dense fish like monkfish cooks more evenly if you first cut it into medallions. You could jazz up this dish with more garlic, but one clove gives a pleasant, subtle flavor to this no-added-fat version.

Preparation time: 10 minutes
Microwave time: 3½–4½ minutes
Servings: 4

1 pound monkfish fillets, skinned and cut into four 1-inch-thick medallions
1 tablespoon fresh lemon juice
1 large clove garlic, peeled, cut in half
4 lemon wedges

1. Arrange monkfish along outside of a plate. Drizzle with lemon juice. Rub fish with cut ends of garlic, then place garlic in middle of dish. Cover with plastic wrap, vented at one corner.
2. MICROWAVE (high) 3½–4½ minutes until thickest portion is almost opaque when tested with a fork. Let stand 5 minutes to finish cooking. Drain. Serve with lemon wedges.

POOR MAN'S LOBSTER

Why not? This is the nickname bestowed upon monkfish, which indeed does resemble the dense, meaty texture of an African lobster tail. Save the expense of lobster by cooking up some monkfish and serving it with great ceremony like lobster, with clarified butter and lemon wedges.

Preparation time: 10 minutes
Microwave time: 4½–6½ minutes
Servings: 4

1 pound monkfish fillets, skinned and cut into four 1-inch-thick medallions
1 tablespoon fresh lemon juice
½ cup (1 stick) butter
4 lemon wedges

1. Arrange monkfish along the outside of a plate. Drizzle with lemon juice. Cover with plastic wrap, vented at one corner. MICROWAVE (high) 3½–4½ minutes until thickest portion is almost opaque when tested with a fork. Let stand 5 minutes to finish cooking. Drain.
2. Put butter in 2-cup measure. MICROWAVE (high), uncovered, 1–2 minutes to melt. Line a sieve with cheesecloth and pour butter through the cheesecloth and into a container. Repeat if necessary to rid butter of its white, foamy, milk solids. Serve fish with lemon wedges and small bowls of clarified butter for dipping.

TIP: Instead of using cheesecloth, you can use a large spoon to skim off and discard most of the foamy, white solids. Let the butter stand for 3 minutes on the counter to allow the rest of the milk solids to settle to the bottom. Skim or carefully pour the clear, or clarified, butter into a container. Discard the remaining white solids. Clarified butter looks neater than melted butter and can be heated to a higher temperature without burning.

TIP: Store unused clarified butter in the refrigerator for several months.

MONK CAESAR SALAD

A warm anchovy dressing drizzled over romaine lettuce and chunks of cooked monkfish makes an unusual appetizer or luncheon entree.

Preparation time: 15 minutes
Microwave time: 4½–6 minutes
Servings: 4–6

1 **pound monkfish fillets, skinned and cut into four 1-inch-thick medallions**
3 **tablespoons fresh lemon juice**
3 **anchovy fillets, chopped coarse**
1 **teaspoon minced garlic**
⅛ **teaspoon salt**
⅛ **teaspoon freshly ground black pepper**
4 **tablespoons olive oil**
2 **tablespoons minced parsley**
1 **head romaine lettuce, torn into 2-inch pieces**
1 **cup fresh croutons (*see* Tip)**

1. Arrange monkfish along outside of a plate. Drizzle with 1 tablespoon lemon juice. Cover with plastic wrap, vented at one corner. MICROWAVE (high) 3½–4½ minutes until thickest portion is almost opaque when tested with a fork. Let stand 5 minutes to finish cooking. Drain. Cut into bite-sized pieces.
2. To make the dressing, put anchovies and garlic in 2-cup measure. Use fork to mash. (Mixture will be lumpy but will smooth out after it has cooked.) Stir in remaining lemon juice, salt, and pepper. MICROWAVE (high) 1–1½ minutes. Whisk in oil and parsley until smooth. To serve, toss lettuce, fish, croutons, and dressing.

TIP: *To make croutons, put 2 tablespoons butter in 8″ × 8″ × 2″ dish. MICROWAVE (high), uncovered, 30 seconds to melt. Stir in 2 tablespoons snipped parsley. Mix in 2 cups of ½-inch-cubed French bread. MICROWAVE (high), uncovered, 3–5 minutes, stirring every minute. Let cool.*

BLACK MONK SOUP

Black beans, beef broth, and red wine provide a deep-colored backdrop for chunks of tender, white monkfish. Serve with crusty bread and a light red wine.

Preparation time: 20 minutes
Microwave time: 18–22 minutes
Servings: 4

1 cup diced green pepper
¼ cup chopped onion
1 teaspoon minced garlic
1 tablespoon olive oil
1 tablespoon butter
2 tablespoons flour
2 cups beef stock or broth
1 can (15 ounces) black beans, drained
2 medium tomatoes, peeled, seeded, and diced
2 tablespoons dry red wine
¼ teaspoon salt
⅛ teaspoon freshly ground black pepper
⅛ teaspoon cayenne pepper
1 ¾-pound monkfish fillet, skinned and cubed
2 tablespoons minced fresh cilantro

1. Put green pepper, onion, garlic, olive oil, and butter in 2½-quart casserole. Cover. MICROWAVE (high) 4–5 minutes until vegetables are tender. Blend in flour.
2. Puree beef broth and half the beans in food processor or blender, and add to vegetable mixture. Stir in tomatoes, wine, salt, pepper, and cayenne. MICROWAVE (high), uncovered, 10–12 minutes until soup thickens.
3. Stir in monkfish and remaining black beans. Cover. MICROWAVE (high) 4–5 minutes until center of fish cubes are opaque. Serve topped with cilantro.

MONKFISH WITH NAPA-WALNUT ROLLS

Tender napa cabbage cooks quicker than standard green cabbage, so it is ideal to team it with quick-cooking fish. Plan on two cabbage rolls per person. Serve with rice.

Preparation time: 20 minutes
Microwave time: 11–15 minutes
Servings: 4

8 large napa leaves
¼ cup minced onions
2 tablespoons butter
½ cup chopped walnuts
1 tablespoon fresh thyme *or* **½ teaspoon dried**
½ teaspoon salt
⅛ teaspoon freshly ground black pepper
1 pound monkfish fillet, skinned and cut into eight ½-inch by 3-inch strips
1 tablespoon fresh lemon juice
1 cup chicken stock or broth
1 teaspoon cornstarch dissolved in 1 tablespoon water

1. Cut out firm white base of napa and save for another use. Put leaves on a plate. Cover with plastic wrap, vented. MICROWAVE (high) 30 seconds to 1 minute to soften slightly. Let stand, covered, 1 minute.
2. Put onions and butter in 4-cup measure. MICROWAVE (high), uncovered, 2–3 minutes to soften onions. Stir in walnuts, thyme, salt, and pepper.
3. Put a monkfish piece in center of each napa leaf. Drizzle with lemon juice. Top with a tablespoon of the onion-walnut mixture. Roll, starting at the thicker end and tucking in sides. Fasten with a toothpick. Arrange rolls in 2-quart flat casserole with the largest rolls to the outside. Pour chicken broth over rolls. Cover with plastic wrap, vented.
4. MICROWAVE (high) 7–9 minutes until fish is almost opaque. Let stand, covered, 3 minutes.
5. Use a slotted spoon to lift rolls onto a serving platter, reserving cooking broth. Stir cornstarch mixture into cooking broth. MICROWAVE (high), uncovered, 2–3 minutes until broth thickens. Pour over cabbage rolls.

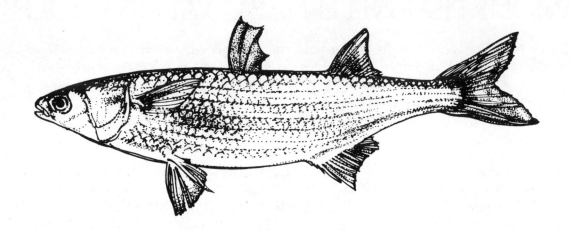

MULLET

If you've eaten mullet and didn't like it because it was too muddy-tasting, you probably didn't have real mullet.

One of the charms—and frustrations—of selecting fresh fish is the colorful names given to different species—and sometimes the same species. Unfortunately for mullet, the name generally is used to refer to almost any manner of sucker fishes that indeed can be muddy-tasting depending on the waters.

Real mullet is nutty-tasting, not muddy. It is fat, not lean, and firm-flaked. There are more than 100 species of mullet, but the most important commercial species are the striped mullet and the silver mullet, a large-eyed, small-mouth fish with iridescent silver sides and white belly.

Firm-fleshed mullet hold up well to smoking, and hickory-smoked mullet are a roadside attraction in several states along the Gulf of Mexico. The fish also tastes good with the strong flavors of mustard or garlic and tomato, as in the following recipes.

⌣♥ MULLET WITH MUSTARD

A little mustard, lemon juice, and black pepper are all you need to dress up simple mullet fillets.

Preparation time: 5 minutes
Microwave time: 4–5 minutes
Servings: 4

1 **pound mullet fillets**
1 **tablespoon fresh lemon juice**
2 **teaspoons Dijon mustard**
¼ **teaspoon freshly ground black pepper**

Arrange mullet skin-side down on a plate with thickest portions to the outside. Drizzle with lemon juice. Spread mustard on top of fish. Sprinkle with pepper. Cover with plastic wrap, vented at one corner. MICROWAVE (high) 4–5 minutes until thickest portion is opaque when pulled apart gently with fork. Let stand 3–5 minutes to finish cooking, then drain.

MULLET WITH GARLIC-TOMATO TOPPING

Because the fish cooks so quickly, this chunky topping is made ahead and kept warm until the fish is ready.

Preparation time: 10 minutes
Microwave time: 10–13 minutes
Servings: 2

1 tablespoon olive oil
2 teaspoons minced garlic
¼ cup minced onion
2 tablespoons dry white wine
2 medium tomatoes, peeled,
  seeded, and chopped
⅛ teaspoon salt
Dash freshly ground black
  pepper
Dash red pepper flakes
1 1-pound mullet, whole, gutted
  and cleaned
1 tablespoon fresh lemon juice

1. To make the topping, put olive oil, garlic, and onion in 4-cup measure. MICROWAVE (high) 2–3 minutes to soften. Stir in wine, tomatoes, salt, black pepper, and red pepper. MICROWAVE (high), uncovered, 4–5 minutes to thicken, stirring twice. Keep sauce warm.

2. Put mullet in 2½-quart flat casserole. Drizzle with lemon juice. Wrap head and tail of fish loosely with foil to prevent overcooking, keeping foil smooth and at least 1 inch from the sides of the microwave. Cover dish with plastic wrap, vented. MICROWAVE (high) 4–5 minutes until flesh closest to the bone is just opaque, turning fish over after 1½ minutes. Let stand, covered, 5 minutes. Top fish with garlic-tomato mixture.

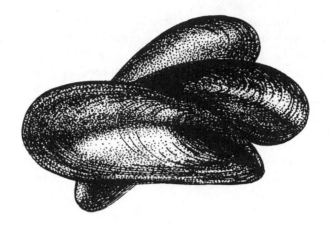

MUSSELS

Long appreciated by Europeans, blue-black mussels only recently have begun to be relished by American cooks. And the discovery is a double pleasure. The plump, pink-orange meat of the mussels is particularly sweet—easier to like for the first time than steamers or hard-shelled clams. Because there is not a large demand for mussels, prices are relatively low.

The bivalve mollusk grows abundantly in New England and eastern Canada in intertidal water, which is the area of water between low and high tide. To anchor itself during heavy waves, a mussel uses its byssus thread, a strong, rough thread that most people yank off before eating the mussels.

Mussel farming is a growing industry in France, Italy, Spain, Holland, and the United States where small mussels, or *spats*, are raised on large oak poles or ropes in shallow bottom waters. Whereas wild mussels tend to be quite sandy, farm-raised mussels are less sandy. They also tend to be more even-sized—a minor convenience in the microwave oven because the cooking time then is more even.

When buying mussels, select only those with shells that are tightly closed when tapped and, when tapped, have a solid, not hollow, sound.

MUSSELS BASICS
Before cooking, scrub the mussels and pull off the stringy beards.

To remove much of the sand, swish mussels in a shallow pan of cold water and lift out of the water. Some sand inevitably remains. Discard any mussels that have opened or cracked shells.

Cook mussels on a plate deep enough to hold the cooking juices; a dozen mussels gives off about ½ cup of natural juices.

For a dozen or fewer mussels, arrange them along the outside of the plate, overlapping if necessary, with hinged sides to the outside. For a dozen or more mussels, use a large casserole, and stir or rotate them carefully. No added liquid is needed, although a little wine or other liquid may be added as flavoring. Cover the plate tightly with plastic wrap. Cook on high power.

Remove mussels just as they open wide, even if this means pulling them out one or two at a time. (Take care: the shells will be hot.) Tender steamed mussels get tough if cooked even 10 seconds too long.

Remaining juices are very flavorful and may be used as a broth or in sauces for the mussels. However, skim the juices, using only the clear broth. Discard the remaining gritty juices.

Timing Guidelines
- ½ pound (12 mussels): 2–3 minutes
- 1 pound (24 mussels): 3–3½ minutes

❤ MUSSELS STEAMED WITH WINE AND HERBS

Mussels get a flavor boost from a little wine and herbs. Serve the mussels in a wide bowl to handle extra juices and with an extra plate for discarded shells.

Preparation time: 10 minutes
Microwave time: 5–7 minutes
Servings: 2–3

1 pound fresh mussels in the shell
¼ cup dry white wine
1 bay leaf, crushed
1 tablespoon fresh tarragon *or* ½ teaspoon dried

1. See Mussels Basics in this chapter for instructions on how to prepare and remove sand from mussels.
2. Put wine, bay leaf, and tarragon in 3-quart casserole. Cover tightly. MICROWAVE (high) 2–3 minutes to soften. Stir in mussels. Cover. MICROWAVE (high) 3–4 minutes until liquid boils and clams open slightly. Remove mussels just as they open wide, even if this means pulling them out one or two at a time. (Take care: the shells will be hot.) Do not overcook. Drain.

MUSSELS WITH FRESH TOMATO SAUCE

Most of the time needed in this recipe is to make a batch of fresh, homemade tomato sauce. You can do that part ahead and simply reheat the sauce. The mussels take a mere 3–4 minutes to cook. Note that the mussels are drained before you add the sauce—this avoids grittiness from the mussels' cooking liquid.

Preparation time: 20 minutes
Microwave time: 20–25 minutes
Servings: 2–3

2 pounds fresh mussels in the shell
1 tablespoon olive oil
1 tablespoon minced garlic
2 pounds fresh tomatoes, peeled, seeded, and chopped coarse
2 teaspoons fresh oregano *or* **½ teaspoon dried**
½ teaspoon salt
⅛ teaspoon freshly ground black pepper
¼ teaspoon cayenne pepper
2 tablespoons minced fresh parsley

1. See Mussels Basics in this chapter for instructions on how to prepare and remove sand from mussels.
2. Meanwhile, put olive oil and garlic in 3-quart casserole. MICROWAVE (high), uncovered, 2–3 minutes to soften but not brown garlic. Stir in tomatoes, oregano, salt, pepper, and cayenne. MICROWAVE (high), uncovered, 15–18 minutes until sauce thickens, stirring every 5 minutes.
3. Put mussels in 3-quart casserole. Cover. MICROWAVE (high) 3–4 minutes until mussels open. Remove mussels just as they open wide, even if this means pulling them out one or two at a time. (Take care: the shells will be hot.) Do not overcook. Drain. Spoon the hot tomato sauce over the mussels and sprinkle with parsley.

OCTOPUS

Frankly, I was beginning to worry about this chapter after the first five or so octopuses—tough, rubbery specimens—were pathetically lifted from the microwave. But I've found the secret.

The secret is that you have to rely on old tricks to make octopus work in a modern microwave oven. The microwave will help decrease the cooking time, but you can't sidestep time-honored methods for first rendering the octopod tender.

The Japanese pound raw octopus into submission to make it tender enough for even sashimi. The Spanish twice dip raw octopus briefly into boiling water, letting it cool between dips. This relaxes the muscles and helps keep them tender.

I tried both techniques and found that the more important of the two is the pounding. After just three minutes under the receiving end of a heavy veal pounder, octopus is decidedly more tender. You can feel the difference when you squeeze the meat with your fingers before and after pounding.

It takes 1–3 hours to properly cook octopus by conventional methods. In the microwave, you can finish an octopus in 40 minutes, but on medium-low power. If you try to speed up the process with high power, the octopus will turn tough.

Like squid, octopus has a black ink that is used to confuse its enemies. Although the ink is edible—indeed, considered a delicacy—it is usually removed from the octopus that you purchase at the fish department. If you have a fresh, uncleaned octopus, use scissors or a knife to remove the eyes, the yellowish inner pouch, any membranes, and the ink sac, which is near the eyes.

Why all this bother? Because octopus is truly delicious—mild, nonfishy, meatlike, low-fat—and fun to serve. Even if you cut it up into bite-sized pieces, the telltale suction cups reveal its identity as one of the delicacies from the deep.

SIMMERED OCTOPUS

These are the basic ingredients used by the Greek Islands restaurants in Chicago in preparing a large, 6-pound octopus. By the restaurant's conventional, low-heat cooking techniques, the octopus needs 3 hours; here, we do a smaller, 1–2 pound octopus on medium-low power in 40 minutes. Larger octopuses, particularly those from Spain, are more tender and yield more meat, says George Koutsogiorgas, general manager of Greek Islands. However, the more commonly found, smaller octopuses work beautifully in the microwave.

Preparation time: 10 minutes
Microwave time: 40–50 minutes
Servings: 4

1 small whole octopus (1–2 pounds), cleaned
¼ cup vegetable oil
¼ cup wine or cider vinegar
1 rib celery, chopped
1 medium carrot, chopped
3 sprigs parsley
2 tablespoons orange juice

1. Spread octopus on a board or counter. Use a veal pounder or other heavy tool to pound and tenderize octopus for 3 minutes.
2. Put octopus and then the rest of the ingredients in 2½-quart casserole. Cover. MICROWAVE (medium-low) 40–50 minutes or until fork easily pierces octopus. Let stand, covered, 15 minutes.
3. Lift out octopus and cut into bite-sized pieces. Serve warm or cold, or use for other recipes.

TIP: The purplish skin of the cooked octopus is edible, and I leave it on. However, you may rub it off with your fingers while the cooked octopus is still warm.

TIP: Store cooked octopus in its cooking juices in the refrigerator for up to 3 days.

OCTOPUS AND CELERIAC SALAD

Celeriac, or celery root, which tastes a bit like celery with a tang, provides a crisp contrast to meatlike octopus.

Preparation time: 10 minutes
Microwave time: 6–8 minutes
Servings: 4

1 ¾-pound celeriac, peeled and
  julienned
¼ cup water
½ cup mayonnaise
2 tablespoons fresh lemon juice
1 1–2-pound octopus, precooked
  (see Simmered Octopus in
  this chapter) and cut into
  1-inch slices

1. Put celeriac and water in 1-quart casserole. Cover. MICROWAVE (high) 6–8 minutes until just tender. Let stand 2 minutes. Drain. Set on counter to cool.
2. Mix mayonnaise and lemon juice. Stir into celeriac, and add octopus. Serve immediately or refrigerate, covered, for an hour.

☙ OCTOPUS OVER GREEN RICE

Simmered octopus stars atop a plate of rice, mixed with fresh spinach and parsley.

Preparation time: 10 minutes
Microwave time: 21–29 minutes
Servings: 4

1 cup uncooked converted rice
2 cups chicken stock or broth
⅔ cup washed, stemmed,
  chopped spinach
⅓ cup chopped parsley
1 1–2-pound octopus, precooked
  (see Simmered Octopus in
  this chapter) and cut into
  bite-sized pieces

Put rice and stock in 2½-quart casserole. Stir. Cover. MICROWAVE (high) 5–7 minutes until boiling. Cover. MICROWAVE (medium) 15–20 minutes until rice is tender. Stir in spinach and parsley. Cover. MICROWAVE (high), uncovered, 1–2 minutes to warm greens. Put rice on a serving dish and arrange warm octopus on top.

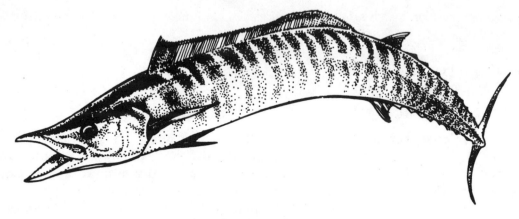

O N O

Ono, or *wahoo*, is one of the "new" Hawaiian fish found increasingly in larger fish stores. The fairly large fish, typically 25–30 pounds, is actually found around the world in tropical and subtropical waters but only recently has it been marketed here, primarily through Hawaii.

A member of the mackerel family, grey-blue ono is most typically sold in narrow steaks, a reflection of the fish's long, narrow shape. The steaks are very firm with a hard, thick skin that cuts away easily after cooking. The light-colored meat turns even lighter once cooked and is leaner and lighter-tasting than the Atlantic or king mackerel. Don't overcook this fish, or it will dry out fast.

❤ ONO WITH FRESH DILL AND MUSTARD

Mustard and dill add color as well as taste to this very fast dish that has no added fat.

Preparation time: 5 minutes
Microwave time: 4–5 minutes
Servings: 4

1 pound ono steaks
1 tablespoon fresh lemon juice
1 tablespoon smooth, Dijon mustard
1 tablespoon fresh dill *or* ½ **teaspoon dried**

1. Arrange ono on plate with thickest portions to the outside. Drizzle with lemon juice. Spread mustard on top of fish. Sprinkle with dill. Cover with plastic wrap, vented at one corner.
2. MICROWAVE (high) 4–5 minutes until thickest portion is opaque when pulled apart gently with fork, rotating fish once if necessary. Let stand 3–5 minutes to finish cooking. Drain.

⌇♥ SKEWERED ONO WITH RED PEPPER PUREE

Chunks of white ono on a bed of bright red bell-pepper puree is as dramatic as it is healthful. When the fish is cut into chunks, it needs less cooking time in the microwave: only 3 minutes per pound instead of the usual 4 minutes.

Preparation time: 10 minutes
Microwave time: 13–16 minutes
Servings: 4

2 red bell peppers
1 pound ono steaks
1 tablespoon fresh lemon juice

1. Stem, seed, and roughly chop red peppers; put in 2½-quart casserole. Cover. MICROWAVE (high) 10–12 minutes until very soft. Let stand until cool enough to handle. Put peppers and cooking juices through a food mill or in a food processor, and process until smooth. Keep puree warm.

2. Cut off and discard ono skin. Cut fish into 1-inch chunks. Toss with lemon juice. Space chunks on four wooden skewers so that pieces don't touch. Arrange skewers in the same direction on a dinner plate. Cover, vented, with plastic wrap. MICROWAVE (high) 3–4 minutes until centers of the chunks are almost opaque, rotating and turning the skewers every minute. Let stand 2 minutes. To serve, spoon pepper puree on individual plates and place a kabob on top.

TIP: The puree can be made the night before and stored, covered, in the refrigerator, to be reheated on medium power. The ono can be skewered hours before and stored, covered, in the refrigerator.

TIP: The food mill will remove the skin and make the puree smooth. The processor chops the skin as well, which makes the puree less smooth, but still quite nice for a quick sauce.

TIP: For a different effect, try making the puree with yellow bell peppers. By the way, those beautiful blue-black bell peppers cook up green.

ONO SALAD WITH MANGO CHUTNEY

This chutney is so versatile that I've given you a double recipe. Enjoy it warm one night with pork chops, then chilled for another meal with ono and vegetables in a salad entree.

Preparation time: 30 minutes
Microwave time: 11–15 minutes
Chilling time: 2 hours
Servings: 4

CHUTNEY
- 2 large ripe mangos
- ¼ cup minced onion
- 1 teaspoon minced garlic
- 2 teaspoons minced fresh ginger
- ½ cup lightly packed brown sugar
- 1 small tomato, peeled, seeded, and chopped fine
- ½ cup walnuts, chopped fine
- 1 teaspoon mustard seeds
- ½ teaspoon ground cinnamon
- ⅛ teaspoon ground cloves
- ⅛ teaspoon cayenne pepper
- 2 tablespoons fresh lime juice

SALAD
- 1 pound ono steaks
- 1 tablespoon fresh lemon juice
- 2 cups shredded romaine lettuce
- 1 small zucchini, sliced thin
- 1 medium carrot, cut on an angle into 2-inch-long, thin slices
- 2 green onions, white and first 2 inches of green, sliced

1. To make chutney, peel mangos, remove seeds, and finely chop remaining flesh. Mix with onion, garlic, ginger, brown sugar, tomato, walnuts, mustard seeds, cinnamon, cloves and cayenne in 3-quart casserole. Cover with waxed paper. MICROWAVE (high) 2–3 minutes until quite hot. Stir.

2. MICROWAVE (high), uncovered, 5–7 minutes, until fruit is soft. Stir in lime juice. Cover and chill in refrigerator at least two hours.

3. To make salad, arrange ono on a plate with thickest portions to the outside. Drizzle with lemon juice. Cover with plastic wrap, vented at one corner.

4. MICROWAVE (high) 4–5 minutes until thickest portion is opaque when pulled apart gently with fork, rotating fish once if necessary. Let stand 3–5 minutes to finish cooking. Drain. Cut off and discard skin; wrap fish and chill in refrigerator at least 1 hour.

5. Cut fish into bite-sized pieces. Arrange lettuce, zucchini, carrot, and ono on serving plates. Spoon ¼ cup of chutney on the salad and sprinkle with green onions. Serve any remaining chutney on the side or save for another meal.

O P A H

"How do they work the price on this fish? Charge by the odds?" asked Chicago cabbie John A. Van Kleef as we sped away (eight dollars for the round-trip) from the Chicago Fish House with the first catch of opah (eleven dollars a pound) to land in Chicago in ten days.

He was pretty close.

Opah is what is called an incidental catch. That is, the ocean fish travels alone rather than in packs or schools and shows up when fishermen are actually scouting other prey. Fishermen don't know when they're going to catch an opah, so the retail fish department doesn't know when it's going to get one. You place an order, play the odds—and pay the price.

Is opah worth this suspense?

"Ooooh, opah," starts Nancy Abrams, Chicago Fish House Marketing/Culinary Director, and Chairman of the National Fish and Seafood Promotional Council, and not a woman who gushes easily. "I think maybe I was an opah in a previous life."

"I love the color—a deep midnight blue then rose-red toward the belly—and its bright orange lips, little tiny lips that want to kiss you," she said. Tell us more.

"The flesh is firm and orange but cooks up to a beige," she said. "Treat it like swordfish, and you'll be home free."

We did just that, and now we understand the mystique of the opah. Opah is juicy and sweet, a fatty, rich, yet mellow-tasting fish.

Opah is common in the Hawaiian islands where it is called *moonfish*, most likely from its large, round shape. Old-time fishermen, who thought it was a lucky catch, would give it away as a gesture of goodwill.

142

Because opah is such an unusual treat for most people, I recommend cooking your first batch plain with just a touch of lemon and butter so that you can concentrate on the fish itself. The second time around, consider a luscious sauce, such as a hollandaise, or a warm raspberry vinaigrette. Opah fillets tend to be thick, so you may need an extra minute of cooking time.

OPAH WITH LEMON AND A TOUCH OF BUTTER

A touch of butter—literally a quick rub over the top of a just-cooked steak—is all you need with this wonderfully moist, sweet-tasting fish.

Preparation time: 1 minute
Microwave time: 4–5 minutes
Servings: 4

1 pound opah steaks
1 tablespoon fresh lemon juice
1 teaspoon butter

1. Arrange opah on a dinner plate with thickest portions to the outside. Drizzle with lemon juice. Cover with plastic wrap, vented.
2. MICROWAVE (high) 4–5 minutes until thickest portion turns from orange to a pale pink-beige and is almost opaque when tested with a fork, rearranging fish once. Let stand 5 minutes. Drain. Use a fork to stab a teaspoon of refrigerator-hard butter, and lightly run the butter over the top of the steaks to melt.

OPAH WITH WARM RASPBERRY VINAIGRETTE

A light raspberry vinaigrette, enhanced with a taste of honey and almonds, is drizzled over just-cooked opah steaks. For menu suggestions see page 24.

Preparation time: 5 minutes
Microwave time: 5–6 minutes
Servings: 4

1 pound opah steaks
1 tablespoon fresh lemon juice
2 tablespoons raspberry vinegar
1 tablespoon vegetable oil
1 teaspoon honey
¼ teaspoon almond extract

1. Arrange opah on a dinner plate with thickest portions to the outside. Drizzle with lemon juice. Cover with plastic wrap, vented. MICROWAVE (high) 4–5 minutes until thickest portion turns from orange to a pale pink-beige and is almost opaque when tested with a fork, rearranging fish once. Let stand 5 minutes. Drain.
2. Put rest of ingredients in 2-cup measure. Whisk. MICROWAVE (high) about 1 minute until hot. Whisk again. Drizzle over fish.

OPAH WITH HOMEMADE HOLLANDAISE

Rich hollandaise and extra-sweet opah are a very special combination.

Preparation time: 5 minutes
Microwave time: 5–6 minutes
Servings: 4

1 pound opah steaks
2½ tablespoons fresh lemon
    juice
½ cup (1 stick) unsalted butter
3 large egg yolks

1. Arrange opah on plate with thickest portions to the outside. Drizzle with 1 tablespoon lemon juice. Cover with plastic wrap, vented. MICROWAVE (high) 4–5 minutes until thickest portion is just opaque when tested with a fork, rearranging fish once. Let stand 5 minutes to finish cooking.
2. Put butter in 4-cup measure. MICROWAVE (high), uncovered, 20 seconds to soften but not melt. (Butter straight from the refrigerator may need up to a minute.)
3. In a small bowl, mix egg yolks and remaining lemon juice. Add to butter. MICROWAVE (high), uncovered, 1 minute, whipping with whisk every 15 seconds. Sauce is done when it is smooth and thick. Present fish with a tablespoon of hollandaise atop each serving and the rest of the sauce on the side.

TIP: The hollandaise may curdle if you cook it longer than 1 minute or forget to whisk. But it can be fixed. Put 2 tablespoons milk in 1-cup measure. MICROWAVE (high) 30 seconds to boil. Slowly whisk the milk into the curdled sauce until sauce is again smooth.

TIP: To make half the sauce, follow Steps 2 and 3, using 4 tablespoons butter, 1 egg yolk, and 2 teaspoons lemon juice. Cook in Step 3 for 40–50 seconds.

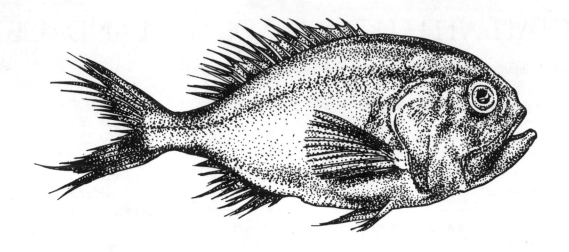

ORANGE ROUGHY

Orange roughy is the kiwi of the fish department, a very easy-to-like fish hardly known 10 years ago but now very popular on American tables. Like the kiwifruit, orange roughy hails from New Zealand, in this case from the very deep waters where commercial fishermen have expanded their livelihood. And like the brown, furry kiwi that hides a delicious, bright green flesh, the ugly orange roughy is more hospitable-tasting than it looks.

American shoppers snap up this fish for two main reasons: its sweet, very mild flavor, and its thick but flaky white fillets. When it was first introduced, orange roughy also was inexpensive, a kind of poor man's sole. But shoppers now have to seek newer fish to find such bargains.

Because orange roughy is such a popular family fish, I designed the first three recipes to be particularly easy on the palate as well as easy to make. The last recipe, an Indian-spiced version, is a bit more adventuresome—perhaps just what's needed to jolt attention at dinner time.

❤ ORANGE-ORANGE ROUGHY

A fresh orange and lemon flavor garnish the orange roughy fillets, and the natural juices are thickened with a little cornstarch. For menu suggestions see page 24.

Preparation time: 10 minutes
Marinating time: 10 minutes
Microwave time: 6–8 minutes
Servings: 4

1 orange
1 lemon
1 pound orange roughy fillets
¼ cup orange juice
**½ teaspoon cornstarch dissolved
   in 1 tablespoon water**
**2 tablespoons chopped pecans
   (optional)**

1. Finely grate zest from orange and lemon; reserve. Use paring knife to remove and discard remaining white peel from orange; cut orange horizontally into ¼-inch slices. Reserve.
2. Put orange roughy on a plate. Drizzle with the orange juice and with juice from one half of the lemon. Let fish stand on counter 10 minutes to marinate, turning once.
3. Arrange fish on plate with thickest portions to the outside and any thin ends turned under. Cover with plastic wrap, vented at one corner. MICROWAVE (high) 2 minutes.
4. Rearrange fish to put less-cooked portions to the outside. Arrange reserved orange slices on top. Cover with plastic, vented. MICROWAVE (high) 2–3 minutes until thickest portion is opaque when tested with a fork. Pour juices into 2-cup measure, and let fish stand on counter 5 minutes to finish cooking.
5. Meanwhile, stir cornstarch mixture into fish juices. Stir in reserved orange and lemon zest. MICROWAVE (high) 2–3 minutes until thick. Stir in pecans. Spoon a little sauce over the fish, serving the rest on the side.

ROUGHY-AND-RICE SOUP

Using sesame oil is the real trick in making this simple soup that can be whipped up with a little fish and kitchen staples. If you happen to have a cup of cooked rice in the refrigerator, you could just heat it up with the chicken broth and proceed to Step 2.

Preparation time: 5 minutes
Microwave time: 17–21 minutes
Servings: 4

¼ **cup uncooked white rice**
4 **cups chicken stock or broth**
½ **pound orange roughy, cut into**
½-inch chunks
1 **tablespoon fresh lemon juice**
¼ **teaspoon sesame oil**
1 **green onion, white and first 2**
inches of green, chopped

1. Put rice and chicken stock in 2½-quart casserole. Cover. MICROWAVE (high) 10–12 minutes to boiling. MICROWAVE (medium), covered, 5–6 minutes until rice is almost tender.
2. Add orange roughy. Cover. MICROWAVE (high) 2–3 minutes until fish almost flakes. Stir in lemon juice and sesame oil. Let stand 3 minutes to finish cooking. Serve garnished with chopped green onion.

ORANGE ROUGHY WITH WHITE WINE AND MUSHROOMS

This recipe is generous with mushrooms and stingy with the olive oil. You don't, of course, need the oil at all because the fish won't stick in the microwave, but the oil does add a nice flavor.

Preparation time: 10 minutes
Microwave time: 8–10 minutes
Servings: 4

½ **pound fresh mushrooms, cut into ¼-inch slices**
1 **tablespoon olive oil**
¼ **cup dry white wine**
¼ **teaspoon salt**
⅛ **teaspoon freshly ground black pepper**
1 **pound orange roughy fillets**

1. Put mushrooms, olive oil, wine, salt, and pepper in 2½-quart casserole. MICROWAVE (high), uncovered, 4–5 minutes until mushrooms are tender.

2. Arrange orange roughy on a plate with a lip (a 10-inch pie plate is good), with thickest parts to the outside and any thin ends tucked under. Pour mushroom mixture over fish. Cover with plastic wrap, vented. MICROWAVE (high) 4–5 minutes until thickest part of fish is almost opaque when tested with fork. Let stand 5 minutes to finish cooking. Spoon mushrooms over the fish.

INDIAN-SPICED ORANGE ROUGHY

This exotically flavored dish was inspired by Yamuna Devi, author of The Art of Indian Vegetarian Cooking. *As practiced in India, seeds, nuts, and spices are first crushed and then cooked in hot butter to develop flavor. Next, vegetables are added to simmer and absorb the wonderful juices. Here I have added orange roughy to give this mild-tasting fish an exciting presentation. Serve over a bed of rice.*

Preparation time: 15 minutes
Microwave time: 5–8 minutes
Servings: 4

1 **hot green chili, seeded** *or* ⅛ **teaspoon red pepper flakes**
1 **¾-inch slice fresh ginger, scraped, chopped rough**
¼ **cup cashews**
2 **teaspoons coriander seeds**
½ **teaspoon cumin seeds**
¼ **teaspoon fennel seeds**
¼ **cup water**
1 **tablespoon butter**
1 **medium tomato, peeled, seeded, and chopped**
½ **teaspoon turmeric**
½ **teaspoon salt**
1 **pound orange roughy fillets, cubed**
3 **tablespoons chopped fresh cilantro**

1. Combine chili, ginger, cashews, coriander seeds, cumin, fennel, and water in food processor or blender, and process until smooth.
2. Put butter in 2-quart casserole. MICROWAVE (high), uncovered, 1–2 minutes until melted and quite hot. Pour in spice puree. Do not cover. MICROWAVE (high) 1–2 minutes until puree thickens.
3. Stir in tomato, turmeric, salt, orange roughy, and 1½ tablespoons cilantro. Cover. MICROWAVE (high) 3–4 minutes until fish is almost ready to flake. Let stand 5 minutes. Serve fish and juices over rice; sprinkle with remaining cilantro.

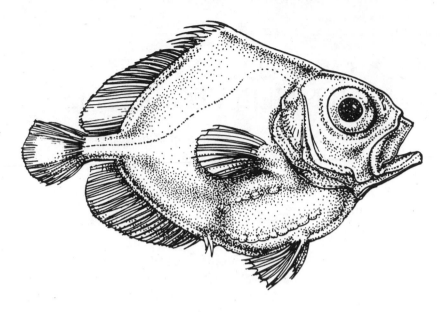

OREO DORY

A relatively new fish on the American market, oreo dory hails from the deep waters of New Zealand where it has been caught regularly only in recent years.

The white-fleshed fish has a mild flavor and medium to firm texture. It may be used as a substitute for orange roughy, another New Zealand fish. Before cooking, check for bones by running your finger down the center of the fillet.

Oreo dory doesn't flake as easily as most fish, so when testing for doneness look for an almost opaque look, not flakiness, as a guide.

❥ OREO DORY WITH JULIENNED VEGETABLES

Thin strips of yellow squash and zucchini cook just as quickly as the oreo dory and make an attractive—and healthful—addition to this no-added-fat entree.

Preparation time: 5 minutes
Microwave time: 4–5 minutes
Servings: 4

1 medium zucchini
1 medium yellow squash
1 pound oreo dory fillets
1 tablespoon fresh lemon juice
2 teaspoons fresh oregano *or* ½
teaspoon dried

1. Julienne vegetables. Arrange in center of a plate. Place oreo dory around vegetables, turning thin ends under or rolling fillets, if necessary. Drizzle fish and vegetables with lemon juice.
2. Cover with plastic wrap, vented. MICROWAVE (high) 4–5 minutes until thickest portion of fish is almost opaque when tested with a fork. Let stand 5 minutes to finish cooking. Drain. Sprinkle fish and vegetables with oregano.

OREO-SHRIMP SALAD

With some help from herbs and colorful shrimp and crab, mild-tasting oreo dory can be turned into a salad for stuffed tomatoes or sandwiches. To help reduce fat, yogurt replaces some of the mayonnaise.

Preparation time: 10 minutes
Microwave time: 2–3 minutes
Chilling time: 2 hours
Servings: 4

½ **pound oreo dory fillets**
1 **tablespoon fresh lemon juice**
1 **6-ounce package frozen shrimp and crab meat, defrosted**
1 **stalk celery, chopped fine**
⅓ **cup mayonnaise (reduced calorie, if desired)**
¼ **cup plain low-fat yogurt**
2 **tablespoons chopped fresh basil**
2 **tablespoons chopped fresh parsley**
2 **tablespoons chopped chives**

1. Arrange oreo dory on a plate, turning thin ends under, if necessary. Drizzle with lemon juice. Cover with plastic wrap, vented. MICROWAVE (high) 2–3 minutes until thickest portion is just opaque when tested with a fork. Let stand 2 minutes to finish cooking. Drain. Flake or chop.
2. Mix fish with rest of ingredients. Cover and chill in refrigerator for at least 2 hours. Mix again before serving.

OREO DORY WITH LEMON VELOUTE

There is an extra portion of this pretty, pale sauce to go with some accompanying yellow rice. Garnish with twists of lemon rind.

Preparation time: 10 minutes
Microwave time: 12–17 minutes
Servings: 4

2 tablespoons butter
2 tablespoons flour
1 cup chicken stock or broth
½ cup whipping cream
2 teaspoons grated lemon zest
2 tablespoons fresh lemon juice
¼ teaspoon salt
⅛ teaspoon freshly ground black
or white pepper
1 pound oreo dory fillets

1. Put butter in 4-cup measure. MICROWAVE (high), uncovered, 2–3 minutes until the butter melts and is very hot. Whisk in flour. MICROWAVE (high), uncovered, 2–3 minutes until the mixture bubbles furiously.
2. Whisk in broth and cream. MICROWAVE (high), uncovered, 2–3 minutes until bubbles that start at the edge of the sauce fill in and completely cover the top of the sauce. Thoroughly whisk.
3. MICROWAVE (High), uncovered, 2–3 minutes until sauce thickens enough to coat a spoon. Thoroughly whisk in lemon zest and 1 tablespoon lemon juice. Taste. Add salt and pepper. Keep sauce warm.
4. Arrange oreo dory on a dinner plate, turning thin ends under or rolling fillets, if necessary. Drizzle fish with remaining lemon juice. Cover with plastic wrap, vented. MICROWAVE (high) 4–5 minutes until thickest portion of fish is almost opaque when tested with a fork. Let stand 5 minutes to finish cooking. Drain. Drizzle sauce over fish.

TIP: For a lower-calorie version, omit cream and increase broth to 1½ cups. Add an extra 7–8 minutes of cooking time in the last step to reduce broth to a creamy texture. Be sure to taste before adding salt, because the reduction will intensify the saltiness of the broth.

OYSTERS

In the cold, quiet waters of the Damariscotta River in coastal Maine, occasional seals seem to be the only living creatures around. But deep in these salty waters, resting and feeding in specially designed nets, are literally thousands of tiny Belon oysters.

Flat, fanlike Belon oysters are a famous product of the French Brittany coast. But they also thrive in Maine. Oystermen like Gil Jaeger of Dodge Cove Maine Farm in Newcastle, Maine, purchase minuscule, hatchery-raised oyster seeds in the spring and lower them into the Damariscotta River to feed on plankton. After about three years, the oysters are harvested by divers and shipped around the country.

Elsewhere in the country, other varieties of oysters are favored with regional chauvinism, from the Wellfleet and Cotuit of Cape Cod to the tiny Olympias from the Pacific Northwest. They all share the fresh, briny taste—and stone-hard shells—that make oysters both a delight and challenge to eat.

If you've never developed the skill of opening fresh oysters, the microwave can help—but with some limitations. If you put a whole oyster in the microwave, the adductor muscle that holds the shells together will weaken and the shells will pop open. However, the oyster meat will be almost cooked. This is fine for hot dishes such as Oysters Stuffed with Mushrooms in this chapter, but not for eating oysters raw on the half shell. (Hard-shelled clams such as Littlenecks and Cherrystones open faster in the microwave, leaving the meat uncooked and suitable for eating raw.)

Oysters normally are purchased in the shell by the dozen or already shucked and in their own liquor by the pint and quart. If oysters have been shucked by your fish store, they must be eaten as soon as possible. Keep fresh whole oysters cold in the refrigerator or atop ice, but not in water.

The adage to eat oysters only in months that have *R*s has merit. The months without *R*s (May, June, July, and August) are the traditional summer spawning months when the oyster uses its stored glycogen to make eggs and sperm. The oysters are edible, but the excess, milky glycogen dulls the flavor of the oyster. Exceptions to the "R" rule are oysters from cold northern waters which spawn later and recover earlier than warmer weather ones.

OYSTER BASICS

Cook oysters on a plate deep enough to hold the cooking juices; a dozen oysters gives off about ⅓ cup of natural juices.

Arrange oysters on a deep plate or pie plate, overlapping if necessary, with hinged sides to the outside. Cover with plastic wrap, vented. No water is necessary because oysters give off natural juices as they cook. The steam from heating these juices causes the muscle on the hinged portion to weaken and the oysters to open.

When steaming, keep a steady eye on the plate of oysters, and remove oysters one at a time, just as they open. Do not wait for them to open wide—just enough to slip in a sturdy knife to finish the job is all you want. (If you let them all cook until the last one is opened, the first to open will be quite overcooked and tough.)

Timing Guidelines:
- 6 oysters: 2–3 minutes
- 12 oysters: 3–4 minutes

OYSTER BROTH

Homemade oyster broth is an extra bonus that comes when you cook fresh oysters. Follow the cooking instructions and time guidelines in Oyster Basics in this chapter to cook the oysters. A dozen oysters yield ⅓ cup oyster broth.

⌒❤ OYSTERS STEAMED WITH WINE AND THYME

If you remove the oysters from the microwave before they cook too long, they will be tender and have just a touch of extra flavor from the wine and thyme.

Preparation time: 5 minutes
Microwave time: 3–4 minutes
Servings: 2

12 fresh oysters in the shell
1 tablespoon dry white wine
1 teaspoon fresh thyme *or* **¼ teaspoon dried**

1. Arrange oysters with hinges to the outside on a deep dinner plate or pie plate. Add wine and thyme. Cover with plastic wrap, vented. MICROWAVE (high) 3–4 minutes, removing oysters as they open just wide enough to slip in a knife, even if this means pulling them out one or two at a time. (Take care: the shells will be hot.)
2. Use a knife to finish opening oysters. Loosen oyster meat and return to the deeper of the two shell halves to serve. Spoon in a little broth.

OYSTER AND ARTICHOKE SOUP

This smooth soup uses kitchen staples plus a pint of fresh half-and-half. Instead of canned oysters, you could substitute a dozen freshly shucked oysters.

Preparation time: 10 minutes
Microwave time: 17 minutes
Servings: 4

1 **5-ounce can oysters with juices**
1⅓ **cups chicken broth**
1 **tablespoon butter**
1 **tablespoon flour**
¼ **teaspoon dried thyme**
½ **teaspoon salt**
⅛ **teaspoon freshly ground black pepper**
1 **10-ounce package frozen artichoke hearts, defrosted and drained**
2 **cups half-and-half**
1 **green onion, white part and first 2 inches of green, sliced**

1. Drain oyster juice into 2-cup measure. Add enough chicken broth to make 1½ cups liquid. Reserve liquid and oysters.
2. Put butter in 2½-quart casserole. MICROWAVE (high), uncovered, 15–30 seconds to melt. Blend in flour until smooth. Whisk in thyme, salt, pepper, and the oyster-chicken liquid.
3. Cover. MICROWAVE (high) 4–5 minutes until it boils, whisking twice. Stir in artichokes. Cover. MICROWAVE (high) 4–5 minutes.
4. Stir in half-and-half and oysters. Cover. MICROWAVE (medium-high) 4–6 minutes to heat thoroughly. Serve sprinkled with green onion.

OYSTERS STUFFED WITH MUSHROOMS

Use your microwave to open oysters, then fill them with a mushroom-cheese mixture that is put under the broiler briefly to brown.

Preparation time: 15 minutes
Microwave time: 6–8 minutes
Broiler time: 2–3 minutes
Servings: 3–4

½ **pound chopped fresh mushrooms**
1 **tablespoon butter**
1 **tablespoon minced shallots**
2 **tablespoons fresh lemon juice**
1 **tablespoon chopped fresh parsley**
¼ **cup freshly grated Parmesan**
12 **oysters in the shell**

1. Put mushrooms, butter, and shallots in 4-cup measure. Do not cover. MICROWAVE (high) 3–4 minutes until very tender, stirring once. Stir in lemon juice, parsley, and half the Parmesan. Set aside.

2. Arrange oysters with hinges to the outside on a deep dinner plate or pie plate. Cover with plastic wrap, vented. MICROWAVE (high) 3–4 minutes, removing oysters when they open just wide enough to slip in a knife, even if this means pulling them out one or two at a time. (Take care: the shells will be hot.)

3. Use knife to finish opening oysters. Loosen oyster meat and return to the deeper of the two shell halves. Spoon mushroom mixture with juices onto the oysters. Sprinkle with remaining Parmesan. Put under the broiler, and broil until cheese melts, 2–3 minutes.

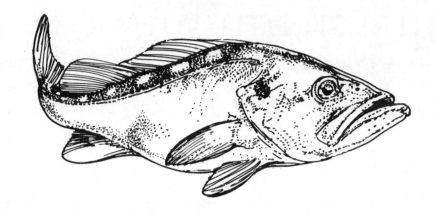

PACIFIC ROCKFISH

This low-fat saltwater fish is very popular on the West Coast, where it often is erroneously labeled red snapper. Indeed, if you look at just the skinned fillets, thick Pacific rockfish fillets look similar to red snapper. However, when cooked, Pacific rockfish has a softer texture and milder flavor.

To complicate matters, Pacific rockfish—of which there are more than 50 species—is sold under names such as rock cod, rosefish, Pacific Ocean perch, and black sea bass. And in a kind of reverse discrimination, in parts of the South *rockfish* is the name given to striped bass.

If you have a choice, select a whole rockfish that is more round than elongated. These species tend to have firmer and better-tasting flesh. Good Chinese restaurants, particularly on the West Coast, favor these Pacific rockfish to steam or serve whole and fried. In the following recipes we have given the fish a lighter treatment, moistened with herbs, marinated in cognac, or topped with a California-style avocado mixture.

⌒❤ PACIFIC ROCKFISH WITH BASIL AND THYME

There are no added fats here, just lemon juice to moisten the herbs and flavor the rockfish.

Preparation time: 5 minutes
Microwave time: 4–5 minutes
Servings: 4

2 tablespoons fresh lemon juice
1 tablespoon minced fresh basil
   or **½ teaspoon dried**
1 tablespoon fresh thyme *or* **½ teaspoon dried**
1 pound Pacific rockfish fillets

1. Put lemon juice on a plate that will hold the Pacific rockfish. Stir in basil and thyme. Put fish on plate and turn twice to coat with juice and herbs. Let stand 5 minutes.
2. Arrange fish with thickest portions to the outside and any thin ends tucked under, if necessary. Cover with plastic wrap, vented. MICROWAVE (high) 4–5 minutes until thickest portion is just opaque when tested with a fork. Let stand 5 minutes. Drain.

ॐ PACIFIC ROCKFISH MARINATED IN ORANGE BRANDY

Brandy and citrus juices are heated to blend and burn off the alcohol, then are used to marinate Pacific rockfish fillets.

Preparation time: 10 minutes
Microwave time: 5–6 minutes
Servings: 4

1 tablespoon fresh lemon juice
1 tablespoon fresh orange juice
2 tablespoons brandy or cognac
1 pound Pacific rockfish fillets
1 teaspoon grated orange zest
**1 tablespoon minced fresh
   parsley**

1. Put lemon juice, orange juice, and brandy on a plate large enough to hold the fillets. MICROWAVE (high), uncovered, 30 seconds to 1 minute until hot. Put Pacific rockfish on plate and turn twice to coat with liquids and herbs. Let stand 5 minutes.
2. Arrange fish with thickest portions to the outside and any thin ends tucked under, if necessary. Cover with plastic wrap, vented. MICROWAVE (high) 4–5 minutes until thickest portion is just opaque when tested with a fork. Let stand 5 minutes.
3. Pour juices over fish. Sprinkle with orange zest and parsley.

PACIFIC ROCKFISH WITH AVOCADO TOPPING

West Coast Pacific rockfish gets a California treatment here with a topping of fresh avocado and tomatoes.

Preparation time: 10 minutes
Microwave time: 7–9½ minutes
Servings: 4

1 pound Pacific rockfish fillets
1 tablespoon and 2 teaspoons fresh lemon juice
½ teaspoon minced garlic
1 teaspoon vegetable oil
1 tomato, peeled, seeded, and chopped
1 tablespoon minced fresh cilantro
1 avocado, peeled, pitted, and chopped coarsely at the last moment

1. Arrange Pacific rockfish with thickest portions to the outside and any thin ends tucked under, if necessary. Drizzle with 1 tablespoon lemon juice. Cover with plastic wrap, vented. MICROWAVE (high) 4–5 minutes until thickest portion is just opaque when tested with a fork. Let stand 5 minutes. Drain.
2. Put garlic, oil, and tomato in 4-cup measure. Cover with plastic wrap, vented. MICROWAVE (high) 2–3 minutes to soften tomato and draw out juices.
3. Stir in cilantro and avocado. Do not cover. MICROWAVE (high) 1–1½ minutes to soften and warm avocado, stirring once. Stir in remaining lemon juice. Serve fish topped with avocado mixture.

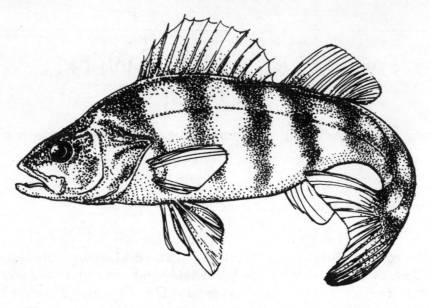

PERCH

Barefoot summer days and a string of yellow perch are a timeless image of innocent pleasure, and with excellent reason: anyone can catch a perch—a string of perch—with a short line and a few wriggly minnows. They make wonderful eating.

Larger walleye and sauger are both members of the perch family, but perch typically means yellow perch, a 5- to 7-inch freshwater catch.

Fresh perch are most abundant in spring or in winter, when they are pulled from the ice. However, they are also easily found in the frozen food section of the grocery. Frozen perch that come in boxes are a bit of a nuisance because the fillets are cut off at odd spots to make them fit neatly into a rectangular pack. The fish, of course, taste fine, but the irregular shapes are not as attractive and the pieces need to be rearranged while in the microwave oven to cook evenly.

Perch flesh is very firm and white, and the little fish or fillets cook up very quickly. Although the usual rule of thumb for cooking fish in the microwave is 4 minutes per pound, I find that perch typically needs only 3 minutes. And this is one fish you really don't want to overcook, or the little fillets will curl up and toughen.

✠ PERCH WITH LEMON AND CHIVES

Simple, sweet-tasting perch needs only a dash of lemon juice and a touch of chives. The microwave cooking will keep it moist and juicy. Be sure to cook the perch skin-side down to keep the fillets from curling up.

Preparation time: 5 minutes
Microwave time: 3–4 minutes
Servings: 4

1 pound perch fillets
1 tablespoon fresh lemon juice
2 tablespoons chopped fresh chives

Arrange perch skin-side down on a plate or in a flat casserole. Drizzle with lemon juice. Cover with plastic wrap, vented. MICROWAVE (high) 3–4 minutes, rearranging once, until thickest portion of fish is opaque when tested with a fork. Let stand 1 minute to finish cooking. Drain. Top with chives.

PERCH MEUNIERE

Meunière is basically browned butter with lemon juice and parsley. The butter is first strained, or clarified, to make it clear, then browned to a fine, nutty flavor.

Preparation time: 10 minutes
Microwave time: 9–12 minutes
Servings: 4

4 tablespoons (½ stick) butter
1 tablespoon fresh lemon juice
1 tablespoon minced fresh
  parsley
1 pound perch fillets

1. Put butter in 4-cup measure. MICROWAVE (high), uncovered, 1–2 minutes to melt. Line a sieve with cheesecloth and pour the butter through the cheesecloth and into a container. Repeat if necessary to rid the butter of foamy milk solids. Return clarified butter to measure. MICROWAVE (high) 5–6 minutes until butter is light brown. Strain butter again, if necessary. Stir in ½ teaspoon of the lemon juice and all of the parsley. Set aside.
2. Arrange perch skin-side down on a plate or in a flat casserole. Drizzle with remaining lemon juice. Cover with plastic wrap, vented. MICROWAVE (high) 3–4 minutes, rearranging once, until thickest portion of fish is opaque when tested with a fork. Let stand 1 minute to finish cooking. Drain. To reheat butter sauce, MICROWAVE (high) 30 seconds. Serve sauce over fish.

TIP: Clarified butter can be stored in the refrigerator for several months.

TIP: Instead of using cheesecloth, you can use a large spoon to skim off and discard most of the foamy, white solids. Let the butter stand for 3 minutes on the counter to allow the rest of the milk solids to settle to the bottom. Skim or carefully pour the clear, or clarified, butter into a container. Discard the remaining white solids. Clarified butter looks neater than melted butter and can be heated to a higher temperature without burning.

PERCH IN TANGY MUSTARD SAUCE

A thick mustard sauce, made extra-tangy with anchovy paste, works well on perch.

Preparation time: 15 minutes
Microwave time: 5–7 minutes
Servings: 4

2 tablespoons minced onion
3 tablespoons olive oil
½ cup ketchup
¼ cup Dijon mustard
2 teaspoons anchovy paste
1 pound perch fillets
1 tablespoon fresh lemon juice

1. Put onion and olive oil in 2-cup measure. MICROWAVE (high), uncovered, 1–2 minutes to soften. Stir in ketchup, mustard, and anchovy paste. MICROWAVE (high), uncovered, 30 seconds to 1 minute to warm through.

2. Arrange perch skin-side down on a plate or in a flat casserole. Drizzle with lemon juice. Cover with plastic wrap, vented. MICROWAVE (high) 3–4 minutes, rearranging once, until thickest portion of fish is opaque when tested with a fork. Let stand 1 minute to finish cooking. Drain. Spoon sauce over fish to serve.

⌣♥ PERCH-AND-POTATO SOUP

This thick, satisfying soup has no added fat—just healthful vegetables and an economical use of fish.

Preparation time: 20 minutes
Microwave time: 15–19 minutes
Servings: 4

2 russet potatoes, peeled and sliced thin
1 small onion, peeled and quartered
2 cups fish or chicken stock
¼ pound mushrooms, sliced thin
1 tablespoon fresh thyme *or* ¼ teaspoon dried
⅛ teaspoon freshly ground black pepper
½ pound perch, cut into 1-inch squares
1 tablespoon fresh lemon juice
2 green onions, white and first 2 inches of green, chopped

1. Put potatoes, onion, and stock in 2½-quart casserole. Cover. MICROWAVE (high) 8–10 minutes until vegetables are very tender. Pour into food processor or blender, and process until smooth.

2. Return potato mixture to casserole. Stir in mushrooms, thyme, and pepper. Cover. MICROWAVE (high) 5–6 minutes until mushrooms are tender. Stir in perch. Cover. MICROWAVE (high) 2–3 minutes until fish just flakes. Stir in lemon juice. Top with green onions.

PIKE

With its long mouth and mass of pointed teeth, pike looks like the Doberman pinscher of fish. Fortunately, this feisty sport fish has a deliciously tame taste that makes it one of my favorite freshwater fish.

Actually, it's not just the sweet, mild taste that makes pike a favorite, but its texture. The firm white meat holds together in nice large flakes when cooked and cold, so leftovers are easily turned into a tempting salad or cold plate.

Indeed, unless you have a large family, you can usually count on leftovers from a whole pike because the two most common varieties tend to be fairly large fish. Northern pike typically comes to market at 4–10 pounds, and muskellunge, a game fish, is even larger at 10–30 pounds. The largest fish are much too big for a microwave oven, but a 4- to 5-pounder can be curved a bit to fit in a full-sized microwave oven.

Fresh pike is most common in spring, when catches come in from the Great Lakes states and Canada. One drawback to pike is its numerous Y-shaped bones, but they are fairly easy to spot, especially in the larger fish.

PIKE AND PEA PODS

Crisp slices of fresh snow pea pods add crunch and a pretty bright green color to this simple fish dish, which has only ½ teaspoon added fat for four people. For menu suggestions see page 23.

Preparation time: 5 minutes
Microwave time: 4–5 minutes
Servings: 4

8–10 **fresh snow pea pods**
  ½ **teaspoon sesame oil**
  1 **pound pike fillets**
  1 **tablespoon fresh lemon juice**

1. Pull off and discard threads from pea pods. Slice pea pods into very fine strips. Toss with sesame oil.
2. Arrange pike on a dinner plate with any thin ends tucked under, if necessary. Drizzle with lemon juice. Top with pea pod strips. Cover with plastic wrap, vented. MICROWAVE (high) 4–5 minutes until thickest portion of fish is almost opaque when tested with a fork. Drain.

PIKE BEURRE BLANC

Pike with a wine-and-shallot-enhanced butter sauce is a common combination in the Loire area of France.

Preparation time: 10 minutes
Microwave time: 7–9 minutes
Servings: 4

1 pound pike fillets
1 tablespoon fresh lemon juice
2 tablespoons dry white wine
2 tablespoons white vinegar
2 teaspoons minced shallots
8 tablespoons (1 stick) butter,
  diced, room temperature
Dash of salt

1. Arrange pike on a plate with thickest portions to the outside and any thin ends tucked under, if necessary. Drizzle with lemon juice. Cover with plastic wrap, vented. MICROWAVE (high) 4–5 minutes until thickest portion is almost opaque when tested with a fork. Let stand 5 minutes. Drain.
2. Put wine, vinegar, and shallots in 4-cup measure. MICROWAVE (high), uncovered, 3–4 minutes until liquid is reduced to about 1 tablespoon.
3. Add butter gradually while whisking. Sauce should be creamy and foamy. Strain if desired to remove shallot. Serve fish atop sauce.

TIP: If beurre blanc gets too hot, it gets oily; too cold, it turns to hard butter. Make beurre blanc just before serving, or make ahead and store in an insulated bottle.

PIKE AND VEGETABLE VINAIGRETTE SALAD

Firm pike fillets hold up beautifully in a cold salad, and this vegetable-enhanced vinaigrette adds to a lovely summer entree. Use any extra vinaigrette in a tossed vegetable salad. This dish can also be served immediately as a warm salad.

Preparation time: 15 minutes
Microwave time: 6–8 minutes
Chilling time: 1 hour or overnight
Servings: 4

1 pound pike fillets
3 tablespoons fresh lemon juice
1 teaspoon minced garlic
¼ cup diced green pepper
¼ cup diced sweet red pepper
½ cup peeled, diced cucumber
2 tablespoons cider vinegar
1 tablespoon sugar
1 tablespoon Dijon mustard
½ teaspoon salt
⅛ teaspoon freshly ground black pepper
½ cup vegetable oil
1 tablespoon roughly chopped capers

1. Arrange pike on a dinner plate with thickest portions to the outside and any thin ends tucked under, if necessary. Drizzle with 1 tablespoon lemon juice. Cover with plastic wrap, vented. MICROWAVE (high) 4–5 minutes until thickest portion is almost opaque when tested with a fork. Let stand 5 minutes. Drain. Cover and chill in refrigerator for an hour or overnight.

2. Put garlic, green pepper, red pepper, and cucumber in 4-cup measure. MICROWAVE (high) 2–3 minutes to just soften vegetables, stirring once.

3. In a small bowl, whisk remaining lemon juice, vinegar, sugar, mustard, salt, and pepper. Whisk in oil. Stir in capers. Add mixture to vegetables. Cover and store in refrigerator for up to a week. To serve, spoon vegetables with a little of the dressing over the fish.

TIP: Capers add distinct flavor and tang, but if you don't like them you may substitute a tablespoon of vinegar or chopped dill pickle.

WHOLE STUFFED PIKE WITH LEEK

You could add some onions and parsley, if you like, but this simple version works very well with a whole fish such as pike. Save any leftover fish to serve in a fish salad.

Preparation time: 10 minutes
Microwave time: 20–25 minutes
Servings: 6

1 leek
1 4–5-pound whole pike, cleaned and scaled
2 tablespoons fresh lemon juice

1. Cut off and discard root end of leek. Trim dark green portion; wash, and spread on base of 4-quart flat casserole. Slice white portion of leek in half lengthwise; wash well under running water, separating stalk sections to remove dirt. Chop; reserve.
2. Rinse pike well. Place on top of dark green leek stalks. Drizzle lemon juice inside cavity and over fish. Place chopped white portion of leek in cavity of fish. Wrap head and tail loosely with smooth foil wrap to prevent these areas from overcooking. (Keep foil at least 1 inch from microwave sides.) Cover casserole with plastic wrap, vented at one corner.
3. MICROWAVE (high) 20–25 minutes until thickest portion of fish near the spine is almost opaque when tested with a fork. Let fish stand 10 minutes on counter to finish cooking. Serve fish topped with chopped leeks and some of the juices.

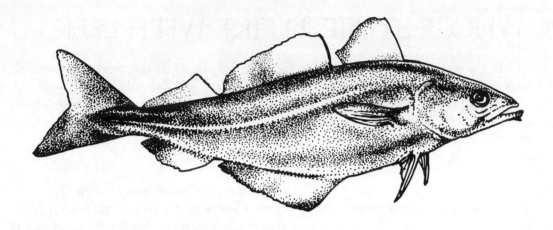

POLLACK

A fish of many names, pollack is marketed around the country as blue cod, green cod, or Boston blue, the names referring to its distinctive deep-blue to olive-green skin.

Atlantic pollack is a close relative of cod and haddock and is caught in abundance by sport fishermen on both sides of the Atlantic Ocean. Its flesh ranges from tan to light pink, with a deep-red lining next to the skin.

Because pollack isn't as well known as its cousins cod and haddock, you'll find pollack at a better price. But the lower price doesn't mean lower quality. When cooked, pollack is very much like cod: white, mild-tasting, and flaky—albeit slightly softer. Use pollack as a substitute for cod and haddock in other recipes.

POLLACK WITH BLOODY MARY TOPPING

The essence of a Bloody Mary (without the vodka) is piled on pollack fillets for a spicy, low-fat entree.

Preparation time: 10 minutes
Microwave time: 7–9 minutes
Servings: 4

2 medium tomatoes, peeled, seeded, and chopped *or* **½ cup canned tomatoes, drained and chopped**
2 tablespoons minced celery
2 teaspoons fresh lemon juice
4 drops Tabasco sauce
¼ teaspoon Worcestershire sauce
Dash salt
Dash freshly ground black pepper
1 pound pollack fillets

1. Put all ingredients except pollack in 2-cup measure. MICROWAVE (high), uncovered, 3–4 minutes to slightly soften celery.
2. Arrange fish on a plate with thickest portions to the outside. Spoon topping over fish. Cover with plastic wrap, vented. MICROWAVE (high) 4–5 minutes until thickest portion of fish is just opaque when tested with a fork. Let stand 5 minutes to finish cooking.

POLLACK WITH FISH VELOUTE

This light, mild-tasting sauce pairs easily with pollack, and there is enough leftover sauce to moisten a rice side dish.

Preparation time: 20 minutes
Microwave time: 15–21 minutes
Servings: 4

2 tablespoons butter
2 tablespoons flour
2 tablespoons minced onion
¼ cup minced carrot
¼ cup minced celery
¼ cup minced mushroom stems
1 cup fish stock or bottled clam broth
⅛ teaspoon salt
⅛ teaspoon freshly ground white or black pepper
1 pound pollack fillets
1 tablespoon fresh lemon juice

1. Put butter in 4-cup measure. MICROWAVE (high), uncovered, 2–3 minutes until the butter melts and is very hot. Thoroughly whisk in flour. MICROWAVE (high), uncovered, 2–3 minutes until the mixture bubbles furiously. Whisk.
2. Stir in onion, carrot, celery, and mushrooms. MICROWAVE (high) 3–4 minutes until soft. Thoroughly whisk in broth. MICROWAVE (high), uncovered, 2–3 minutes until bubbles that start at the edge of the sauce fill in and completely cover the top of the sauce. Whisk.
3. MICROWAVE (high) 2–3 minutes until sauce thickens enough to coat a spoon. Whisk. Add salt and pepper. (Taste before adding salt if using bottled clam broth.) Set sauce aside.
4. Put pollack on a plate with thickest portions to the outside. Drizzle with lemon juice. Cover with plastic wrap, vented. MICROWAVE (high) 4–5 minutes until thickest portion is just opaque when tested with a fork. Let stand 5 minutes to finish cooking. Drain. Serve fish atop sauce.

TIP: *For a smooth sauce, strain before serving and present the cooked, minced vegetables as a bonus side dish.*

⌀♥ POLLACK-AND-LENTIL SOUP

This hearty, healthful soup features a little fish, a lot of vegetables and dried lentils, and little fat. It does take time to cook, but there is little fussing once the soup is in the microwave. Serve with a loaf of crusty bread.

Preparation time: 15 minutes
Microwave time: 47–67 minutes
Servings: 6

1 cup washed lentils
½ pound mushrooms, chopped
1 small onion, chopped
1 carrot, chopped
1 celery rib, chopped
2 cups beef broth
2 cups water
½ teaspoon fresh thyme
⅛ teaspoon cayenne pepper
1 teaspoon salt
¼ teaspoon black pepper
¾ pound pollack, cubed

1. Put all ingredients except pollack in 4-quart casserole. Cover. MICROWAVE (high) 14–18 minutes until boiling. Stir.
2. Cover. MICROWAVE (medium) 30–45 minutes until lentils are tender. Ladle half of the soup into a food processor, and process until smooth. Return to casserole and mix.
3. Add fish. Cover. MICROWAVE (high) 3–4 minutes until centers of cubes are just opaque when tested with a fork.

TIP: *Note that the soup is cooked on high power to bring it up to a boil, then on medium power to develop flavor.*

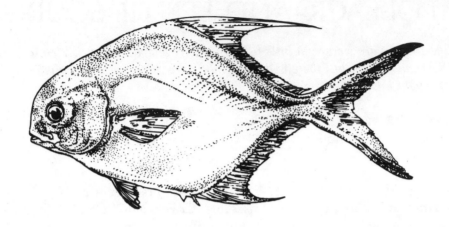

POMPANO

Florida pompano—the common name—is an entree that appears at upscale restaurants at upscale prices. The fish is truly special and elegant-tasting, full-flavored yet sweet.

And it's anything but dull in the water, too. "It's one of the most active swimmers, almost hyper in its swimming pattern," says Dr. Steven Otwell, a professor of Seafood Technology at the University of Florida.

During winter and early spring when tourists flock to the warmth of Florida and the Gulf of Mexico, pompano fishing reaches its height. And so do the pompano. The small—usually only about 2 pounds—silvery fish literally skim the surface of the warm Gulf waters, appearing to walk around and mock the fishermen trying to land them for dinner. Visitors wading in the waters are apt to find pompano scurrying in the water, especially if the water is active with waves.

Pompano just seem to love action. "Some people have tried to cultivate pompano," Dr. Otwell says, "but they couldn't. When pompano are confined, they become stressful."

Unless you live in a large urban area or near the warm Atlantic or Gulf waters, you are not likely to find pompano behind the fish department counter. But because it sells well in fine restaurants, you are likely to have luck with a special order. Be prepared to pay a good price and to give it special treatment at home. Included here are two recipes worthy of the fine, delicate, white fillets: Pompano with Skinny Asparagus, and Pompano in Parchment.

POMPANO WITH SKINNY ASPARAGUS

The first thin wisps of spring asparagus cook very quickly in the microwave and, teamed with pompano, create a light, healthful entree. Instead of butter, we top the pompano and asparagus with lemon juice and tarragon.

Preparation time: 5 minutes
Microwave time: 4–5 minutes
Servings: 4

¼ **pound thin asparagus**
1 **pound pompano fillets**
2 **tablespoons fresh lemon juice**
2 **teaspoons grated lemon zest**
2 **teaspoons fresh tarragon** *or* ½
   teaspoon dried

1. Arrange asparagus in the center of a plate. Place pompano around asparagus with thickest portions to the outside. Drizzle fish and asparagus with lemon juice.
2. Cover with plastic wrap, vented. MICROWAVE (high) 4–5 minutes until thickest portion of fish is almost opaque when tested with a fork. Let stand 5 minutes to finish cooking. Drain. Sprinkle pompano and asparagus with lemon zest and tarragon.

POMPANO IN PARCHMENT

Cooking and presenting fish in individual paper wrapping is especially appropriate with delicate-tasting pompano and is especially easy in the microwave. Be sure to have the rest of the meal ready so that guests can enjoy the first wonderful burst of aroma when they cut into the paper wrapping. For menu suggestions see page 24.

Preparation time: 20 minutes
Microwave time: 5–7 minutes
Servings: 4

1 small leek
1 pound pompano fillets, cut into four equal pieces
2 tablespoons fresh lime juice
1 tablespoon chopped fresh thyme *or* ¼ teaspoon dried
½ teaspoon salt
⅛ teaspoon freshly ground black pepper
½ cup cherry tomatoes, cut in half or in quarters
1½ tablespoons butter

1. Cut off root end of leek. Trim all but 2 inches of green. Slice in half lengthwise. Wash well under running water, separating stalk sections to remove dirt. Save thicker, white outer stalk sections for soup or other use. Julienne more tender, green inner sections. Set aside.
2. Spread a large piece of parchment paper on flat surface. Invert a 12-inch-round cake pan on paper and trace around it with a sharp knife to make a 12-inch circle. Repeat to make four circles.
3. Place one pompano fillet on each parchment circle, slightly below the center, leaving enough margin to fold over. Drizzle each fillet with lime juice, then thyme, salt, and pepper. Scatter tomatoes on fish. Top with fanlike arrangement of leeks. Dot with butter.
4. Fold paper tightly to enclose contents, leaving a little room for expansion. Arrange packages on a round platter. MICROWAVE (high) 5–7 minutes until fish is almost opaque when tested with fork. (You may briefly open one package to check for doneness.) Serve packages on dinner plates and allow guests to slit them open themselves.

TIP: Extra leeks can be cooked easily in the microwave and make a wonderful accompaniment to other fish dishes or chicken. For best results, use only the tender, inner sections, and either julienne or chop the leeks. Add 2 tablespoons water to 2 leeks, cover with plastic wrap, vented at one corner. MICROWAVE (high) 2–4 minutes until tender, stirring once. Drain. Do not overcook leeks, or they will become mushy.

PORGY

Fat little porgies are one of the first fish I ever caught, so the oval, silvery species was my early definition of a fish. They seemed to taste better than larger, store-bought fish, and this, of course, was not simply a romantic notion. Freshly caught fish do taste best. And these easy prey porgies are particularly sweet.

The New England variety that I knew best is an oval-shaped, pretty, silvery fish that Indians along the Atlantic coast used for fertilizer. Other varieties of this saltwater fish range from grey-green to reddish-silver.

Porgy, also called *scup* or *sea bream*, is an easy fish to catch and to keep. It tolerates a little time in the boat before it hits the table. The fish are usually small, about ¾ pound each, enough so that two fit neatly into a flat 2½-quart casserole.

The delicately flavored, coarse-textured fish is, however, cursed with many small bones, and the scales are firm and tough to remove. If you are buying the fish, ask the fish department to scale it for you.

WHOLE PORGY WITH FENNEL SEEDS

Just a few fennel seeds softened in a little butter add a special flavor to porgies. Because the fish need so little time to cook in the microwave, little slits are made in the fish before cooking so that the seeds can be slipped in for optimum flavor. For menu suggestions see page 24.

Preparation time: 10 minutes
Microwave time: 8–10 minutes
Servings: 4

1 tablespoon butter
½ teaspoon fennel seeds
2 whole porgies, about ¾ pound each, cleaned and scaled

1. Put butter in 1-cup measure. MICROWAVE (high), uncovered, about 1 minute to melt. Stir in seeds. MICROWAVE (high), uncovered, 1 minute to warm seeds and let them start softening. Let stand 5 minutes to soften more.

2. Arrange porgies in 2½-quart flat casserole, with thicker back sides to the outside. Use a sharp knife to make three vertical 2-inch slits in the fillet portion of each fish, cutting right down to, but not through, the bones. Holding slits open with your fingers or a fork, spoon softened fennel seeds into the slits. Drizzle the last few seeds and drops of butter over the whole fish.

3. Cover with plastic wrap, vented at one corner. MICROWAVE (high) 6–8 minutes until thickest portion of fish is just opaque when tested gently with a fork. Drain.

QUICK CAJUN FISH STEW

When the refrigerator is harboring too many small leftovers, combine them into a quick stew. This recipe uses an ear of corn, a handful of potatoes, and some leftover fish, but you may easily substitute lima beans or carrots for the corn, and rice or turnips for the potatoes. The few extra minutes needed to make a dark roux add extra color and flavor to this Cajun version.

Preparation time: 10 minutes
Microwave time: 14–20 minutes
Servings: 4

2 tablespoons butter
2 tablespoons flour
4 cups chicken stock or broth
½ cup cooked corn
½ cup cooked, diced potatoes
½ cup ½-inch chunks cooked porgy
½ teaspoon minced fresh basil *or* **⅛ teaspoon dried**
¹⁄₁₆ teaspoon (dash) cayenne
2 green onions, white and first 2 inches of green, sliced

1. Put butter in 2½-quart casserole. MICROWAVE (high), uncovered, 1–2 minutes until melted and hot. Thoroughly whisk in flour. MICROWAVE (high), uncovered, 6–8 minutes until roux turns a rich brown color.
2. Thoroughly whisk in half of chicken stock. MICROWAVE (high), uncovered, 3–4 minutes until mixture bubbles and thickens. Thoroughly whisk.
3. Stir in remaining chicken stock and the rest of ingredients, except for green onions. Cover. MICROWAVE (high) 4–6 minutes to heat through. Garnish each serving with sliced green onions.

TIP: Thorough whisking in Steps 1 and 2 helps make a smooth stew base.

RED SNAPPER

If you put three food stylists in a room and ask them to name a beautiful, dramatic, yet friendly-looking fish, you will hear a quick chorus of "red snapper." Indeed, the large red fish on the cover photograph of this cookbook was no haphazard choice.

Red snapper is the fish that has everything: great looks, great taste, and a wealth of chefs writing odes in the form of recipes. Best-known member of the large snapper family, the moderately sized—usually 4–6 pounds—red snapper is found readily in the Gulf of Mexico and the warm, shallow ocean waters off the coast of the Carolinas and Florida and down to Brazil.

Red snapper has a warm, red color on the top that tapers to almost white at the belly, and large, red eyes. The rest of the snapper family is quite colorful, too, with other varieties in shades of yellow, orange, green, grey, and brown, and can also be used in these recipes.

After it is scaled, the skin of a red snapper bears a distinctive red netting that is particularly attractive in dishes such as Red Snapper and Tortilla-Lime Soup at the end of this chapter.

RED SNAPPER ON APPLE SLICES

Fresh apple, apple juice, and apple butter—but no added fat—provide an intense and pleasantly sweet accompaniment to snapper fillets.

Preparation time: 10 minutes
Microwave time: 5–9 minutes
Servings: 4

1 Granny Smith apple, cored and cut into ½-inch slices
1 tablespoon fresh lemon juice
1 pound snapper fillets
¼ cup apple juice
1 tablespoon apple butter

1. Arrange apple slices flat on a dinner plate or pie plate. Drizzle with ½ tablespoon lemon juice. Arrange snapper on top of apple slices, skin-side down with thickest portions to the outside. Drizzle with remaining lemon juice. Pour apple juice over fish. Cover with plastic wrap, vented.
2. MICROWAVE (high) 4–8 minutes until thickest portion of fish is almost opaque when tested with a fork. Let stand 5 minutes on counter.
3. Lift out fish and apple slices. Stir apple butter into cooking juices. MICROWAVE (high), uncovered, about 1 minute to warm sauce thoroughly. Spoon sauce over fish and apples.

RED SNAPPER WITH SESAME-GINGER MARINADE

I love the peppery-spicy taste of fresh ginger in this marinade. If some of your guests have timid tastes, scrape off the excess ginger and garlic before serving.

Preparation time: 10 minutes
Microwave time: 5–6 minutes
Servings: 4

1 tablespoon sesame seeds
½ teaspoon sesame oil
2 tablespoons soy sauce
1 tablespoon white wine vinegar
2 tablespoons minced fresh ginger
1 teaspoon minced garlic
¼ teaspoon cayenne
1 pound snapper fillets

1. Spread sesame seeds in a cup. MICROWAVE (high), uncovered, about 1 minute to toast. Set aside.
2. Mix sesame oil, soy sauce, vinegar, ginger, garlic, and cayenne in a cup. Arrange snapper on a dinner plate skin-side down with the thickest portions to the outside. Pour marinade over fish and let stand 10 minutes.
3. Cover with plastic wrap, vented. MICROWAVE (high) 4–5 minutes until thickest portion is just opaque when tested with a fork. Let stand 5 minutes to finish cooking. Spoon some of the juices over fish. Sprinkle with sesame seeds.

RED SNAPPER AND ORANGE SALAD

Red-flecked red snapper adds a colorful touch to this light salad entree.

Preparation time: 10 minutes
Microwave time: 4–5 minutes
Chilling time: 3 hours or overnight
Servings: 4–6

1 **pound red snapper fillets** 1 **tablespoon fresh lemon juice** 4 **cups torn romaine lettuce, rinsed, dried, and chilled** 3 **oranges** 4 **thin slices red onion** 1 **cup diagonally sliced celery** ¼ **cup and 2 tablespoons olive oil** 2 **tablespoons red wine vinegar** 1 **teaspoon walnut oil** 1 **tablespoon minced fresh mint leaves** ¼ **teaspoon salt** ⅛ **teaspoon freshly ground black pepper**	1. Arrange snapper skin-side down on a plate with thickest portions to the outside. Drizzle with lemon juice. Cover with plastic wrap, vented. MICROWAVE (high) 4–5 minutes until thickest portion is almost opaque when tested with a fork. Let stand 5 minutes to finish cooking. Drain. Refrigerate, covered, 3 hours or overnight. 2. Just before serving, arrange lettuce on plates. Peel oranges and cut into wheel-like slices. Cut snapper into bite-sized pieces. Arrange oranges, snapper, and red onion on top of lettuce. Sprinkle with celery. 3. For the dressing, put the remaining ingredients in a small bowl and whisk until thick and blended. Drizzle dressing over salad.

RED SNAPPER AND TORTILLA-LIME SOUP

This colorful soup has a nice bite from cumin, chili, and cayenne, plus tortilla strips for added texture. Instead of deep-frying the tortilla strips, they are dried in the microwave without any added fat. To keep a good contrast in textures, be sure to serve the soup immediately after the tortillas and avocados are added. For menu suggestions see page 23.

Preparation time: 20 minutes
Microwave time: 13–17 minutes
Servings: 4

6 6-inch corn tortillas
1 tablespoon vegetable oil
1 teaspoon minced garlic
¼ cup minced onion
2 medium tomatoes, peeled, seeded, and chopped
¼ teaspoon cumin seeds
½ teaspoon chili powder
1 bay leaf, broken in half
2 cups chicken stock or broth
¼ teaspoon salt
Dash of cayenne
¾ pound red snapper fillets, cut into 1-inch chunks
1 tablespoon fresh lime juice
1 small avocado, peeled, seeded, and cubed
½ cup shredded cheddar cheese

1. Cut tortillas into ¾-inch strips. Spread tortillas on paper-towel-lined floor of microwave oven. Do not cover. MICROWAVE (high) 1–2 minutes until tortillas start to curl up and dry out a little. Spread on counter to cool.
2. Put oil, garlic, onion, and tomatoes in 2½-quart casserole. Cover. MICROWAVE (high) 2–3 minutes to soften vegetables.
3. Stir in cumin, chili powder, bay leaf, chicken stock, salt, and cayenne. Cover. MICROWAVE (high) 6–7 minutes to boiling.
4. Stir in snapper. Cover. MICROWAVE (high) 4–5 minutes until centers of chunks are just opaque. Stir in lime juice and tortilla strips. Top with avocado and cheese, and serve immediately.

TIP: Don't substitute light-colored wheat tortillas for yellow-colored corn tortillas. The wheat ones will get limp and soggy.

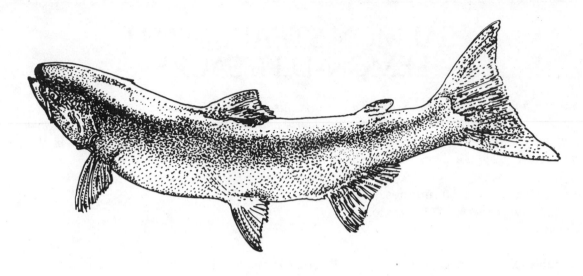

SALMON

With its beautiful pink to deep-red color and unique, rich taste, salmon easily stands apart from mainstream fin fish.

Salmon is expensive—often twice the price of lesser fish in the fish department. But the demand is still so strong that farm-raised salmon is a sizable business in Canada, Maine, and our Pacific Northwest.

Among the most common species enjoyed in this country are Atlantic salmon, and three Pacific varieties: Sockeye, Chinook, and Coho. The last two are also caught in the Great Lakes and other freshwater bodies. The flavor of the salmon depends on how the salmon has dined, and those from the oceans are considered the most prime.

Fresh salmon can be quite large, 4–10 pounds for a Coho and 6–25 pounds for a Chinook or King salmon. These very large salmon will be too large to even fit in your microwave oven, but the smaller ones will do just fine.

Because salmon is recognizable party fare, I have included in this chapter two recipes—Salmon Quenelles and Salmon Benedict with Orange Hollandaise—that are rich, time-consuming, and delicious.

SALMON STEAKS WITH LEMON-DILL SAUCE

Salmon and dill are a classic combination, and this lemon-dill sauce has a smooth, rich texture—but no butter or cream. The sauce starts with a low-fat white sauce, using margarine and skim milk instead of butter and whole milk. Because the salmon cooks so quickly in the microwave oven, the sauce is made first and kept warm.

Preparation time: 10 minutes
Microwave time: 16–22 minutes
Servings: 4

2 tablespoons margarine
2 tablespoons flour
1 cup skim milk
4 tablespoons fresh lemon juice
1 tablespoon fresh dill *or* 1 teaspoon dried
¼ teaspoon salt
⅛ teaspoon ground white pepper
4 salmon steaks, 6–7 ounces each

1. For the sauce, put margarine in 4-cup measure. MICROWAVE (high), uncovered, about 1 minute until margarine melts and is very hot. Whisk in flour. MICROWAVE (high), uncovered, 1–2 minutes until mixture bubbles. Whisk in milk.

2. MICROWAVE (high), uncovered, 2–2½ minutes until bubbles cover the top of the sauce. Whisk. MICROWAVE (high) about 2 minutes until sauce thickens, stirring twice to avoid spillover. Thoroughly whisk in 2 tablespoons of lemon juice, dill, salt, and pepper. Keep sauce warm.

3. Arrange salmon on a plate with the base of the U-shape to the outside. Sprinkle with remaining lemon juice. Cover with plastic wrap, vented at one corner. MICROWAVE (high) 10–15 minutes until the thickest portion near the bone is almost opaque when tested with a fork, rearranging fish once. Let stand 2 minutes. Drain. Spoon sauce over fish to serve.

✖ POACHED WHOLE SALMON

Poached in wine with vegetables and no added fat, salmon has enough rich flavor to stand alone, without a sauce. This recipe calls for a pretty big salmon—4½ pounds without the head. Enjoy most of it as a warm entree one night and the rest in a glorious cold salad with a horseradish cream sauce (see the Tip below) or a dill vinaigrette.

Preparation time: 10 minutes
Microwave time: 20–29 minutes
Servings: 6–8

¼ **cup dry white wine**
1 **carrot, chopped**
1 **celery rib, chopped**
¼ **cup roughly chopped onion**
3 **sprigs parsley**
1 **4½-pound salmon (weighed with head off and tail intact), cleaned and scaled**
2 **tablespoons fresh lemon juice**

1. Put wine, carrot, celery, onion, and parsley in a flat casserole or deep dish large enough to hold the fish. Cover with plastic wrap and MICROWAVE (high) 3–4 minutes to soften vegetables.
2. Rinse salmon well. Place on top of vegetables. Drizzle with lemon juice. Wrap foil smoothly around end of tail to keep it from overcooking. Be sure foil is at least 1 inch from the sides of the microwave. Cover plate with plastic wrap, vented at one corner. MICROWAVE (high) 5 minutes to start cooking but before fish is too soft to turn.
3. Turn fish over on the plate. Cover. MICROWAVE (high) 12–15 minutes until thickest portion of fish is opaque when pulled apart gently with fork. Let stand covered 10 minutes. Gently lift out onto serving platter.

TIP: A whole fish with head intact takes a little longer per pound to cook in the microwave. See Index for How to Cook Whole Fish.

TIP: If salmon is to be chilled, cool first in cooking liquids. Use two large spatulas to carefully lift fish onto platter. Mop up excess liquid with paper towel. Use a small knife to carefully scrape off skin. Cover, and put in refrigerator.

TIP: For the horseradish cream sauce, mix ½ cup sour cream or yogurt with ½ cup mayonnaise and 1–2 tablespoons prepared horseradish. Keep covered in refrigerator until ready to use.

SALMON-STUFFED POTATOES

These hearty potatoes make a great lunch and also look pretty as a hot buffet dish. Serve two halves for each person. The amount of milk in the recipe is approximate and will depend on the size and variety of potato. Add enough milk until the potatoes progress from sticky to fluffy but not mushy. You want a little less milk than you would for mashed potatoes so that the filling mounds well.

Preparation time: 30 minutes
Microwave time: 18–22 minutes
Servings: 4

4 large baking potatoes
2 tablespoons butter
½ cup milk, or as needed
**1 tablespoon chopped fresh
    tarragon *or* 1 teaspoon dried**
¼ teaspoon salt
**¼ teaspoon freshly ground black
    pepper**
1 cup shredded cheddar cheese
**1 15½-ounce can pink salmon,
    drained**
**2 green onions, white and first
    2 inches of green, chopped**
**2 tablespoons minced fresh
    parsley**

1. Scrub potatoes well. Prick tops with fork. Put potatoes on corners of a paper towel. MICROWAVE (high) 15–18 minutes until potatoes are just soft when squeezed, turning towel 180 degrees after 6 minutes. Let stand 3 minutes.

2. Cut potatoes in half horizontally. Scoop out centers, leaving a ½-inch-thick shell. Mash the scooped-out portion of potatoes. Mix in the butter, milk, tarragon, salt, pepper, and ½ cup of the cheddar. Mix until the cheese and butter have melted and mixture is fluffy. Crumble salmon into mixture, and stir. Spoon mixture into potato shells.

3. Arrange potatoes in spokelike fashion on plate. Cover loosely with waxed paper. MICROWAVE (high) 3–4 minutes to heat through. Sprinkle with onions, reserved cheese, and parsley. Serve immediately.

SALMON QUENELLES

Fish quenelles, which look like little dumplings, often are served with a generous amount of rich cream sauce, such as Mornay or a hollandaise. But because these salmon quenelles are already rich with cream, try them on a bed of cooked chopped spinach with some lemon wedges.

Preparation time: 15 minutes
Microwave time: 4–5 minutes
Chilling time: 15 minutes to 1 hour
Yield: 20–25 quenelles

1 pound very cold salmon fillets, skinned and cut into chunks
2 egg whites
1 tablespoon chopped fresh dill *or* **1 teaspoon dried**
1 teaspoon salt
⅛ teaspoon ground white pepper
½ cup heavy cream, very cold
2 tablespoons fresh lemon juice

1. Put salmon in food processor, and process about 10 seconds until pureed. With fish still in processor, add egg whites, dill, salt, and pepper. Process about 10 seconds until mixed. With machine running, add cream and lemon juice through the top of the machine, and process until mixed. Put the whole bowl of the processor in the refrigerator for 15 minutes to 1 hour.

2. Use two serving spoons to shape quenelles (see Tip below), about 3 tablespoons each in size. Arrange 6–8 quenelles in spoke fashion on a plate so they don't touch. Add 2 tablespoons water. Cover with plastic wrap, vented, leaving enough room so that the plastic doesn't flatten the quenelles.

3. MICROWAVE (high) 50 seconds to 1½ minutes until salmon turns from deep pink to light pink and the quenelles spring back when touched lightly with a finger. Do not overcook, or they will feel like plastic. Repeat with remaining mixture.

TIP: Quenelles shape best if the salmon mixture is well chilled. For a smooth look, take a scoop with one spoon, then transfer the scoop, bottoms up, onto the second spoon. Round or shape the scoop, if necessary, then gently scrape it off the second spoon and onto a plate.

TIP: Note that white pepper is used instead of black to avoid dark speckles.

SALMON BENEDICT WITH ORANGE HOLLANDAISE

This takeoff on eggs Benedict is glorious fare for brunch or a special luncheon. Instead of a poached egg and ham on an English muffin, I use fresh salmon rounds and artichoke bottoms on an English muffin, topped with a rich orange hollandaise, or maltaise, sauce. The medallions are cut from a fillet, so for even cooking it is best to have a fillet with a fairly even thickness. After cutting, there will be leftover scraps of fresh salmon which can be saved for quenelles or a fish salad.

Preparation time: 20 minutes
Microwave time: 3–5 minutes
Servings: 4

1 12-ounce salmon fillet, ½- to ¾-inch-thick, skinned

4 artichoke bottoms, fresh cooked (*see* Tip below), or defrosted, or canned and rinsed

2 tablespoons fresh lemon juice

4 tablespoons (½ stick) unsalted butter

2 large egg yolks

1 tablespoon orange juice

⅛ teaspoon salt

4 English muffin halves, toasted

1. Use 2½-inch-diameter round cookie cutter to cut four medallions from the salmon fillet (see Tip below).
2. Trim base of artichoke bottoms to ½-inch-thick and flat. Arrange artichokes around edges of a plate. Drizzle ½ tablespoon lemon juice over the artichokes. Place a salmon medallion on top of each artichoke. Drizzle ½ tablespoon lemon juice over salmon. Cover with plastic wrap, vented.
3. MICROWAVE (high) 2–4 minutes until fish turns from reddish to pink. If fillets are of different thicknesses, remove the thinner ones as they finish cooking. Drain. Cover fish lightly and keep in a warm spot.
4. To make the sauce, put butter in 4-cup measure. MICROWAVE (high), uncovered, 20 seconds to soften but not melt. (Cold butter straight from the refrigerator may need up to a minute.)
5. In a small bowl, mix egg yolks and remaining lemon juice. Add to butter. MICROWAVE (high) 45 seconds to 1 minute, whipping with whisk every 15 seconds. Sauce should be smooth and thick. Stir in orange juice and salt.

6. To serve, use a spatula to lift artichoke and salmon onto each muffin half. Drizzle with sauce, and serve rest of sauce on the side.

TIP: *If the fourth medallion looks skimpy because it was cut from a thinner part of the fillet, you can squeeze a big scrap of salmon under the cookie cutter and mold a medallion; the fish pieces will stick together once they are cooked. To make medallions, you can also trace around a circle of paper and cut with a knife.*

TIP: *To cook four large, fresh globe artichokes, cut each stem flush with the bottom of the artichoke. Sit artichokes on a plate, leaving an inch between artichokes. Cover with plastic wrap, vented. MICROWAVE (high) 14–16 minutes, rotating a quarter-turn every 4 minutes. Artichokes are done when a middle leaf pulls out easily or the bottom can be pierced easily with a knife. Let artichokes cool. Pull off outer leaves, scrape off thistlelike choke, and sprinkle artichoke bottom with lemon juice to keep from discoloring.*

TIP: *The sauce can be made with half butter and half margarine and still be thick and creamy.*

TIP: *The sauce can be made a day ahead and stored, covered, in the refrigerator. To reheat, cover and MICROWAVE (low) 1–2 minutes until warm. Stir well.*

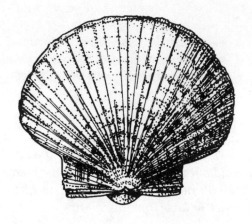

SCALLOPS

Inhale the scent of very fresh scallops and your life as a seafood lover is crystallized. Sweet and perfumy, with a hint of ocean, a deep breathful of scallops—or *Coquilles St. Jacques*, as they are called in France—is as tantalizing as just-ground coffee beans or sizzling butter. Scallops are seafood at its finest.

Most of the scallops in this country are taken from the East Coast: large, full-flavored sea scallops from the cold Atlantic coast off Maine; small, delicately flavored bay scallops from the warmer waters around the Carolinas, Florida, and the Gulf of Mexico; and equally small calico scallops, also from the Florida-area waters. Though I suspect most won't agree, I prefer the larger scallops for their fuller, briny flavor.

In the water, scallops are almost comical-looking, swimming by rapidly clapping together their beautiful, fluted shells. Like clams, all of the meat in a scallop is edible, but typically we eat only the thick, ivory-colored adductor muscle that holds the shells together. The reason is quite practical. Whole scallops are not easily transported because the bivalves don't completely close their shells. Instead, scallop fishermen shuck the mollusks immediately, storing only the large, tender muscle.

Tender scallops are quite edible raw, so when in doubt it is better to slightly undercook rather than overcook the delicate meat.

SCALLOPS BASICS
Delicate scallops cook very quickly in the microwave and require more attention than most seafood to keep them from overcooking and getting tough.

I find that scallops cook best on high power. The meat is slightly more juicy than when cooked on medium power. However, just 20 seconds too long on high power and the scallops will be overcooked.

To avoid overcooking, start by having all the scallops approximately the same size. This is usually no problem with the small bay scallops. Some large sea scallops, however, may need to be cut in half to match the rest of the batch.

An equal weight of small bay scallops or larger sea scallops takes the same amount of time to cook in the microwave. I prefer the taste of the larger scallops, and it is a little easier to avoid overcooking them; however, they are more expensive and harder to obtain.

A small, ¼-pound batch of scallops is easier to monitor in the microwave than a full pound.

To cook scallops, spread them on a dinner plate and drizzle with lemon juice (a teaspoon for a ¼-pound batch or a tablespoon for a 1-pound batch). Cover with plastic wrap, vented. MICROWAVE (high), using time guidelines given below.

Check the scallops several times while cooking, and rearrange them to put uncooked portions to the outside. Scallops are ready to come out of the microwave when the centers of the scallops are almost opaque; scallops that finish cooking first—usually the smallest ones of the batch—should be removed as they are ready.

Allow scallops to stand for several minutes to finish cooking. If undercooked, return them to microwave and check every 10 seconds.

Timing Guidelines
- ¼ pound scallops: 50 seconds–1 minute
- ½ pound scallops: 1½–2 minutes
- 1 pound scallops: 2½–3 minutes

⌇❤ SCALLOPS IN SCALLION-FLAVORED BROTH

This delicate-tasting, pastel yellow soup makes a pretty first course, particularly if presented in shallow soup bowls. It's very easy to make and has an extra bonus: no added fat.

Preparation time: 5 minutes
Microwave time: 13–15 minutes
Servings: 4

4 cups chicken stock or broth
3 scallions, sliced
½ pound bay scallops
⅛ teaspoon ground white pepper
8 very thin, round lemon slices

1. Put chicken stock and scallions in 2½-quart casserole. Cover. MICROWAVE (high) 7–8 minutes to boiling.

2. Stir in scallops with any juices, and the pepper. MICROWAVE (high), covered, 6–7 minutes or until stock boils again and scallops are just opaque. Serve in shallow bowls and float lemon slices on top.

TIP: *Note that white pepper is used instead of black to avoid unattractive speckles.*

❤ SCALLOPS WITH OYSTER SAUCE

This dish is remarkably easy and fast.

Preparation time: 5 minutes
Microwave time: 3–4 minutes
Servings: 4

1 pound sea scallops
1 tablespoon fresh lemon juice
¼ cup oyster sauce

1. Arrange scallops on a dinner plate. Drizzle with lemon juice. Cover with plastic wrap, vented. MICROWAVE (high) 2½–3 minutes until centers of scallops are just opaque, rearranging twice to put uncooked portions to the outside. Let scallops stand on counter for 3 minutes to finish cooking.
2. Drain juices into 2-cup measure. Stir in oyster sauce. MICROWAVE (high), uncovered, 30 seconds to 1 minute to heat. Stir into scallops.

SCALLOP AND CILANTRO SALAD

This colorful salad makes a lovely first course for six people or a light summer entree for four. The scallops will cook a little in the marinade, so take extra care to avoid overcooking them in Step 1.

Preparation time: 10 minutes
Microwave time: 2–3 minutes
Chilling time: 2 hours
Servings: 4–6

1 pound bay scallops
3 tablespoons fresh lemon juice
¼ cup olive oil, preferably extra virgin
1 teaspoon grated lemon zest
1 teaspoon Dijon mustard
¼ teaspoon salt
2 tablespoons minced fresh cilantro
1 tomato, peeled, seeded, and diced

1. Spread scallops evenly on a large plate. Drizzle with 1 tablespoon lemon juice. Cover with plastic wrap, vented. MICROWAVE (high) 2–3 minutes, stirring every minute, until centers are almost opaque. Drain.
2. In a small bowl, whisk olive oil, remaining lemon juice, lemon zest, mustard, and salt. Stir in cilantro. Combine dressing with scallops. Refrigerate, covered, for at least 2 hours. Just before serving, mix in tomato.

SCALLOPS WITH PASSION FRUIT SAUCE

Announce ahead of time that this will be the first course, and your guests are likely to arrive with a particularly fine bottle of wine. Exotic, tropical-tasting passion fruit make this dish as wonderful as it sounds, and with very little effort.

Most passion fruit are imported from tropical climates and when ripe look like large, dimpled, brittle prunes—not very romantic to look at. Indeed, according to Elizabeth Schneider, author of Uncommon Fruits and Vegetables, *the passion in the fruit's name refers to the Passion of Christ, as the various parts of the fruit's flower represent Christ's wounds, crucifixion nails, and crown of thorns, and the Apostles.*

Although I prefer the taste of sea scallops, smaller bay scallops look prettier in this dish, dotted with tiny passion-fruit seeds. For menu suggestions see page 23.

Preparation time: 5 minutes
Microwave time: 3½–4 minutes
Serves: 4–6

1 pound bay scallops or sea scallops
1 tablespoon fresh lemon juice
1 teaspoon sugar
Pulp and seeds from 2 passion fruit (*see* Tip, following)
2 tablespoons butter

1. Spread scallops evenly on a large plate. Drizzle with lemon juice. Cover with plastic wrap, vented. MICROWAVE (high) 2½–3 minutes, stirring every minute, until centers are almost opaque. Lift out scallops, leaving juices (about ½ cup) in plate.
2. Stir sugar and passion fruit pulp into juices. MICROWAVE (high), uncovered, 1–2 minutes until hot. Stir in butter. Pour over scallops. Dot scallops with passion-fruit seeds.

TIP: Passion fruit are ripe when dimply and brittle. Cut fruit in half and use a spoon to scoop out mustard-colored pulp and seeds.

TIP: To reduce fat, you can eliminate the butter, but the sauce will not be as smooth.

SHARK

Maybe it's the appeal of man-bites-dog, but shark is showing its teeth at an increasing number of restaurant and home tables. And once consumers pass the psychological barrier of eating shark, they typically discover that shark makes a fine dish: firm, meaty, sweet-tasting, and mild.

A variety of shark, including spiny dogfish (called *harbor halibut* in Maine), blacktip, and porbeagle, is caught by net or longline in the Atlantic and Pacific oceans. The most prized, however, are the white-fleshed blue shark and the mako, which is often used as a substitute for more expensive swordfish. Cooked shark does resemble swordfish, but it is softer in texture.

Those who shy away from shark may well have eaten shark without knowing better. Shark is a common fish, along with haddock or cod, that is battered and fried for fish-n-chips plates. And authentic shark's-fin soup in Chinese restaurants indeed uses the fins, which provide little flavor but plenty of gelatinous body.

Sharks retain urea in their bodies, and this needs to be neutralized before it turns to ammonia. To neutralize shark fillets, the shark meat must be soaked for about an hour in salted water, or marinated in lemon juice, vinegar, or milk for 20 minutes. Fish merchants typically soak shark before it is sold, so you don't need to repeat this step.

⟨♥ MUSTARD-MARINATED SHARK

Shark is marinated in lemon and mustard and then cooked quickly with no added fat.

Preparation time: 5 minutes
Marinating time: 20 minutes
Microwave time: 4–5 minutes
Servings: 4

1 pound shark steaks
2 tablespoons fresh lemon juice
2 tablespoons Dijon mustard
Lemon wedges

1. Arrange fish on a dinner plate with thickest portions to the outside. Drizzle lemon juice on both sides of fish. Spoon mustard on top. Let stand 20 minutes to marinate.
2. Cover with plastic wrap, vented. MICROWAVE (high) 4–5 minutes until thickest portion is almost opaque when tested with a fork. Let stand 5 minutes. Drain. Serve with lemon wedges.

SHARK WITH SHIITAKE MUSHROOMS AND SPINACH

Meaty-textured shiitake mushrooms are mixed with just-softened fresh spinach leaves to top shark fillets.

Preparation time: 15 minutes
Microwave time: 8–11 minutes
Servings: 4

1 pound shark fillets
1 tablespoon fresh lemon juice
½ pound fresh shiitake mushrooms (or porcini, morel, or button mushrooms)
1 tablespoon olive oil
1 tablespoon white wine vinegar
⅛ teaspoon salt
⅛ teaspoon freshly ground black pepper
2 cups (packed) fresh spinach leaves, cleaned and chopped
2 green onions, white part and first 2 inches of green, sliced

1. Arrange fish on a dinner plate with thickest portions to the outside. Drizzle with lemon juice. Cover with plastic wrap, vented. MICROWAVE (high) 4–5 minutes until thickest portion is almost opaque when tested with a fork. Let stand 5 minutes. Drain.
2. Wipe dirt off mushrooms and chop medium-fine. Put mushrooms and oil in 2½-quart casserole. Cover. MICROWAVE (high) 3–4 minutes to soften.
3. Stir in vinegar, salt, pepper, spinach, and green onions. Cover. MICROWAVE (high) 1–2 minutes until spinach wilts. Top shark generously with mushrooms and spinach mixture.

CHILI-MARINATED SHARK WITH AVOCADO TOPPING

Shark fillets are marinated in hot pepper, cooked, then topped with a cool guacamole-style mixture. To keep the avocado bright green, make the sauce just before you serve it.

Preparation time: 15 minutes
Marinating time: 20 minutes
Microwave time: 9–11 minutes
Servings: 4

1 **jalapeño pepper, seeded and minced**
2 **tablespoons vegetable oil**
3 **tablespoons fresh lemon juice**
1 **pound shark fillets**
1 **tomato, peeled, seeded, and chopped**
1 **avocado, peeled, pitted, and chopped rough at the last moment**
1 **tablespoon minced fresh cilantro**

1. Put pepper, oil, and 2 tablespoons lemon juice in 1-cup measure. MICROWAVE (high), uncovered, 1 minute to heat. Pour mixture on fish and use two forks (not your fingers—those pepper pieces are hot!) to turn the fillets several times. Let stand 20 minutes to marinate.
2. Arrange fish with pepper and oil on a dinner plate with the thickest portions of fish to the outside. Cover with plastic wrap, vented. MICROWAVE (high) 4–5 minutes until thickest portion is almost opaque when tested with a fork. Let stand 5 minutes. Drain.
3. Put tomato in 4-cup measure. Cover with plastic wrap. MICROWAVE (high) 3–4 minutes to soften tomato and draw out juices. Stir in avocado and cilantro. Do not cover. MICROWAVE (high) 1 minute to heat through. Stir in remaining lemon juice. Serve shark topped with avocado mixture.

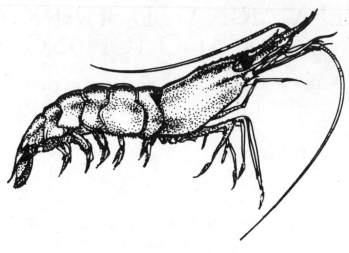

SHRIMP

Here is America's Georgia peach, California sunshine, and party at the Ritz all tied up in a tiny pink curl. If people don't like fish they still like shrimp, and they rarely just like shrimp—they love it.

Shrimp are found in waters all over the world, and the more than 300 varieties range from tiny thumbnail size to jumbos. Although shrimp turn pink when cooked, raw shells may start from grey, brown, pink, purple, and even blue and white.

Unless you live near the Gulf Coast, fresh shrimp have probably been a rare treat. However, air-transported fresh shrimp—often with heads still intact—are becoming more common throughout the country.

Most shrimp that you find in fish departments has been frozen, then thawed for display. For best results, cook thawed shrimp within 24 hours and don't refreeze it. When you refreeze fish, and especially delicate shrimp, the protein breaks down and the texture becomes mushy. If you want to keep frozen shrimp at home, ask the fish department to sell you still-frozen—not thawed—shrimp, and take it home immediately.

Shrimp are graded and sold by unit number, and that number tells how many beheaded shrimp it takes to make a pound: U-250/500 are so tiny that 250 or more are needed to make a pound; U-36/40 are the variety often found on sale in supermarkets and yield about 10 shrimp per pound; and U-21/25 are jumbo shrimp typically found in shrimp cocktails.

Extra-jumbo shrimp (U-15/20) sometimes are presented in restaurants as scampi, but this is a misnomer. Scampi are not shrimp. Scampi is the Italian name for a small clawed lobster whose tail is about the size of an extra-jumbo shrimp.

To defrost shrimp, put them in a colander with a bowl underneath to catch the water, and place in the back of the refrigerator overnight. You can start cleaning them when they are semifrozen, and they likely will be completely thawed by the time you are ready to cook.

To peel shrimp, hold the tail in one hand. With the other hand, slip your thumb under the shell between the swimmerets and peel off the shell. To remove the tail shell, squeeze the tail with your thumb and forefinger. Use your other hand to gently pull out the shrimp.

You don't have to devein or remove the black intestinal tract from the shrimp, but it does look nicer if you do. It is easier to do this before the shrimp are cooked.

To devein, use a sharp knife to cut a ⅛-inch-deep line along the curve of the shrimp. Remove the intestinal tract with a toothpick under running water, or rinse afterwards.

To butterfly shrimp, use a small knife to cut in about ¼ inch along the back edge, stopping at the tail; press shrimp body flat. When the shrimp cook, they will curl into a butterfly-like shape.

SHRIMP SIZES

Name	Number per Pound
Giant	10–14
Extra-Jumbo	15–20
Jumbo	21–25
Extra-Large	26–30
Large	31–35
Medium-Large	36–40
Medium	41–50
Small	51–70
Tiny	70–150
Midgets	150–250
Titi	250–500

SHRIMP BASICS

To cook a batch of plain shrimp, arrange the shrimp on a plate with tails facing in, cover with plastic wrap, and MICROWAVE (high), using the following timing guidelines, until shrimp just turn pink.

A ¼ pound of shrimp doesn't need to be rearranged on a plate; just rotate the plate a couple of times. You'll have the most consistent cooking results in the microwave with this small amount of shrimp.

For a ½ pound of medium-sized shrimp, make concentric circles of shrimp on the plate, and rotate the shrimp after a minute, then again after 30 seconds, also rotating the plate.

A pound of shrimp needs to be tossed and rearranged at least every minute to get evenly cooked. And still, I often find two or three undercooked shrimp—particularly shelled shrimp—hidden under the pile. Don't overcook the majority of the shrimp just to get these last few; instead, put the wayward shrimp on a small plate, and give them another 20 seconds, or as needed, in the microwave.

The size of the shrimp doesn't matter; ½ pound of jumbo shrimp take the same time as ½ pound of medium shrimp. Note, however, that butterflied shrimp need less time per pound.

Timing Guidelines
- **Unshelled:**
  ¼ pound: 45 seconds–1 minute
  ½ pound: 2–2½ minutes
  1 pound: 3–3½ minutes
- **Shelled:**
  ¼ pound: 1–2 minutes
  ½ pound: 2–3 minutes
  1 pound: 2½–3 minutes
- **Butterflied:**
  ¼ pound (dinner plate): 30–35 seconds
  ½ pound (dinner plate): 1–1½ minutes
  1 pound (2½ quart casserole): 2½–3 minutes

⌣♥ COLD SHRIMP WITH SPIKED CHILI SAUCE

With just a little help, a bottle of chili sauce makes a fine, traditional cocktail sauce for cold shrimp. A touch of horseradish, lemon juice, and Worcestershire sauce provide the extra oomph.

Preparation time: 5 minutes
Microwave time: 2½–3 minutes
Chilling time: 2 hours or overnight
Servings: 4–6 appetizers

1 pound raw shrimp, shelled and deveined
1 12-ounce bottle chili sauce
2 tablespoons prepared horseradish
2 tablespoons fresh lemon juice
¼ teaspoon Worcestershire sauce

1. Put shrimp in 2½-quart casserole. Cover tightly. MICROWAVE (high) 2½–3 minutes until shrimp are just pink, tossing and rearranging shrimp after the first minute, then every 30 seconds. If two or three shrimp are still not cooked, put them back alone to cook more, checking every 20 seconds. Drain. Refrigerate, covered, for 2 hours or overnight.
2. To make sauce, mix remaining ingredients in a medium-sized bowl. Serve chilled, cooked shrimp with sauce on the side.

TIP: For even prettier shrimp, butterfly before cooking. Use a small knife to cut in about ¼-inch along the back edge, stopping at the tail; press shrimp body flat. When the shrimp cook, they will curl into a butterfly-like shape. Because butterflied shrimp are thinner, they take less time per pound to cook than regular, shelled shrimp. A ½ pound of butterflied shrimp needs only 1–1½ minutes.

GINGER-MARINATED SHRIMP

Shrimp marinate in Oriental herbs and oil just long enough to absorb enticing flavors—ideal for a light appetizer.

Preparation time: 5 minutes
Marinating time: 15 minutes
Microwave time: 2–3 minutes
Servings: 2–4

1 teaspoon minced garlic
1 teaspoon minced fresh ginger
2 tablespoons soy sauce
2 tablespoons dry white wine
¼ teaspoon sesame oil
¼ teaspoon freshly ground black pepper
½ pound raw shrimp, shelled and deveined

1. Mix all ingredients except for shrimp in 4-cup measure. Add shrimp. Let marinate 15 minutes.

2. Arrange shrimp in concentric circles on a dinner plate with tails pointing in. Cover with plastic wrap. MICROWAVE (high) 2–3 minutes until shrimp are just pink, rotating the shrimp after a minute, then again after 30 seconds; also rotate the plate, if necessary, for more even cooking. Drain and serve warm or cold.

SWEET SESAME SHRIMP SALAD

The shrimp and dressing can be prepared a day ahead of time, then assembled in a quick, beautiful salad.

Preparation time: 15 minutes
Microwave time: 5–8 minutes
Chilling time: 2 hours or overnight
Servings: 6

1 **pound raw shrimp, shelled and deveined**
2 **tablespoons sesame seeds**
1 **teaspoon minced garlic**
3 **tablespoons white wine vinegar**
⅛ **teaspoon red pepper flakes**
⅛ **teaspoon dried oregano**
¼ **teaspoon salt**
⅛ **teaspoon freshly ground black pepper**
¼ **cup vegetable oil**
¼ **cup honey**
2 **quarts shredded romaine lettuce**
½ **pound fresh snow peas, top and bottom threads removed**
1 **11-ounce can mandarin orange sections, drained**
½ **cup slivered almonds**

1. Put shrimp in 2½-quart casserole. Cover tightly. MICROWAVE (high) 2½–3 minutes until shrimp are just pink, tossing and rearranging shrimp after the first minute, then every 30 seconds. If two or three shrimp are still not cooked, put them back alone to cook more, checking every 20 seconds. Drain. Refrigerate, covered, for 2 hours or overnight.
2. For the dressing, put sesame seeds on a small plate and shake to spread them. Do not cover. MICROWAVE (high) 2–3 minutes to heat well. Set aside.
3. Put garlic, vinegar, red pepper, oregano, salt, and black pepper in 4-cup measure. MICROWAVE (high), uncovered, 1–2 minutes to soften garlic and dried spices. Whisk in oil and honey, then sesame seeds.
4. Line serving platter or plates with lettuce. Arrange shrimp, pea pods, orange sections, and almonds on top. Drizzle with dressing.

TIP: For even prettier shrimp, butterfly before cooking. Use a small knife to cut in about ¼-inch along the back edge, stopping at the tail; press shrimp body flat. When the shrimp cook, they will curl into a butterfly-like shape. Because butterflied shrimp are thinner, they take less time per pound to cook than regular, shelled shrimp. A ½ pound of butterflied shrimp needs only 1–1½ minutes of cooking.

SHRIMP-STUFFED WONTONS

These flavorful wontons, or dumplings, make a wonderful appetizer, side dish, or wonton soup in homemade chicken stock. The filling is prepared in the microwave, then the stuffed wontons are cooked in boiling water over the stove—it takes too long to boil a large amount of water in the microwave. The little dumplings are time-consuming to prepare, but as the first 12 are boiling, you have just enough time to fold the second batch.

Preparation time: 1 hour
Microwave time: 4–6 minutes
Yields: 60 dumplings

1 tablespoon butter
4 green onions, white and first 2 inches of green, sliced
1 tablespoon minced garlic
1 tablespoon flour
1 pound raw shrimp, shelled, deveined, and minced
2 teaspoons minced fresh ginger
1 cup napa (Chinese cabbage) white portion, minced
3 tablespoons soy sauce
¼ teaspoon sesame oil
¼ teaspoon freshly ground black pepper
1 teaspoon cornstarch dissolved in 1 tablespoon water
15 egg roll skins, *or* 60 wonton skins

1. Put butter, green onions, and garlic in 2½-quart casserole. Cover with plastic wrap, vented. MICROWAVE (high) 2–3 minutes, stirring after 1 minute. Stir in flour, shrimp, ginger, and napa. Do not cover. MICROWAVE (high) 2–3 minutes until shrimp just turn pink, stirring three or four times to help the shrimp cook evenly. Mix in soy sauce, sesame oil, and pepper. Let mixture cool a little.
2. Bring 4 quarts of water to a boil in a stockpot on the stove. Set cornstarch mixture on work counter.
3. Cut three of the egg roll skins into quarters to make a total of 12 little rectangles. Put a scant teaspoon of filling in center of one rectangle. Use your finger to paint the edges with the cornstarch mixture. (This helps the skins stick together.) Fold the long sides together so that it looks like a long ravioli, and press edges firmly to seal. The dumplings may be cooked like this, or you may continue to paint, fold, and press the bottom of the short sides to form little wontons.
4. Drop stuffed dumplings 12 at a time into boiling water. Cook for 5 minutes until the egg roll skin or wonton is soft like cooked pasta. Remove with a slotted spoon, set in a single layer on a plate, and cover with plastic wrap. Repeat Steps 3 and 4 with remaining

egg roll skins until all of dumplings are ready.
(You may need to reheat the first few batches.
See Tip, following.)

TIP: *Egg roll skins may be purchased in Oriental markets and in many supermarkets, wrapped in clear plastic, in the produce or other refrigerated section.*

TIP: *The wonton skins stick together when wet, so arrange the finished dumplings on a plate in a single layer without touching. Cover with plastic wrap to reheat.*

✺ SPICY SHRIMP BOIL

This makes a wonderfully spicy and messy bowl of shrimp, perfect for sharing with friends. Guests have to peel their own cooked shrimp, so have plenty of napkins—and cold beer—on hand.

Preparation time: 10 minutes
Microwave time: 7–9 minutes
Servings: 4

  1 cup water
  1 cup chopped celery
10 allspice berries
  ¼ teaspoon ground mace
  5 cloves
  1 bay leaf, crushed
  2 sprigs fresh parsley
  ½ teaspoon fresh thyme
  ½ teaspoon red pepper flakes
  ¼ teaspoon cayenne pepper
  2 tablespoons salt
  ¼ teaspoon freshly ground
    black pepper
  1 pound unshelled raw shrimp

1. Put all ingredients except for shrimp in 2½-quart casserole. Cover. MICROWAVE (high) 5–6 minutes until boiling.
2. Stir in shrimp, then push shrimp to outer edges of dish. Cover tightly. MICROWAVE (high) 2–3 minutes or until shrimp are just pink, stirring after first minute, then every 30 seconds. Let stand, covered, 2–3 minutes. Serve shrimp in a large bowl or individual bowls, with the liquid.

SHRIMP MOUSSE WITH BEURRE ROUGE

This delicate shrimp-pink mousse on a pink-toned butter sauce makes a stunning first course or luncheon entree. And it's so easy in the microwave—no conventional water bath is necessary, and there is no need to butter the custard cups. It is important to use small, round molds or bowls, such as custard cups, to assure even cooking. Have the shrimp and cream well chilled so they won't stick in the food processor.

Preparation time: 20 minutes
Microwave time: 9–12 minutes
Standing time: 15 minutes
Servings: 4

MOUSSE
1 pound very cold raw shrimp, shelled and deveined
1 cup whipping cream, chilled
2 tablespoons fresh lemon juice
½ teaspoon grated lemon zest
⅛ teaspoon ground nutmeg
⅛ teaspoon cayenne pepper
1 teaspoon salt
⅛ teaspoon ground white pepper
Twisted lemon zest strips, for garnish
½ teaspoon minced fresh parsley, for garnish

BEURRE ROUGE
1 tablespoon red wine vinegar
1 teaspoon minced shallots
4 tablespoons (½ stick) butter, diced, room temperature
Dash of salt

1. Put shrimp in food processor and process until chopped coarse. With shrimp still in processor, add cream, lemon juice, grated zest, nutmeg, cayenne, salt, and pepper. Process only until mixed.
2. Fill 6-ounce glass custard cups three-fourths full with the shrimp mixture. Cover each loosely with plastic wrap. Using the bottom of a glass, press shrimp mixture down to fill in most of the larger air holes for a prettier shape when the mousse is unmolded. Cover tightly with plastic wrap.
3. For easier handling, place covered cups on a plate. MICROWAVE (medium) 2 minutes. Turn plate and cups half a turn. MICROWAVE (low) 4–6 minutes until edges are firm to the touch, the center is almost firm, and a toothpick inserted into the center comes out almost dry. Let stand 15 minutes. Use a knife to loosen edges, if necessary, and turn onto a plate to unmold.
4. To make the sauce, put the vinegar and shallots in 4-cup measure. MICROWAVE (high) 1–2 minutes until liquid is reduced by half. Add butter and salt gradually while whisking. Sauce should be creamy and foamy. Strain to remove shallots.

5. To serve, spoon sauce onto salad-sized serving plates. Use a spatula to lift unmolded mousse onto each plate. Garnish with twisted zest strips and just a few pieces of minced parsley.

TIP: Mousses can be made up to two days ahead and kept in their molds, covered, in the refrigerator. To serve, let stand for 10 minutes, then unmold. The mousse will taste lighter and fuller if at room temperature, not cold.

TIP: This butter sauce is too thin if made with all or half margarine. To reduce some of the fat and calories, skip the sauce and serve the mousse with lemon wedges on colorful appetizer plates or serve on a bed of green lettuce with thinly sliced Granny Smith apples.

TIP: Extra guests or need smaller portions? Let mousses cool slightly, then cut into 1-inch slices. You'll still have two generous, overlapping slices each for six people.

FETTUCCINE WITH SHRIMP SAUCE

The sauce here is mostly olive oil (so use a good quality), plus the juices from fresh tomatoes, mushrooms—and shrimp. The fettuccine is better cooked the conventional way, on the stove.

Preparation time: 10 minutes
Microwave time: 12–15 minutes
Servings: 4–6

¼ **cup and 2 tablespoons olive oil**
2 **tablespoons minced garlic**
2 **medium tomatoes, peeled, seeded, and cubed**
½ **cup chopped fresh mushrooms**
1 **pound raw shrimp, shelled and chopped coarse**
3 **tablespoons fresh lemon juice**
¼ **cup chopped parsley**
5–6 **drops hot sauce**
½ **teaspoon salt**
⅛ **teaspoon freshly ground black pepper**
1 **pound fettuccine, cooked, drained, and hot**

1. Put ¼ cup olive oil, garlic, tomatoes, and mushrooms in 2½-quart casserole. Do not cover. MICROWAVE (high) 10–12 minutes until the vegetable juices partially evaporate and the sauce thickens.
2. Stir in the shrimp. Cover. MICROWAVE (high) 2½–3 minutes until shrimp just turn pink. Stir in lemon juice, parsley, hot sauce, salt, and pepper.
3. Toss remaining 2 tablespoons olive oil into hot fettuccine. Mix most of the shrimp mixture into the fettuccine, leaving about ¼ cup to sprinkle on top. Serve immediately.

TIP: Note the microwave cooking techniques here: the vegetables are cooked uncovered to let the juices evaporate and the sauce thicken; the shrimp and vegetables then are covered to help the shrimp cook evenly.

TIP: Cooked pasta is a food that reheats particularly well in the microwave. Cover with plastic wrap and MICROWAVE (medium) until heated. (When you touch the top of the wrapped dish with your palm and you feel the heat, it is done.)

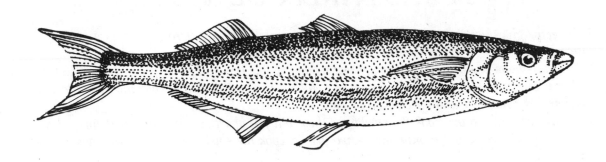

SMELTS

Smelts are like licorice candies—you love 'em or hate 'em. Those who love the small, finger-length fish no doubt relish the number of fish as well as the taste. Eyes widen and mentally count the little silvery fish like a six-year-old with a dumped piggy bank counts pennies.

Those who don't like smelts, I suspect, don't like the bones. It is a matter of bravura that one eats the whole thing—sans head, of course, and the very tip of the tail. Removing the bones is removing the heart of the fish. That's the fun, the crunch—and the calcium.

Fresh smelts are most common in spring, when the ocean fish run from the sea into fresh water. Lakebound smelts are also caught at this time, also during their spawning run. When buying fresh smelts, check the batch carefully. Each little fish will have a slit in its belly and its insides removed. Finish cleaning any errant smelts before placing them in the refrigerator.

Flash-frozen smelts are available all year and have an excellent texture. Defrosting a pound of smelts takes only about 15 minutes on the counter if you first run the smelts under running cold water several times.

❧ SMELTS WITH SHARP TEXAS BARBECUE SAUCE

This recipe gives you basic instructions for cooking smelts in the microwave, plus a favorite sauce.

Tiny smelts stand up well to a big-tasting sauce, like this spicy-sharp barbecue. The recipe makes a generous 3 cups of barbecue sauce, which stores well in the refrigerator for at least a week and is equally useful on chicken or ribs.

Take care not to overcook the smelts, or they will fall apart as you transfer them to dinner plates. If you're cooking for only one or two people, cook the smelts right on a microwave-proof dinner plate.

Preparation time: 15 minutes
Microwave time: 14–18 minutes
Servings: 4

1 **cup finely chopped onion**
2 **teaspoons minced garlic**
1⅓ **cups cider vinegar**
1¾ **cups ketchup**
1⅓ **cups Worcestershire sauce**
3 **tablespoons light or unsulfured molasses**
¼ **cup fresh lemon juice**
2 **tablespoons dry mustard**
1 **bay leaf, crushed**
2 **teaspoons fresh oregano** *or* ½ **teaspoon dried**
½ **teaspoon freshly ground black pepper**
1 **pound smelts (5–6 inches long), cleaned and gutted, tails intact**

1. To make the sauce, put onion, garlic, and about 3 tablespoons of the vinegar in 2½-quart casserole. MICROWAVE (high), uncovered, 2–3 minutes to soften the vegetables. Stir in rest of the ingredients except smelts. Do not cover. MICROWAVE (high) 8–10 minutes to thicken. (Sauce may be made up to a week ahead and stored, covered, in the refrigerator.)

2. Arrange fish in a single layer on a large plate or casserole, placing the largest pieces to the outside. Cover. MICROWAVE (high) 4–5 minutes until the slit edges of the smelts start to curl and the fish are almost ready to flake. Let stand 5 minutes. Serve smelts on plate, with barbecue sauce on the side.

TIP: Sulfur is a concentrated brownish syrup that is a residue of sugar refining. "Sulfured" molasses contains sulfur from the sugar-making process and comes in either dark or light versions. Unsulfured is made without the use of sulfur and in cooking is comparable to light molasses.

MARINATED SMELTS

Smelts are covered with a hot oil mixture, cooked slightly, then left to marinate three days in the refrigerator. Serve them like sardines, on crusty black bread with a slice of red onion.

Preparation time: 10 minutes
Microwave time: 3–5 minutes
Chilling time: 3 days
Servings: 4–6

1 **medium onion, sliced thin**
¼ **cup olive oil, preferably extra virgin**
2 **tablespoons white wine vinegar**
2 **bay leaves, crushed**
¼ **teaspoon salt**
⅛ **teaspoon freshly ground black pepper**
1 **pound smelts, cleaned and gutted**

1. Put onion and olive oil in 4-cup measure. MICROWAVE (high) 2–3 minutes to soften onion. Stir in vinegar, bay leaves, salt, and pepper.
2. Put smelts in 2-quart flat casserole. Pour oil mixture over fish and use two spoons to gently toss. Cover. MICROWAVE (high) 1–2 minutes until smelts are warm to the touch but still very firm, stirring once. Gently toss. Let stand on counter 15 minutes. Refrigerate, covered, 3 days to marinate. To serve, bring smelts to room temperature. Lift out smelts and discard sauce. Serve smelts in salads or on lightly buttered black bread.

INDIAN-SPICED SMELTS AND ZUCCHINI

Eastern spices—coriander, cumin, and fennel—are cooked in butter to intensify their flavors and then are mixed with the smelts and vegetables. This colorful dish spreads less than a pound of smelts to serve three or four people.

Preparation time: 15 minutes
Microwave time: 8–12 minutes
Servings: 3–4

1 ¾-inch-thick slice of fresh ginger, scraped and chopped rough
1 teaspoon coriander seeds
½ teaspoon cumin seeds
¼ teaspoon fennel seeds
¼ cup water
1 tablespoon butter
¾ pound smelts, cleaned and gutted, tails intact
½ teaspoon turmeric
½ teaspoon salt
1 medium tomato, peeled, seeded, and chopped
½ pound (2 small) zucchini, cut into ¼-inch slices
2 tablespoons chopped fresh cilantro

1. Put ginger, coriander, cumin, fennel, and water in food processor, and process until smooth.
2. Put butter in 2½-quart casserole. MICROWAVE (high), uncovered, 1–2 minutes until melted and quite hot. Pour in spice puree. Do not cover. MICROWAVE (high) 1–2 minutes until spices thicken and give off a good aroma. Roll smelts in the mixture; lift out and set aside.
3. Stir turmeric and salt, then the tomato and zucchini, into the spice mixture. Cover. MICROWAVE (high) 2–3 minutes until vegetables start to soften.
4. Arrange smelts on top in a single layer, putting the largest to the outside. Cover. MICROWAVE (high) 4–5 minutes until the slit edges of the smelts start to curl and the fish are almost ready to flake. Let stand 5 minutes. Sprinkle with fresh cilantro.

TIP: Turmeric, a natural dye, will temporarily stain your counter a lovely yellow if you carelessly set down the mixing spoon.

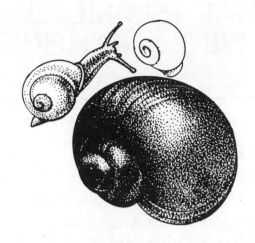

S N A I L S

Snails are mollusks that are found both in fresh and salt waters and on land. Although it is the terrestrial snails, specifically the Bourgogne, that we eat most commonly, snails are identified more with fish than meat, and so I think they are appropriate for a fish cookbook.

Although snails are gathered in the Greek Islands and scooped up by children along the Italian seaside, the mollusks are most closely identified in this country with France and French cooking.

Escargot, bathed in garlicky butter, is a dish that almost defines a traditional French restaurant here. More recently, restaurants touting lighter fare have adopted the snails but dropped the butter, perhaps mixing snails with olive oil and a touch of intense-tasting sun-dried tomatoes.

Snails themselves have a very mild flavor and so depend on spices, herbs, wine, and butter to gild their soft, meaty texture.

Most snails in this country are sold precooked and canned, so cooking a snail dish is really making a sauce and reheating the snails—a perfect job for the microwave.

Snails Simmered in Wine and Herbs, the first recipe in this chapter, is very basic and light and lends only the flavors of wine, basil, and parsley to the snails. Snails de Jonghe tips its hat to Chicago, French restaurants, and the irresistible leadership of butter and garlic. And Snails with Sun-Dried Tomatoes on Linguine updates snails with a California touch.

☙ SNAILS SIMMERED IN WINE AND HERBS

Because canned snails are precooked, all you really have to do is rinse and drain them. However, they will taste even better if briefly simmered in wine and herbs. If not using them immediately, let the snails marinate in the cooking liquids overnight in the refrigerator.

Preparation time: 5 minutes
Microwave time: 1–2 minutes
Servings: 2

1 **7-ounce can snails (about 12 snails), rinsed and drained**
¼ **cup dry white wine**
1 **tablespoon chopped fresh basil** *or* **1 teaspoon dried**
1 **tablespoon chopped fresh parsley**

Put all ingredients in 1-cup measure. MICROWAVE (high), uncovered, 1–2 minutes until hot but not boiling. Let stand 10 minutes. Arrange and serve with the cooking liquids, or drain and use in other recipes.

SNAILS DE JONGHE

This is a takeoff on Shrimp de Jonghe, a restaurant menu cliché that travels back to Henri de Jonghe and his turn-of-the-century Loop restaurant. The butter-rich treatment doesn't fit the modern style of low-fat eating, but it's Chicago. And I like it.

Preparation time: 10 minutes
Microwave time: 2–3 minutes
Broiling time: 5 minutes
Servings: 2–3

¼ cup dry white wine or sherry
1 ¼-inch slice of onion
1 bay leaf, crumbled
5 peppercorns
1 7-ounce can snails (1 dozen), rinsed and drained
8 tablespoons (1 stick) butter
1 teaspoon fresh lemon juice
1 teaspoon minced garlic
1 tablespoon minced shallots
2 tablespoons minced fresh parsley
⅛ teaspoon cayenne pepper
⅛ teaspoon freshly ground black pepper
½ cup fresh French bread crumbs

1. Put white wine, onion, bay leaf, and peppercorns in 1-quart casserole. Cover. MICROWAVE (high) about 1 minute until hot but not boiling. Mix in snails. Let stand 10 minutes to absorb flavors. Drain, reserving 2 tablespoons liquid.

2. Put butter in 2-cup measure. MICROWAVE (high), uncovered, 1–2 minutes to melt. Stir in lemon juice, garlic, shallots, parsley, cayenne, pepper, and all but 1 tablespoon of the bread crumbs.

3. Top snails with butter-bread crumb mixture. Sprinkle with remaining bread crumbs. Put under broiler about 5 minutes until bread crumbs are lightly browned.

SNAILS WITH SUN-DRIED TOMATOES ON LINGUINE

For an unusual topping on pasta try a quick mixture of snails and tasty sun-dried tomatoes. The pasta is best made conventionally on the stove.

Preparation time: 10 minutes
Microwave time: 6–9 minutes
Servings: 4

1 **7-ounce can snails, rinsed and drained**	1. Mix snails and wine in a small bowl. Let stand 10 minutes.
2 **tablespoons dry red wine**	2. Cut off root end of leek. Trim all but 2 inches of green. Slice in half lengthwise, and wash well under running water, separating stalk sections to remove dirt. Chop. Put leek, butter, and 2 tablespoons of the olive oil in 1-quart casserole. Cover. MICROWAVE (high) 2–3 minutes to soften.
1 **medium leek**	
1 **tablespoon butter**	
3 **tablespoons olive oil**	
½ **cup canned plum tomatoes, chopped coarse**	
1 **tablespoon minced garlic**	
2 **teaspoons finely chopped fresh oregano** *or* ½ **teaspoon dried**	3. Stir in plum tomatoes, garlic, oregano, and pepper. Cover. MICROWAVE (high) 2–3 minutes to heat through. Stir in sun-dried tomatoes and snails. Cover. MICROWAVE (high) 2–3 minutes to heat through. Toss linguine with remaining tablespoon olive oil. Spoon snail mixture on top and sprinkle with parsley.
⅛ **teaspoon freshly ground black pepper**	
2 **ounces sun-dried tomatoes, chopped coarse**	
12 **ounces linguine, cooked, drained, and hot**	
2 **tablespoons chopped fresh parsley**	

TIP: If sun-dried tomatoes are not packed in oil, reconstitute them in warm water to cover.

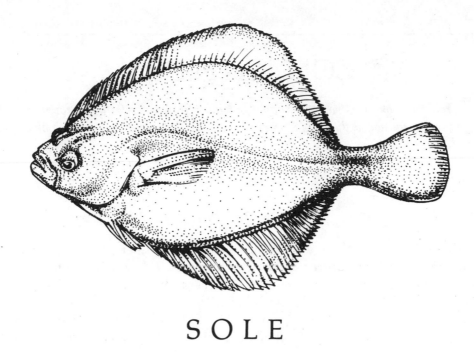

S O L E

Fillet of sole is the standard-bearer against which lesser white fish are compared. Orange roughy can be hailed as similar to but not as delicate as fillet of sole, flounder as a coarser fillet of sole, and lemon sole as a flounder good enough to borrow the sole surname.

One reason for its high esteem is that sole is a fish that doesn't taste like fish. Its flavor is delicate and light, very fine and inoffensive. For this reason, it's best to keep recipes for sole fairly simple and avoid overpowering herbs and sauces.

Because the name *sole* carries the weight of quality, numerous flatfish are marketed as sole. However, authentic sole refers only to a variety of flatfish found from the Mediterranean to Denmark, particularly off the coasts of England and France. Authentic sole is listed as English sole or Dover sole and typically arrives in this country frozen, though sometimes it is flown in fresh. Either way, it is quite expensive.

Realistically, when you buy what is called sole from the fish store you will be buying one of the finer-tasting flounders that borrow the sole name. Among these flounders are grey sole, or witch flounder, and lemon or winter sole. The latter is a good-sized fish, about 3 pounds, commonly found in New England. From the West Coast, you will be offered butter sole and petrale sole, firm-tasting flounder caught in the Pacific from Mexico to Alaska.

Delicate, thin sole or flounder fillets cook a little faster in the microwave oven than other fish fillets. For a 600- to 700-watt oven, count on about 3–5 minutes per pound.

⌇❤ SOLE WITH DILL

Because microwave cooking is so moist, you don't have to use any fat at all when cooking fish. For this simple, no-fat-added dish, you simply drizzle the fish with lemon juice and sprinkle with fresh dill.

Preparation time: 2 minutes
Microwave time: 3–5 minutes
Servings: 4

1 pound sole fillets
2 tablespoons fresh lemon juice
2 teaspoons fresh dill *or* ½
teaspoon dried

Arrange sole on a dinner plate with thickest portions to the outside and thin ends tucked under, if necessary. Drizzle with lemon juice. Sprinkle with dill. Cover with plastic wrap, vented. MICROWAVE (high) 3–5 minutes until thickest portion is almost opaque when tested with a fork. Let stand 5 minutes. Drain.

SOLE WITH LEMON-LIME VELOUTE

This creamy but light-tasting sauce is a smooth natural with sole. Note that white pepper is used instead of black pepper to avoid tiny black speckles in the sauce.

Preparation time: 10 minutes
Microwave time: 7–13 minutes
Servings: 4

1 tablespoon butter
1 tablespoon flour
½ cup chicken stock or broth
¼ cup whipping cream
1 tablespoon and 1 teaspoon fresh lemon juice
1 teaspoon fresh lime juice
Dash salt
Dash ground white pepper
1 pound sole fillets
2 tablespoons minced fresh parsley

1. Put butter in 4-cup measure. MICROWAVE (high), uncovered, 1–2 minutes until the butter melts and is very hot. Whisk in flour. MICROWAVE (high), uncovered, 1–2 minutes until the mixture bubbles furiously.
2. Thoroughly whisk in broth and cream. MICROWAVE (high), uncovered, 1½–2 minutes until bubbles that start at the edge of the sauce fill in and completely cover the top of the sauce. Thoroughly whisk.
3. MICROWAVE (high), uncovered, 1–2 minutes until sauce thickens enough to coat a spoon. Thoroughly whisk in 1 teaspoon lemon juice and lime juice. Taste. Add salt, if desired, and pepper. Keep sauce warm.
4. Arrange sole on a dinner plate with thickest portions to the outside and thin ends tucked under, if necessary. Drizzle with remaining lemon juice. Cover with plastic wrap, vented. MICROWAVE (high) 3–5 minutes until thickest portion is almost opaque when tested with a fork. Let stand 5 minutes. Drain. Top with lemon-lime veloute. Sprinkle with parsley.

TIP: To double the sauce, double all sauce ingredients and add about 1 minute to each of the cooking times.

TIP: You probably won't need to add salt in Step 3 if using canned broth.

SOLE WITH TANGY SPINACH SAUCE

A fresh spinach sauce, smoothed with tangy yogurt, makes a fine accompaniment to sole fillets.

Preparation time: 10 minutes
Microwave time: 14–20 minutes
Servings: 4

2 tablespoons butter
2 tablespoons flour
½ cup dry white wine
½ cup fish stock or clam broth
½ cup chopped fresh spinach
1 tablespoon minced fresh parsley
1 tablespoon minced fresh chervil
1 tablespoon minced fresh chives
¼ teaspoon salt
⅛ teaspoon freshly ground black pepper
4 tablespoons plain yogurt
1 pound sole fillets
1 tablespoon fresh lemon juice

1. Put butter in 4-cup measure. MICROWAVE (high), uncovered, 2–3 minutes until butter melts and is hot. Whisk in flour. MICROWAVE (high) 2–3 minutes until bubbly and hot. Whisk.
2. Stir in wine and stock. MICROWAVE (high), uncovered, 6–7 minutes until thick and hot, whisking twice. Stir in spinach, parsley, chervil, chives, salt, and pepper. MICROWAVE (high) 1–2 minutes to wilt spinach. Stir in yogurt. Keep sauce warm.
3. Arrange sole on a dinner plate with thickest portions to the outside and thin ends tucked under, if necessary. Drizzle with lemon juice. Cover with plastic wrap, vented. MICROWAVE (high) 3–5 minutes until thickest portion is almost opaque when tested with a fork. Let stand 5 minutes. Drain. Serve topped with spinach sauce.

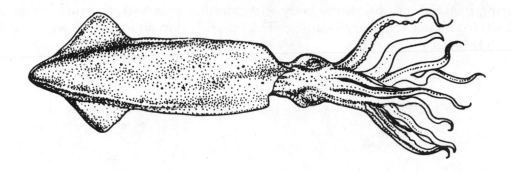

S Q U I D

Think of s-q-u-i-d as calamari, the melodious name that Italians bestow on this ocean delicacy. It's easier for guests to swallow.

With the exception of Monterey, California—the self-proclaimed calamari capital of the world, where about 10,000 tons of squid are harvested from Monterey Bay every year, most of it bound for Japan and Europe—squid is still a minor character on American plates.

When diners shy away from squid, it's more from the image of wriggling tentacles or from an experience with overcooked, tough portions than from taste. Squid has a very mild, inoffensive taste, but it can be tough and rubbery if cooked incorrectly.

The trick to cooking squid in the microwave is to use medium or medium-low power. This keeps the squid from getting tough.

Squid is a mollusk with ten arms and a long, slender body with fins and a small, internal shell. It's a crafty creature, able to swim backward or forward and armed with dark ink that it shoots when it needs to hide itself from enemies. The ink is edible—indeed, considered a delicacy, especially in Spain.

Squid are most commonly purchased fresh or frozen, and the frozen squid are very good quality. Count on about 10 small squid to the pound. The meat is very lean and high in protein.

Cleaning squid is easy but time-consuming. Often I find it more convenient to clean squid one night after dinner to have them ready to cook up the next night.

To clean squid, first pull the head and tentacles from the body; a long mantle will come out with the head. Cut the tentacles from the head, just in front of the eyes; discard head and mantle. Remove the small, hard beak from the middle of the tentacles.

Use fingers to pull out the "pen," or thin rudimentary shell, the ink sac, and any remaining material; discard. Rinse body with running water; larger squid bodies can be turned inside out for easier cleaning. The purplish skin and the two winglike fins may be left on or pulled off.

⌒ꓸ SQUID SOUP WITH SPINACH

This simple soup provides an easy introduction to squid and a creative start to dinner. A mere ¼ pound of squid does the trick—the tentacles are the most dramatic-looking, so make sure that each person gets at least one. Most of the cooking time is needed to heat the stock; the squid take only 2–3 minutes to cook.

Preparation time: 10 minutes
Microwave time: 8–11 minutes
Servings: 4

¼ **pound squid (3 small)**
4 **cups chicken stock or broth**
1 **quarter-sized slice fresh ginger**
½ **cup fresh spinach, cut into ½-inch-wide strips**
2 **green onions, white and first 2 inches of green, chopped**

1. Clean squid (see the introduction to this chapter). Cut body into ½-inch strips. Roughly chop tentacles, leaving smallest ones whole. Set aside.
2. Put chicken stock and ginger in 2-quart casserole. Cover. MICROWAVE (high) 6–8 minutes to boiling. Remove ginger.
3. Stir in squid. Cover. MICROWAVE (medium) 2–3 minutes until tender. Ladle broth into bowls. Stir in spinach leaves to wilt. Sprinkle with onions.

TIP: Note that the squid are cooked on medium power to keep them tender.

↶♥ SWEET PICKLED SQUID

Make this recipe a day ahead and the squid will get even softer from marinating. For this dish, leave the skin on for a pretty, mottled purple look.

Preparation time: 15 minutes
Microwave time: 7–10 minutes
Servings: 6–8 appetizers

1 pound squid
1 small onion, sliced thin
¼ cup cider vinegar
¼ cup water
2 tablespoons sugar
¼ teaspoon ground allspice
½ teaspoon mustard seed
½ teaspoon celery seed
Pinch of ground cloves
½ teaspoon salt

1. Clean squid (see the introduction to this chapter). Cut bodies into ½-inch strips. Roughly chop tentacles.
2. Put rest of ingredients in 2-quart casserole. Cover. MICROWAVE (high) 2–3 minutes to just boiling, stirring once. Stir in squid. Cover. MICROWAVE (medium-low) 5–7 minutes until squid are tender, stirring twice. Let stand 15 minutes to cool, then refrigerate. Drain and serve chilled as an appetizer or in salad.

MONTEREY SQUID CHOWDER

The inspiration for this dish was a thick squid chowder that we enjoyed at Abalonetti, a unique restaurant on Old Fisherman's Wharf in Monterey, California, that specializes in squid dishes. I like to leave the purple skin on the squid, which adds a pretty color to the chowder. For menu suggestions see page 22.

Preparation time: 20 minutes
Microwave time: 18–24 minutes
Servings: 4

2 slices uncooked bacon
¾ cup chopped onion
¾ cup diced celery
2 tablespoons flour
1 cup diced potato
2 tablespoons dry white wine
1 cup clam broth
1 pound squid, cleaned (see the introduction to this chapter), skin intact, cut into ½-inch rings
1 cup heavy cream
2 teaspoons fresh thyme *or* ½ teaspoon dried
2 teaspoons fresh sage *or* ½ teaspoon dried
½ teaspoon salt
¼ teaspoon freshly ground black pepper
⅓ cup fresh croutons (*see* Tip at end of this recipe)

1. Put bacon in 2-quart casserole. Cover. MICROWAVE (high) 1–2 minutes until cooked but not crisp. Remove bacon, leaving bacon fat in casserole. Dice bacon and set aside.
2. Add onion and celery to fat in casserole. Cover. MICROWAVE (high) 3–4 minutes until celery starts to get tender. Blend in flour.
3. Stir in potato, wine, clam broth, and reserved bacon. Cover. MICROWAVE (HIGH) 3–4 minutes to boiling. MICROWAVE (medium) 8–10 minutes until potato is tender.
4. Stir in squid. Cover. MICROWAVE (medium) 3–4 minutes until squid is tender. Do not overcook, or squid will be tough. Stir in cream, thyme, sage, salt, and pepper. Reheat, if necessary, on medium power for 2–3 minutes. Serve with croutons on top.

TIP: To make croutons, put 2 tablespoons butter in 8" × 8" × 2" dish. MICROWAVE (high), uncovered, 30 seconds to melt. Stir in 2 teaspoons snipped parsley. Mix in 2 cups of ½-inch-cubed French bread. MICROWAVE (high), uncovered, 3–5 minutes, stirring every minute. Let cool.

PINE NUT–STUFFED SQUID

There is quite a bit of preparation here, particularly if you clean the squid yourself, so other cooks, especially, will appreciate being served these pretty squid!

Preparation time: 45 minutes
Microwave time: 6–9 minutes
Servings: 4–6

1⅓ **pound squid (about 12 squid, with 5-inch bodies)**
  2 **tablespoons olive oil**
  2 **tablespoons butter**
  2 **teaspoons minced garlic**
  ¼ **cup minced onion**
  ½ **cup chopped mushrooms**
  ½ **cup fine bread crumbs**
  ¼ **cup pine nuts**
  2 **tablespoons minced fresh parsley**
  2 **teaspoons chopped fresh thyme, *or* ½ teaspoon dried**
  ½ **teaspoon chopped fresh oregano, *or* ⅛ teaspoon dried**
  ¼ **teaspoon salt**
  ⅛ **teaspoon freshly ground black pepper**
  2 **tablespoons dry white wine**

1. Clean squid (see the introduction to this chapter), leaving purple skin on. Chop tentacles; leave bodies whole.
2. Put reserved tentacles, olive oil, butter, garlic, onion, and mushrooms in 1-quart casserole. Cover. MICROWAVE (high) 2–3 minutes to soften. Stir in bread crumbs, pine nuts, parsley, thyme, oregano, salt, and pepper.
3. Stuff squid bodies loosely with mixture. Place in shallow, round plate, with tails to the center. Pour wine over squid. Cover with plastic wrap, vented at one corner. MICROWAVE (medium) 4–6 minutes until tender.

TIP: After you add the first teaspoon of filling, shake the squid sharply to help the filling fall into the base of the body.

TIP: Serve as a warm appetizer, sliced crosswise into ½-inch pieces and drizzled with pan juices and sprinkled with minced, peeled tomato; or serve whole as a cold appetizer, with julienned sweet red pepper and a wedge of lemon, or on top of olive-oil-tossed spinach linguine.

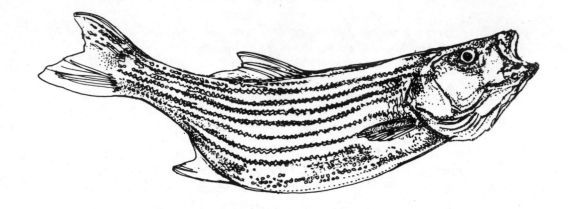

STRIPED BASS

Striped bass is a beautiful creature, black on green-grey, with silvery stripes running the length of its body. Its firm flesh has a moderate amount of fat, which helps create its sweet flavor.

Striped bass is an anadromous fish like salmon that lives in salt water but returns to fresh water to reproduce. It thrives in the Atlantic Ocean between Cape Cod and South Carolina, but some are in the Gulf of Mexico and even landlocked freshwater lakes in the Southwest, though these are considered inferior to saltwater catches. Demand and often dwindling supply keep prices high, but striped bass could be showing up on more dinner plates as interest grows to farm the variety as is done with trout, crayfish, and oysters.

Striped bass is not to be confused with smallmouth or largemouth bass, popular freshwater fish that are not really bass but are members of the sunfish family. In the South, striped bass may be called *rockfish*. And in France, a very close relative goes by *loup*, which doubly delighted my young son during one visit as he frequently ordered his favorite "wolf."

WHOLE STRIPED BASS WITH BASIL

Cooking a whole fish is hardly more complicated than cooking fillets, especially when it is stuffed with a simple handful of fresh herbs. Before starting this recipe, make sure to read How to Cook a Whole Fish (see Index).

Preparation time: 10 minutes
Microwave time: 8–15 minutes
Servings: 4

1 2–2½-pound whole striped bass, gutted and scaled
1 tablespoon fresh lemon juice
¼ cup roughly chopped fresh basil

1. Put bass in casserole or on a large plate. Drizzle with lemon juice. Stuff basil into cavity of fish. Wrap head and tail loosely with smooth foil wrap, kept at least an inch from the sides of the microwave, to keep fish from overcooking. Cover casserole or plate with plastic wrap, vented at one or two corners.
2. MICROWAVE (high) 4–5 minutes until fish starts to cook but is still firm. Turn fish over. MICROWAVE (high) 4–10 minutes until flesh near the bones is almost opaque when tested with a fork. Let stand on counter 5 minutes to finish cooking. Drain. Serve some of the basil with each portion.

STRIPED BASS WITH BEURRE ROUGE

Red wine vinegar gives a pink cast to this simple butter sauce that works well with striped bass.

Preparation time: 10 minutes
Microwave time: 7–9 minutes
Servings: 4

1 pound striped bass fillets
1 tablespoon fresh lemon juice
3 tablespoons red wine vinegar
2 teaspoons minced shallots
8 tablespoons (1 stick) butter,
  diced, room temperature
Dash of salt

1. Arrange bass on a plate with thickest portions to the outside and any thin ends turned under, if necessary. Drizzle with lemon juice. Cover with plastic wrap, vented. MICROWAVE (high) 4–5 minutes until thickest portion is almost opaque when tested with a fork. Let stand 5 minutes. Drain.
2. Put vinegar and shallots in 4-cup measure. MICROWAVE (high) 3–4 minutes until liquid is reduced to about 1 tablespoon.
3. Add butter gradually while whisking. Sauce should be creamy and foamy. Strain if desired to remove shallots. Add salt. Serve fish atop sauce.

S W O R D F I S H

Good ol' swordfish. For years it was the token fish offering on meat-oriented restaurant menus, and now it seems forgotten among the throng of more exciting-sounding—and less expensive—fish.

Swordfish likely never will be inexpensive because the large, dramatic-looking fish with the swordlike upper jaw is caught by time-consuming longline or harpoon rather than nets. Indeed, the high price of swordfish tempts some dealers who pass off very similar-looking mako shark steaks as swordfish.

Swordfish, found on both sides of the Atlantic Ocean, is typically sold in steaks and is available fresh or frozen year-round. Summer and fall are peak seasons for fresh swordfish. The meat, which ranges from white to light pink, darker just under the skin, is oily and rich-tasting.

Cooking fish until it flakes—an old technique that invites overcooking, especially in the microwave—is particularly troublesome with firm-textured swordfish. If swordfish flakes, it is overdone. Instead, make a small incision in the middle of each steak to check for opaqueness. It should still be juicy.

❧ SWORDFISH WITH DARK OYSTER SAUCE

Thick, richly flavored oyster sauce—straight from the bottle—is a great secret to a fast meal. Spoon it on top of the swordfish while it cooks, then mix in the cooking juices just before serving.

Preparation time: 2 minutes
Microwave time: 5–6 minutes
Servings: 4

1 pound swordfish steaks
1 tablespoon fresh lemon juice
2 tablespoons oyster sauce

1. Arrange swordfish on a dinner plate. Drizzle with lemon juice. Spoon oyster sauce on top of fish. Cover with plastic wrap, vented. MICROWAVE (high) 4–5 minutes until middle of steak is almost opaque when tested with a fork, rotating steaks once, if necessary. Let stand 5 minutes to finish cooking.
2. Remove fish from plate. Return plate with juices to microwave and MICROWAVE (high), uncovered, about 1 minute to heat and slightly thicken sauce. Serve sauce over fish.

SWORDFISH WITH SMASHED GARLIC

Garlic turns sweet and nutty when cooked, adding a special flavor to fish. A whole head of garlic is cooked first to make it easier to remove the skin (one of the great tricks of the microwave!), then the cloves are smashed and scattered on top of the swordfish and cooked together with just a pat of butter. For menu suggestions see page 22.

Preparation time: 10 minutes
Microwave time: 5–6 minutes
Servings: 4

1 whole head of garlic
1 pound swordfish steaks
1 teaspoon butter

1. Put the whole head of garlic in the microwave. MICROWAVE (high) 35–50 seconds, turning the head upside down after half the time. Let stand 1 minute to cool. Squeeze the papery skin and let the garlic cloves pop out. Use the broad side of a knife or the back of a spoon to gently smash the cloves.

2. Arrange swordfish on a dinner plate. Scatter smashed garlic on top of the fish. Dot with butter. Cover with plastic wrap, vented. MICROWAVE (high) 4–5 minutes until middle of steak is almost opaque when tested with a fork, rotating steaks once, if necessary. Let stand 5 minutes to finish cooking. Drain.

✂❤ SWORDFISH WITH HOT SAKE

Sake, or rice wine, adds a subtle and sweet flavor to the swordfish.

Preparation time: 2 minutes
Microwave time: 4–5 minutes
Servings: 4

1 pound swordfish steaks
1 tablespoon fresh lemon juice
1 tablespoon sake

Arrange swordfish on a dinner plate. Drizzle with lemon juice and sake. Cover with plastic wrap, vented. MICROWAVE (high) 4–5 minutes until center of steak is almost opaque when tested with a fork, rotating steaks once, if necessary. Let stand 5 minutes to finish cooking. Spoon some of the juices over the fish to serve.

⤳❤ SWORDFISH KABOBS WITH SWEET-AND-SOUR SAUCE

A sweet-and-sour sauce with pineapple chunks lightly coats kabobs of fresh swordfish and green pepper.

Preparation time: 10 minutes
Microwave time: 10–15 minutes
Servings: 4

1 green bell pepper
1 pound swordfish steaks
1 tablespoon fresh lemon juice
1 10½-ounce can pineapple chunks in natural juices
3 tablespoons cider vinegar
¼ cup brown sugar
2 teaspoons soy sauce
1 tablespoon corn starch dissolved in 1 tablespoon water

1. Stem, seed, and cut bell pepper into 1½-inch chunks. Put pepper chunks in 1-quart casserole. Cover. MICROWAVE (high) 1-2 minutes to slightly soften pepper. Drain.
2. Cut off and discard skin from swordfish. Cut fish into 1-inch chunks. Toss with lemon juice. Alternate swordfish and pepper chunks on four wooden skewers, leaving a little space between each item. Arrange skewers in the same direction on a dinner plate. Cover with plastic wrap, vented. MICROWAVE (high) 3–4 minutes until centers of the swordfish chunks are almost opaque, rotating and turning the skewers every minute. Let stand 2 minutes.
3. Drain pineapple, reserving juices. Measure juice and add water if necessary to make 1 cup liquid. Put liquid, vinegar, sugar, and soy sauce in 4-cup measure. MICROWAVE (high) 2–3 minutes to dissolve sugar and boil.
4. Stir in pineapple. MICROWAVE (high) 2–3 minutes to boil. Stir in cornstarch mixture. MICROWAVE (high) 2–3 minutes until thickened. Serve kabobs partially covered with pineapple and sauce.

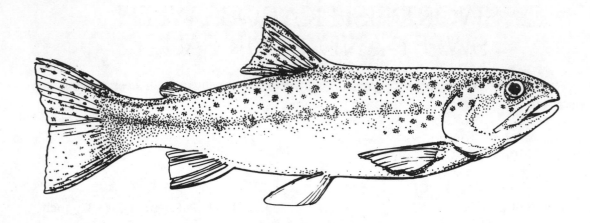

TROUT

Trout is the quintessential game fish, a limber, speckled catch photographed for many a sporting calender and painted in the minds of even more armchair enthusiasts.

Fortunately, trout is so successfully farmed that you don't have to count on high mountain streams for your next meal. Two matching rainbow trout, fresh out of the fish tanks that are popping up in groceries, make an ideal fish dish for the microwave oven. And the fine flavor of trout will hook you on fish in general.

Other trouts worth trying are the fine-tasting brook trout that is very common in the northeastern part of the country and in Canada; the often orange-fleshed brown trout; the cutthroat trout, a sportsman's catch in northern California and into Alaska; the Dolly Varden, an anadromous fish that migrates to fresh water to spawn; and the oilier and large lake trout.

❥ TROUT IN SAFFRON WINE

Strands of red saffron turn golden when they are mixed with warm wine, adding both color and flavor to this low-fat trout dish.

Preparation time: 5 minutes
Microwave time: 6–7 minutes
Servings: 4

¼ cup dry white wine
⅛ teaspoon saffron strands *or*
    pinch saffron powder
1 pound trout fillets
1 tablespoon fresh lemon juice
1 teaspoon cornstarch dissolved
    in 1 tablespoon water
2 tablespoons minced parsley

1. Put wine on a plate large enough to hold the fish. Stir in saffron. MICROWAVE (high), uncovered, about 1 minute until hot.
2. Turn trout several times in the saffron-wine mixture. Arrange fish on plate skin-side down with thickest portions to the outside and any thin ends turned under, if necessary. Drizzle with lemon juice. Cover with plastic wrap, vented.
3. MICROWAVE (high) 4–5 minutes until thickest portion is almost opaque when tested with a fork. Let stand 5 minutes to finish cooking.
4. Use spatula to lift fish from plate. Stir cornstarch into remaining cooking juices and blend well. MICROWAVE (high), uncovered, about 1 minute until juices thicken. Serve sauce drizzled over trout and sprinkle with parsley.

TIP: *Saffron, the dried stigmas of the autumn crocus, is very expensive and you often have to ask for it even in specialty stores. Saffron powder, more readily available, is about four times as powerful as an equivalent amount of saffron strands, so it is a bit more economical.*

CHILLED WHOLE TROUT WITH CUMIN-MAYONNAISE SAUCE

Two whole trout are cooked, then chilled in their own cooking juices and served with a spicy mayonnaise for a lovely summer dinner.

Preparation time: 15 minutes
Microwave time: 5–8 minutes
Chilling time: overnight
Servings: 4

2 whole rainbow trout, 10–12 ounces each, cleaned and scaled
3 tablespoons fresh lemon juice
¼ cup dry white wine
1 cup mayonnaise
½ teaspoon ground cumin
3 finely chopped anchovy fillets
1 tablespoon finely chopped green olives

1. Arrange trout in 2½-quart flat casserole, head to tail, with bellies to the inside. Cover heads and tails with smooth layer of foil, keeping foil at least 1 inch from the sides of microwave. Drizzle fish with 2 tablespoons lemon juice. Add wine to casserole. Cover casserole with plastic wrap, vented.
2. MICROWAVE (high) 5–8 minutes until thickest portion near the bones is almost opaque when tested with a fork. Let stand covered 10 minutes to finish cooking. Drain and save cooking liquids.
3. Remove foil. Use side of fork to gently scrape off skin from both sides of trout. Arrange fish attractively in cooking dish or other platter and cover with reserved cooking liquid. Cover dish and chill in refrigerator overnight.
4. To make cumin-mayonnaise sauce, mix remaining ingredients in a small bowl.
5. Remove trout platter from refrigerator and keep fish in jellied cooking liquids. Serve cumin-mayonnaise sauce on the side.

TROUT AND SHRIMP QUENELLES

Quenelles are light little dumplings held together with egg whites and heavy cream. They shape best if the fish mixture is well-chilled. Serve the quenelles on top of a favorite light tomato sauce.

Preparation time: 15 minutes
Microwave time: 4–5 minutes
Chilling time: 1–3 hours
Yield: 20–25 quenelles

½ **pound very cold trout fillets, skinned and cut into chunks**
½ **pound shelled shrimp, deveined and chopped coarse**
2 **egg whites**
1 **tablespoon chopped fresh tarragon** *or* **1 teaspoon dried**
1 **teaspoon salt**
⅛ **teaspoon ground white pepper**
½ **cup heavy cream, very cold**
2 **tablespoons fresh lemon juice**

1. Put trout and shrimp in food processor, and process about 10 seconds until pureed. With fish still in processor, add egg whites, tarragon, salt, and pepper. Process about 10 seconds until mixed. With machine running, add cream and lemon juice through the top of the machine and process until mixed. Put the whole bowl of the processor in the refrigerator for 1–3 hours until well-chilled.
2. Use two serving spoons to shape quenelles (see Tip below), about 3 tablespoons each in size. Arrange 6–8 quenelles in spoke fashion on a plate so they don't touch. Add 2 tablespoons water. Cover with plastic wrap, vented, leaving enough room so that the plastic doesn't flatten the quenelles.
3. MICROWAVE (high) 50 seconds to 1½ minutes until quenelles spring back when touched lightly with a finger. Do not overcook, or they will feel like plastic. Repeat with remaining mixture.

TIP: For a smooth look, take a scoop with one spoon, then transfer the scoop, bottoms up, onto the second spoon. Round or shape the scoop, if necessary, then gently scrape it off the second spoon and onto a plate.

⌣♥ TROUT WITH BAY AND LIME

A big lake trout makes a fine dinner for 6–8 people. For this version, crushed bay leaves and thyme are heated with lime juice, then spooned into the cavity of the fish to develop a wonderful flavor while the fish cooks. The fish is so moist that you don't need a sauce.

Preparation time: 5 minutes
Microwave time: 20–25 minutes
Servings: 6–8

2 tablespoons fresh lime juice
2 bay leaves, crushed
1 teaspoon fresh thyme *or* ¼ teaspoon dried
1 4–5-pound lake trout, cleaned and scaled, with head and tail intact
Lime wedges

1. Put lime juice, bay leaves, and thyme in 1-cup measure. MICROWAVE (high), uncovered, 15–20 seconds to heat. Let sit 2 minutes.
2. Rinse trout well and place in 4-quart casserole. Spoon and pat lime mixture into cavity of fish. Wrap head and tail loosely with smooth foil wrap to prevent these areas from overcooking. (Keep the foil at least 1 inch from the sides of the microwave.) Cover casserole with plastic wrap, vented at one corner.
3. MICROWAVE (high) 20–25 minutes until thickest portion of fish near the spine is almost opaque when tested with a fork. Let fish stand 10 minutes on counter to finish cooking. Serve with lime wedges.

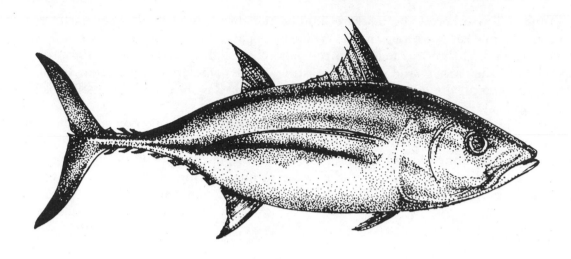

TUNA

Early in the morning, many hours before tourists pack the shops and gift stores along Fisherman's Wharf in San Francisco, Barry Conan is busy at Pier 45, checking his tuna.

The big tuna arrive here daily, hauled onto the wooden wharves directly from fishing boats that don't linger in the famous fog. For the uninitiated, two yellowfin tuna—with bright yellow dorsal tails and called *ahi* in Hawaii—may look alike. But with a quick stab, Barry pierces the skin with a tuna probe and draws out a skinny, red mass of flesh.

"I'm looking for a clarity, a translucent quality," he says, as if describing a red Napa wine. "This one is cloudy. That makes it a Number Two."

If the color had been very dark and dull, it would have been a Number Three, the lowest quality he handles, good only for cooking. Only the most luminescent fish get the ranking of Number One, best-quality tuna, destined for the top sushi bars and restaurants in town.

Age is one factor that affects the quality of fresh tuna. Another is the way the fish are caught and handled. If the fish get scared, they release an enzyme that eventually dulls the flesh. "They will still be wholesome to eat," Barry says, "but they will lose the top-quality grade demanded by the sushi houses."

As Americans learn to appreciate the fresh tuna that the Japanese have long revered, demand increases for more and better tuna. A 1-pound chunk of deep-reddish-brown tuna looks like an expensive beef filet mignon. And indeed, the tuna won't cost you much less. Maybe more.

247

Tuna is a member of the mackerel family, and there are several major varieties that come to market fresh or canned. White-meat packed tuna comes from the albacore tuna. Light meat comes from the yellowfin, slightly darker meat from skipjack, and the darkest and strongest-tasting of the commercial tuna from small bluefin. In general, the lighter tuna will have a milder flavor. Tuna lightens in color as it cooks and tastes somewhat like veal.

It's tricky to cook a very thick fillet or steak evenly in the microwave. If the tuna steak is quite thick, I slice it in half horizontally. If the steaks are cooking and the edges are almost done while the center is almost raw, cut the steak in half, expose the undercooked portion to the outside, and continue cooking. Better yet, start out with four evenly sized ¼-pound servings, and they will cook up perfectly.

☙ TUNA WITH CITRUS SAUCE

This fast and easy sauce adds a sweet interest—but no added fat—to fresh tuna fillets.

Preparation time: 5 minutes
Microwave time: 6–8 minutes
Servings: 4

1 **pound tuna fillets**
2 **tablespoons fresh lemon juice**
½ **cup fresh orange juice**
1 **teaspoon cornstarch**
2 **tablespoons brown sugar**
2 **tablespoons orange marmalade**
Dash ground cinnamon

1. Arrange tuna on a dinner plate with thickest portions to the outside. Drizzle with lemon juice. Cover with plastic wrap, vented. MICROWAVE (high) 4–5 minutes until thickest portion is just opaque when tested with a fork. Let stand 5 minutes to finish cooking.
2. Meanwhile, mix orange juice and cornstarch in 2-cup measure until smooth. Stir in sugar and marmalade. MICROWAVE (high), uncovered, 2–3 minutes until mixture is hot and smooth. Spoon on top of tuna. Sprinkle with ground cinnamon.

TUNA WITH SWEET PEPPER PUREE

A bright-colored, fresh-tasting puree of sweet bell pepper is a tasty and healthful accompaniment to a fresh tuna fillet.

Preparation time: 10 minutes
Microwave time: 12–15 minutes
Servings: 4

3 red bell peppers
¼ cup water
2 tablespoons olive oil
Dash cayenne pepper
¼ teaspoon salt
⅛ teaspoon ground white pepper
1 pound tuna fillets
2 tablespoons fresh lemon juice

1. Seed peppers and cut into 1-inch chunks. Put peppers and water in 2-quart casserole. MICROWAVE (high) 8–10 minutes until quite tender, stirring after 3 minutes. Drain. Puree in blender or food processor. Mix in olive oil, cayenne, salt, and pepper. Keep warm.
2. Arrange tuna on a dinner plate with thickest portions to the outside. Drizzle with lemon juice. Cover with plastic wrap, vented. MICROWAVE (high) 4–5 minutes until thickest portion is just opaque when tested with a fork. Let stand 5 minutes to finish cooking. Spoon puree onto plate and place tuna on top.

TIP: Yellow bell peppers can be substituted for the red.

HOT TUNA MUFFINS

A can of tuna and other kitchen staples turn into a snack or light lunch in minutes. The tuna mixture can be made hours ahead and stored in the refrigerator before heating in the microwave.

Preparation time: 10 minutes
Microwave time: 2–2½ minutes
Servings: 3

1 6½-ounce can white tuna,
  drained and flaked
½ Granny Smith apple,
  unpeeled, cored and chopped
  fine
⅓ cup mayonnaise
1 ounce (¼ cup) shredded
  cheddar cheese
2 green onions, white and first
  2 inches of green, sliced
⅛ teaspoon freshly ground black
  pepper
3 English muffins, split and
  toasted

Combine all ingredients except muffins. Spread mixture on muffin halves. Arrange muffins along edge of a paper-towel-lined round plate. MICROWAVE (high), uncovered, 2–2½ minutes until heated through.

TIP: This sandwich tastes best if eaten while still warm. Take care, however, because the topping is quite hot when just removed from the microwave.

FRESH TUNA WITH HOMEMADE TERIYAKI SAUCE

This homemade teriyaki sauce has a more complex and less salty taste than commonly bottled teriyaki sauce. And it works well with a rich-tasting fish like tuna.

Preparation time: 10 minutes
Microwave time: 4–5 minutes
Servings: 4

1 teaspoon minced garlic
2 teaspoons minced fresh ginger
2 tablespoons mirin
3 tablespoons soy sauce
2 teaspoons sesame oil
1 tablespoon honey
2 tablespoons fresh lemon juice
1 pound tuna fillets
1 green onion, white and first 2 inches of green, chopped fine

1. To make teriyaki sauce, mix all ingredients except for the tuna and onion in 1-cup measure.
2. Arrange tuna on a dinner plate with thickest portions to the outside. Pour teriyaki sauce over tuna. Cover with plastic wrap, vented. MICROWAVE (high) 4–5 minutes until thickest portion is just opaque when tested with a fork. Let stand 5 minutes to finish cooking. Serve sprinkled with green onions.

TIP: Mirin is a sweet rice wine now commonly found in major supermarkets, likely right next to the soy sauce and sesame oil.

FRESH TUNA NIÇOISE SALAD

Instead of the usual canned tuna, buy a pound of fresh tuna for your next Niçoise salad. The fish takes only 4 or 5 minutes to cook in the microwave.

Preparation time: 15 minutes
Chilling time: 2 hours
Microwave time: 12–16 minutes
Servings: 4

1 **pound fresh tuna fillets**
1 **tablespoon fresh lemon juice**
2 **cups fresh green beans, cut into 1½-inch pieces**
¼ **cup water**
2 **cups ¼-inch-sliced red potatoes with skins on**
½ **cup pitted black olives, preferably Mediterranean-style**
6 **tablespoons olive oil**
¼ **teaspoon dry mustard**
2 **tablespoons white wine vinegar**
½ **teaspoon salt**
2 **medium tomatoes, quartered**
6 **thin slices Bermuda onion, separated into rings**
16 **large leaves red leaf lettuce**
1 **hard-boiled egg, peeled and quartered**
8 **anchovy fillets, drained**
2 **tablespoons chopped fresh tarragon *or* 1 teaspoon dried**

1. Arrange tuna on a dinner plate with thickest portions to the outside. Drizzle with lemon juice. Cover with plastic wrap, vented. MICROWAVE (high) 4–5 minutes until thickest portion is just opaque when tested with a fork. Let stand 5 minutes to finish cooking. Drain. Cover and refrigerate at least 2 hours.
2. Put beans and water in 2½-quart casserole. Cover. MICROWAVE (high) 2–3 minutes to give them a head start cooking. Stir in potatoes. Cover. MICROWAVE (high) 6–8 minutes until just tender. Drain. Return to casserole.
3. Mix in olives, olive oil, mustard, vinegar, and salt. Cover. Refrigerate at least 2 hours.
4. Add tomatoes, onion, and cooked tuna, cut into chunks. Toss gently to mix. Arrange lettuce on plates. Arrange tuna and vegetable mixture on top of lettuce. Add eggs, topped with crossed anchovies and sprinkled with tarragon.

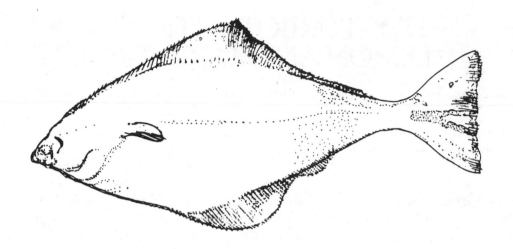

TURBOT

Turbot—the real stuff—is one of the most delicate and elegant of fish. Found primarily in the Eastern Atlantic from the Mediterranean to Norway, the flatfish typically is sold frozen in the United States, and even then at very high prices.

The bargain-priced fish in some markets called turbot or Greenland turbot is not turbot at all but a lesser variety of halibut, specifically Greenland halibut. The thick, white Greenland halibut fillets can have a somewhat "fishy" taste, and the edges and thinner ends of the fillets quickly get tough and show discoloration if improperly stored. It's unfortunate that some people are attracted to the cheap price of Greenland turbot and then decide that turbot—and perhaps fish in general—isn't worth the trouble.

A good-looking and fresh-smelling piece of Greenland halibut can be acceptable if accompanied by a good sauce. See the Halibut chapter for ideas.

Real turbot shouldn't be smothered with highly flavored sauces. Suggested here are two simple approaches: Turbot with Lemon and Tarragon and Turbot with Buttery Shallots.

⌒❤ TURBOT WITH LEMON AND TARRAGON

Tarragon is a pretty strong herb, so very little is needed to flavor this simple fish dish.

Preparation time: 5 minutes
Microwave time: 4–5 minutes
Servings: 4

1 pound turbot fillets
2 tablespoons fresh lemon juice
1 teaspoon chopped fresh
 tarragon *or* ¼ teaspoon dried
Fresh tarragon sprigs for garnish

Arrange turbot on rim of a plate with thickest portions to the outside. Drizzle with lemon juice and sprinkle with chopped tarragon. Cover with plastic wrap, vented at one or two corners. MICROWAVE (high) 4–5 minutes until thickest portion is almost opaque when tested with a fork, rearranging fillets once. Let stand for 2 minutes to finish cooking. Top with sprigs of fresh tarragon and some of the juices.

TURBOT WITH BUTTERY SHALLOTS

A little butter goes a long way here to soften the shallots and then soak into the turbot. To reduce calories, drain the excess butter and juices after cooking—the turbot will still be moist and buttery-tasting.

Preparation time: 5 minutes
Microwave time: 5–7 minutes
Servings: 4

1 tablespoon minced shallots
2 tablespoons butter
1 pound turbot fillet, cut into four serving pieces
4 lemon wedges

1. Put shallots and butter in 1-cup measure. MICROWAVE (high), uncovered, 1–2 minutes until shallots are tender.
2. Arrange turbot on rim of a plate with thickest portions to the outside. Spoon shallots and butter over fish. Cover with plastic wrap, vented at one corner. MICROWAVE (high) 4–5 minutes until thickest portion is almost opaque when tested with a fork, rearranging fish once. Let stand for 2 minutes to finish cooking. Drain excess butter and juices or spoon them over fish. Garnish with lemon wedges.

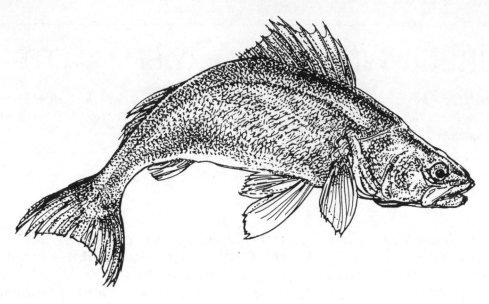

WALLEYE

If a friend offhandedly offers you his last walleye from a recent Canadian fishing trip, don't hesitate—take it. Your guilt will be soothed by one of the finest-tasting freshwater fish, fully in the same league as salmon and trout.

A member of the yellow perch family, walleye gets its popular name from the bulging but cloudy eyes that the nocturnal fish uses to spot food. It is erroneously called walleye pike, probably because of the tiny sharp teeth it shares with the pike family, or yellow pike, because of the golden overtones of its skin.

It has very white, sweet flesh that makes a wonderfully firm and flaky cold salad as well as hot entree. Walleye are good-sized fish, up to 2- or 3-foot-long, so fillets are substantial, usually 10 to 12 ounces each, and easy to work with.

The only difficult part about a walleye is finding it in the fish department. Although it is frequently caught along the East Coast and the Great Lakes, most of the commercial catch comes from the cold Canadian waters. Your most likely source may be that friend with an extra catch stashed away.

⌇❤ WALLEYE WITH HONEY-PAPAYA SAUCE

Ripe papaya—touched with a little honey and ginger—turns into a sauce after just a minute in the microwave. It makes an unusual summer treat atop sweet walleye fillets.

Preparation time: 10 minutes
Microwave time: 5–7 minutes
Servings: 4

1 pound walleye fillets
1 tablespoon fresh lemon juice
½ ripe papaya
2 teaspoons honey
¼ teaspoon ground ginger

1. Arrange walleye skin-side down on a plate with thickest portions to the outside. Drizzle with lemon juice. Cover with plastic wrap, vented at one corner. MICROWAVE (high) 4–5 minutes until thickest portion is almost opaque when tested with a fork. Let stand 5 minutes to finish cooking. Drain.
2. Peel papaya. Scoop out and discard seeds. Chop flesh rough; put in 2-cup measure. Cover. MICROWAVE (high) 1–2 minutes to heat through and soften. Add honey and ginger; mix until blended. Sauce will be thick and pulpy. Top fish with papaya sauce.

WALLEYE-AND-WALNUT SALAD

Sweet-tasting walleye makes an excellent cold salad with nuts and crisp apples.

Preparation time: 10 minutes
Microwave time: 4–5 minutes
Chilling time: 3 hours or overnight
Servings: 4–6

1 pound walleye fillets
1 tablespoon fresh lemon juice
¼ cup and 2 tablespoons olive oil
2 tablespoons red wine vinegar
1 teaspoon walnut oil
1 tablespoon minced fresh basil *or* 1 teaspoon dried
¼ teaspoon salt
⅛ teaspoon freshly ground black pepper
1 Granny Smith or other green, tart apple
1 Red Delicious apple
2 cups red leaf lettuce, rinsed, dried, and chilled
½ cup coarsely chopped walnut meat

1. Arrange walleye skin-side down on a plate with thickest portions to the outside. Drizzle with lemon juice. Cover with plastic wrap, vented at one corner. MICROWAVE (high) 4–5 minutes until thickest portion is almost opaque when tested with a fork. Let stand 5 minutes to finish cooking. Drain. Refrigerate, covered, 3 hours or overnight.
2. To make salad dressing, put olive oil, vinegar, walnut oil, basil, salt, and pepper in a small bowl and whisk until thick and blended.
3. Just before serving, core and slice apples, leaving skin intact. Arrange lettuce leaves on serving plates. Top with chilled fish. Arrange apples and nuts on salads, and drizzle with dressing.

WALLEYE POLONAISE

Polonaise sauce is simply browned and buttery bread crumbs—delicious over fresh walleye fillets. I've made the crumbs quite thick here so they cling to the fish. For a thinner sauce, decrease crumbs to ⅓ cup.

Preparation time: 10 minutes
Microwave time: 12–16 minutes
Servings: 4

1 pound walleye fillets
1 tablespoon and 1 teaspoon
fresh lemon juice
½ pound (2 sticks) butter
½ cup fine, dry bread crumbs

1. Arrange walleye skin-side down on a plate with thickest portions to the outside. Drizzle with 1 tablespoon lemon juice. Cover with plastic wrap, vented at one corner. MICROWAVE (high) 4–5 minutes until thickest portion is almost opaque when tested with a fork. Let stand 5 minutes to finish cooking. Drain.

2. Put butter in 2-cup measure. MICROWAVE (high), uncovered, 2–3 minutes to melt. Line a sieve with cheesecloth, and pour the butter through the cheesecloth and into a container. Repeat if necessary to remove fatty milk solids. This clarified butter looks neater than just melted butter and can be heated to a higher temperature without burning.

3. To make sauce, put clarified butter in 9-inch pie plate. Cover with waxed paper, tucking two ends under to hold firm. MICROWAVE (high) 6–8 minutes until butter is light brown. Strain through cheesecloth, if necessary.

4. Stir 1 teaspoon lemon juice and bread crumbs into browned butter. MICROWAVE (high), uncovered, 2–3 minutes until crumbs are moist and golden. To serve, spoon buttery bread crumbs over fish.

TIP: If you wish, use a large spoon instead of the cheesecloth to carefully remove the foam from the melted butter after allowing it to settle for 3 minutes.

TIP: Store clarified butter in the refrigerator for several months.

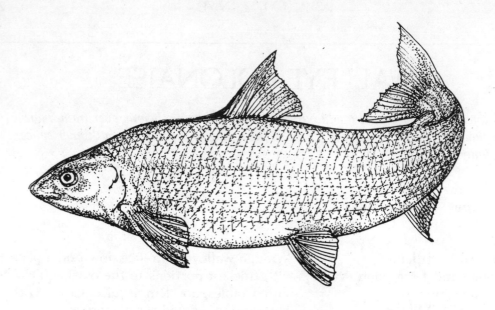

WHITEFISH

Whitefish and gewürztraminer used to be the biggest mysteries of my culinary world. Everyone seemed to love them—except me. Now I'm down to gewürztraminer.

What changed my mind was not whitefish presentations in white-linen restaurants, nor attempts to duplicate them at home. The persuader was a Wisconsin fish boil.

For the uninitiated, a Wisconsin fish boil is a Midwest event, comparable in tempo to a New England clambake. Large fish steaks, onions, and potatoes are boiled in huge pots of briny water and eventually sparked into an explosive boilover. Now *that* is the way to eat whitefish.

Whitefish is a white-fleshed freshwater fish, pulled primarily from the cool lakes of northern Canada, the Midwest, and Maine. It is a relatively inexpensive fish, often sold whole. The fish has a lot of small bones which are not practical to remove even from fillets until after they are cooked; a pair of tweezers will make the job easier.

Plain-tasting whitefish comes alive with the salt used in a Wisconsin fish boil or with a spicy topping or lemony sauce.

For the fun of it, I developed a Wisconsin fish boil—sort of—for the microwave. I think you'll enjoy it. Plus, of course, there are more conventional recipes here, starting with a brown mustard topping, one of the best—and easiest—ways to enjoy a fresh fillet.

✐❤ WHITEFISH FILLETS WITH GRAINY MUSTARD AND PEPPER

This is one of my favorite ways to prepare fish fillets quickly—and without added fat or salt. Brown, grainy mustard and freshly ground black pepper lend finished color as well as flavor to the fish. Very simple. Very good.

Preparation time: 5 minutes
Microwave time: 5 minutes
Servings: 4

1 **pound whitefish fillets**
1 **tablespoon fresh lemon juice**
2 **teaspoons prepared grainy brown mustard**
¼ **teaspoon freshly ground black pepper**

Arrange whitefish skin-side down on a plate with thickest portions to the outside. Drizzle with lemon juice. Spread mustard on top of fillets. Sprinkle with pepper. Cover with plastic wrap, vented at one corner. MICROWAVE (high) 4–5 minutes until thickest portion of fish is opaque when pulled apart gently with fork. Let stand 3–5 minutes to finish cooking.

WHITEFISH WITH CREAMY SPINACH SAUCE

This bright-colored sauce enlivens simple whitefish fillets. The sauce is made first so that the quick-cooking fish can be served immediately.

Preparation time: 10 minutes
Microwave time: 12–16 minutes
Servings: 4

2 tablespoons butter
2 tablespoons flour
1 cup chicken broth
1 cup packed, chopped fresh spinach *or* ½ cup frozen chopped spinach, defrosted and drained
2 tablespoons fresh lemon juice
Pinch ground nutmeg
Pinch salt
Pinch freshly ground black pepper
1 pound whitefish fillets

1. Put butter in 4-cup measure. MICROWAVE (high), uncovered, 2 minutes or until melted and hot but still light yellow in color.
2. Remove butter from oven. Thoroughly whisk in flour. MICROWAVE (high), uncovered, 2 minutes or until mixture bubbles furiously. Whisk in broth. MICROWAVE (high), uncovered, 2–3 minutes or until whole top is covered with small bubbles.
3. Stir in spinach, 1 teaspoon lemon juice, nutmeg, salt, and pepper. MICROWAVE (high) 2–4 minutes until spinach is cooked and sauce is thick. Set sauce aside and keep warm.
4. Arrange whitefish skin-side down on a plate with thickest portions to the outside. Drizzle with remaining lemon juice. Cover with plastic wrap and vent one corner. MICROWAVE (high) 4–5 minutes until thickest portion is opaque when pulled apart gently with fork. Let stand 3–5 minutes to finish cooking. Drain fish, reserving liquid.
5. Mix juices from cooked fish into spinach sauce. Reheat sauce on medium power if necessary. Serve fish partially covered with sauce.

TIP: If you substitute margarine for butter in the sauce, cover lightly with waxed paper in Step 1 to avoid splatters. Margarine takes less time than butter—about 1 minute—to melt.

⌇❤ WHOLE WHITEFISH STUFFED WITH CELERY AND MUSHROOMS

Celery and parsley add a bright color, while mushrooms and sherry provide depth to this simple stuffing.

Preparation time: 20 minutes
Microwave time: 23–29 minutes
Servings: 4–6

¾ **cup thinly sliced celery**
¼ **cup minced fresh parsley**
½ **cup chopped fresh mushrooms**
2 **green onions, white portion and first 2 inches of green, chopped**
½ **cup fresh bread crumbs**
2 **tablespoons dry sherry or white wine**
¼ **teaspoon salt**
⅛ **teaspoon freshly ground black pepper**
1 **2-3-pound whole whitefish, cleaned, with scales removed, head and tail intact**

1. Put celery, parsley, mushrooms, and onions in 1-quart casserole. Cover. MICROWAVE (high) 3–4 minutes until vegetables are soft. Stir in bread crumbs, sherry, salt, and pepper.
2. Place whitefish on a dish or platter. Spoon stuffing into cavity of fish. Secure opening with wooden toothpicks. Wrap foil smoothly around fish head and end of tail to keep from overcooking. Be sure foil is not closer than 1 inch from the sides of the microwave. Cover plate with plastic wrap, turning back one corner to vent. MICROWAVE (high) 5 minutes to start cooking but stop before fish is too soft to turn.
3. Turn fish over on the plate. Replace cover. MICROWAVE (high) 3–13 minutes (see Tip) until thickest portion of fish is opaque when pulled apart gently with fork. Let stand covered 5 minutes. Drain.

TIP: *Because it is usually difficult to order a whole fish in an exact weight, the cooking times above are only a guide. A 2-pound whole fish usually needs a total 8–10 minutes; a 3-pound fish, 15–18 minutes. When in doubt, undercook, then return the whole fish, or even the fillets, to the oven for more cooking time.*

WISCONSIN FISH BOIL

I love the image: masses huddling around a remote microwave oven waiting for fish to boil. It'll never play in Wisconsin, where authentic fish boils start with a wood-stoked fire and 12-gallon pot. But this version will give you a taste of the Midwestern specialty featured in tiny fishing villages of Door County.

Some claim that the secret to the wonderful-tasting fish and potatoes is the last minute boilover, when kerosene added to the open fire causes flames and boiling water to spew at random.

I think it's the salt.

Authentic fish boils call for 2 pounds salt per pot. This elevates the boiling point and shortens the cooking time needed for the fish. It also makes it taste good.

This recipe is designed for a 2–3-pound whitefish, but you may substitute salmon or lake trout, two other fish traditionally used in fish boils. The fish doesn't actually boil; it simmers in briny water.

A little melted butter typically is served with the fish and potatoes, along with coleslaw, beer, and cherry pie for dessert.

For menu suggestions see page 24.

Preparation time: 10 minutes
Microwave time: 27–37 minutes
Servings: 4

4 cups water
¼ cup salt
8 new potatoes *or* 2 large potatoes, peeled and cut into 2-inch chunks
1 bay leaf, crushed
10 peppercorns
4 small whole onions, peeled *or* 1 medium onion, peeled and quartered
1 2–3-pound whitefish, cleaned, scaled, head and tail removed, and cut into 2-inch-thick steaks
¼ cup (½ stick) butter

1. Put water and salt in 3-quart casserole. Stir. Add potatoes, bay leaf, and peppercorns. Cover with plastic wrap, vented. MICROWAVE (high) 15–20 minutes until water boils and a fork almost pierces a potato easily.
2. Add onions. Cover. MICROWAVE (high) 5–8 minutes to boiling.
3. Add whitefish, making sure fish is submerged in liquid. Cover with plastic wrap, vented. MICROWAVE (high) 5–7 minutes until thickest part of fish is opaque when pulled apart gently with fork. Use a slotted spoon to gently lift fish, potatoes, and onions onto serving plate.
4. Put butter in 1-cup measure. MICROWAVE (high), uncovered, 2 minutes or until melted. Pour over fish and vegetables.

FISH STOCK

Turning worthless fish bones and fish heads into rich stock is one of the magical moments of cooking. And it makes small children respect your ways.

For a good-tasting fish stock, use the heads, bones, tails, and skin of the fish, rinsing very well to remove all blood. You should be able to get some from a fish store for free or for a nominal charge. Light-flavored fish make the best-tasting stock. Avoid using salmon, sturgeon, buffalofish, and other strong-tasting fish.

The vegetables for this stock are chopped very fine—a food processor makes this easy—to get the most flavor during the short cooking time. The stock is cooked on high power to get the liquid to boiling, then on medium power to let flavors develop.

Preparation time: 20 minutes
Microwave time: 32–36 minutes
Yield: 3 cups

1 **small onion, peeled and quartered**
2 **peeled shallots**
2 **celery ribs, chopped coarse, with fresh yellow leaves**
2 **medium-sized carrots, chopped coarse**
1 **tablespoon butter**
6 **peppercorns**
¼ **cup chopped fresh parsley**
1 **bay leaf, crushed**
1 **teaspoon fresh thyme** *or* ¼ **teaspoon dried**
2 **whole cloves**
½ **cup white wine**
3½ **cups water**
2 **pounds fish bones and heads, washed**

1. Use a food processor or knife to finely chop the onion, shallots, celery, and carrots. Put vegetables in 3-quart casserole. Add the butter. Cover with plastic wrap, vented. MICROWAVE (high) 4 minutes to soften, stirring after 1 minute.
2. Stir in the rest of the ingredients. Cover tightly. MICROWAVE (high) 18–20 minutes until boiling, stirring after 10 minutes to rearrange bones. MICROWAVE (medium) 10–12 minutes to develop flavor. Strain. Taste, and add salt if needed.

TIP: To reduce fat, the tablespoon of butter may be omitted. You don't need it in the microwave to keep vegetables from sticking, but it does add flavor.

TIP: Keep the fish stock in the refrigerator for up to four days or in the freezer for up to four weeks.

FIVE-MINUTE RECIPES

A new fish recipe doesn't have to take much time—just a little thought and rustling through the refrigerator or herb garden. I've put together here a dozen fast approaches to fish that you can use with a wide variety of species. Some recipes sport a new herb or a different shape for the fish. Others use a vegetable or two varieties of the same vegetable.

Each recipe requires only 5 minutes of preparation time, 5 minutes of cooking, and a minimum of ingredients. Most of them have no added fat—no butter or even olive oil. In the microwave oven, the fish comes out so moist that you don't need the fats to make fish juicy. And the lighter, more healthful taste is worth adopting.

❤ TOMATO-CHIVE FILLETS

Summer-fresh tomatoes and chives make a fine treat over mild-tasting fish fillets. For more robust fish, such as bluefish or mullet, substitute oregano or basil for the delicate chives.

Preparation time: 5 minutes
Microwave time: 5 minutes
Servings: 4

1 pound fish fillets (such as flounder, pompano, or sole)
1 medium tomato, seeded and chopped
1 tablespoon white wine vinegar
1 tablespoon chopped fresh chives
⅛ teaspoon salt
⅛ teaspoon freshly ground black pepper

1. Arrange fish on a dinner plate with thickest portions to the outside and any thin ends tucked under, if necessary. Distribute remaining ingredients evenly over fish.
2. Cover with plastic wrap, vented. MICROWAVE (high) 4–5 minutes until thickest portion is almost opaque when tested with a fork. Let stand 5 minutes to finish cooking. Spoon juices over fish before serving.

TIP: Garlic chives—slim, tender chives with a garlic flavor—are an unusually simple yet exciting addition to a dish.

⌒♥ SPRING ASPARAGUS AND FILLET DINNER

Because asparagus stalks cook quickly in a microwave oven, they are placed in the middle of a plate, with fish fillets arranged around the outside.

Preparation time: 5 minutes
Microwave time: 5 minutes
Servings: 4

¼ **pound thin asparagus stalks**
1 **pound fish fillets (such as flounder, grouper, halibut, or orange roughy)**
2 **tablespoons fresh lemon juice**

1. Arrange asparagus in center of a plate. Place fish fillets around asparagus with thickest portions to the outside and any thin ends tucked under, if necessary. Drizzle asparagus and fish with lemon juice.
2. Cover with plastic wrap, vented. MICROWAVE (high) 4–5 minutes until thickest portion of fish is almost opaque when tested with a fork. Let stand 5 minutes to finish cooking. Drain.

TIP: Hot, buttery bread crumbs taste wonderful on both asparagus and fish fillets. For the topping, put 4 tablespoons butter in 2-cup measure. MICROWAVE (high) 2–3 minutes until melted and hot. Stir in 1 teaspoon lemon juice and ⅓ cup fine, dry bread crumbs. Spoon onto the cooked asparagus and fish.

❤ HONEY-MUSTARD CARROTS AND FISH

Carrots, which take a longer time to cook in the microwave than most other vegetables, are sliced and arranged around the rim of the plate for faster cooking. Fish goes in the center. The fish gets a little mustard; the carrots, a touch of honey.

Preparation time: 5 minutes
Microwave time: 5 minutes
Servings: 4

1 pound fish fillets (such as catfish, grouper, or Pacific rockfish)
2–3 medium carrots
2 teaspoons honey
1 tablespoon mustard

1. Arrange fish in center of a large dinner plate with thickest portions to the outside. Cut carrots into ¼-inch diagonal slices. Scatter around outer rim of plate. Drizzle honey on carrots. Spread mustard on fish.
2. Cover with plastic wrap, vented. MICROWAVE (high) 4–5 minutes until thickest portion of fish is just opaque when tested with a fork. Let stand 5 minutes to finish cooking. Lift fish and carrots onto serving plate.

GINGER-GARLIC STEAKS

Fresh garlic and ginger add a lot of flavor to this dish, which has only a touch of added oil.

Preparation time: 5 minutes
Microwave time: 5 minutes
Servings: 4

1 teaspoon minced fresh ginger
1 teaspoon minced garlic
1 tablespoon soy sauce
⅛ teaspoon sesame oil
1 pound fish steaks (such as mahimahi, swordfish, or tuna)

1. Put ginger, garlic, soy sauce, and sesame oil in 1-cup measure. MICROWAVE (high), uncovered, 30 seconds to 1 minute to soften.
2. Arrange fish on a dinner plate with widest or thickest portions to the outside. Drizzle with ginger mixture. Cover with plastic wrap, vented. MICROWAVE (high) 4–5 minutes until middle of fish is almost opaque when tested with a fork, rotating fish once, if necessary. Let stand 5 minutes to finish cooking.

JUICY MUSHROOM FISH

Natural juices from the mushrooms and fish are enriched with a little butter for a fine, thin sauce. You can't really overcook the mushrooms, so they are placed along the rim for maximum cooking while the fish cook in the center of the plate. Serve over rice.

Preparation time: 5 minutes
Microwave time: 5 minutes
Servings: 4

1 pound fish fillets (such as oreo dory, kingclip, or pollack)
1 tablespoon fresh lemon juice
⅓ pound mushrooms, sliced thin
1 tablespoon butter
Salt
Pepper

1. Arrange fish in center of a plate with thickest portions to the outside. Drizzle with lemon juice. Sprinkle mushrooms around outer rim of plate. Cover with plastic wrap, vented.

2. MICROWAVE (high) 4–5 minutes or until thickest portion of fish is just opaque when tested with a fork. Let stand 5 minutes to finish cooking. Lift out fish. Use a slotted spoon to spoon mushrooms over fish. Swirl butter into juices to melt. Add salt and pepper to taste. Pour over fish.

TIP: For a thicker sauce, let juices cook for a minute right on the plate after you remove the cooked fish, then add the butter.

SHRIMP AND PEA PODS

Both shrimp and snow peas need very little cooking, so take care to not overcook them. If you need to keep the preparation time to 5 minutes, shell and devein the shrimp the night before. Serve with rice and pour cooking juices over the rice.

Preparation time: 5 minutes
Microwave time: 3 minutes
Servings: 4

1 pound raw shrimp, shelled and deveined
¼ pound snow peas
¼ teaspoon sesame oil
1 tablespoon sesame seeds

Put shrimp and pea pods in 2½-quart casserole. Cover tightly. MICROWAVE (high) 2½-3 minutes until shrimp are just pink, tossing and rearranging shrimp after first minute, then every 30 seconds. If two or three shrimp still are not cooked, put them back alone to cook more, checking every 20 seconds. Toss with sesame oil and seeds.

❧ DILLED PEAS AND FISH

Dill is a classic combination with both peas and sweet, tender fish fillets such as sole or flounder. Here they are all cooked on the same plate with still-frozen peas, which need little cooking, in the center.

Preparation time: 2 minutes
Microwave time: 5 minutes
Servings: 4

1 cup frozen baby peas
1 pound fish fillets (such as orange roughy, flounder, or perch—which may need only 3–4 minutes cooking)
2 tablespoons fresh lemon juice
½ teaspoon fresh dill *or* ⅛ teaspoon dried

1. Place peas in center of a large dinner plate. Arrange fish along rim with thickest portions to the outside and any thinner ends tucked under, if necessary. Drizzle with lemon juice. Sprinkle with dill.
2. Cover with plastic wrap, vented. MICROWAVE (high) 4–5 minutes until thickest portion of fish is just opaque when tested with a fork. Let stand 5 minutes to finish cooking.

TIP: *Don't overdose with the dill. A little of this herb goes a long way.*

❦ CHERVIL CHUNKS

One interesting herb and a different shape are all that are needed to enliven your fish dinner. Here I use chervil, a peas-and-licorice-tasting herb that shows up occasionally in grocery produce sections, but you could substitute tarragon or basil. Fish steaks are cut into chunks and slipped onto wooden skewers for a kabob presentation. Because the pieces are smaller, the fish cook even faster in the microwave—only about 3 minutes for a pound of fish.

Preparation time: 5 minutes
Microwave time: 3 minutes
Servings: 4

1 pound fish steaks (such as halibut, mahimahi, shark, or tuna)
1 tablespoon fresh lemon juice
1 small bunch fresh chervil

1. Cut fish into 1½-inch chunks. Slide onto four wooden skewers so that pieces do not touch. Place skewers facing the same direction on a plate. Drizzle with lemon juice. Reserve 4 sprigs of chervil for garnish; chop the rest (about 2 tablespoons) and sprinkle on the fish. Cover with plastic wrap, vented.
2. MICROWAVE (high) 2–3 minutes, rotating skewers twice, until chunks are firm to the touch and the centers are almost opaque. Let stand 3 minutes. Garnish with reserved chervil sprigs.

╳♥ DOUBLE-PEPPER FISH

Strips of green bell pepper and even sweeter yellow bell pepper add color as well as taste to this simple dish. Fast-cooking peppers can be sprinkled all over the plate and come out pretty evenly cooked. However, if you prefer a more crisp texture, keep the peppers to the inside of the plate; for a softer texture, arrange them around the edge of the plate for maximum exposure to the microwaves.

Preparation time: 5 minutes
Microwave time: 5 minutes
Servings: 4

1 **pound fish fillets (such as cod, haddock, orange roughy, or pollack)**
½ **green bell pepper**
½ **yellow bell pepper**
1 **tablespoon fresh lemon juice**
1 **teaspoon minced fresh oregano *or* ¼ teaspoon dried**
⅛ **teaspoon salt**
⅛ **teaspoon freshly ground black pepper**

1. Arrange fish on a plate with thickest portions to the outside and any thin ends tucked under, if necessary.
2. Core, seed, and julienne pepper halves. Sprinkle peppers over and around fish. Drizzle with lemon juice. Sprinkle with oregano. Cover with plastic wrap, vented.
3. MICROWAVE (high) 4–5 minutes until thickest portion of fish is almost opaque when tested with a fork. Let stand 5 minutes. Pour juices over fish and sprinkle with salt and pepper before serving.

✍❤ FISH WITH GRAINY MUSTARD AND PEPPER

This is one of my favorite solutions to a fast meal. It appears as the first recipe in the Whitefish chapter, but almost any fish can be used.

Preparation time: 5 minutes
Microwave time: 5 minutes
Servings: 4

1 pound fish fillets
1 tablespoon fresh lemon juice
2 teaspoons grainy brown mustard
¼ teaspoon freshly ground black pepper

1. Arrange fish on a plate with thickest portions to the outside. Drizzle with lemon juice. Spread mustard on top of fillets. Sprinkle with pepper.
2. Cover with plastic wrap, vented. MICROWAVE (high) 4–5 minutes until thickest portion of fish is almost opaque when tested with a fork. Let stand 5 minutes to finish cooking.

LEEKS AND LIME STEAKS

The tender inner portions of leeks work well in the microwave if you slice or julienne them.
The butter isn't necessary—but it tastes good.

Preparation time: 5 minutes
Microwave time: 5 minutes
Servings: 4

1 leek
1 pound fish steaks (such as
halibut, mahimahi, shark, or
tuna)
2 tablespoons fresh lime juice
1 tablespoon butter, optional
Salt
Pepper

1. Cut off root ends of leek. Trim and discard all but 2 inches of the green portion. Slice in half lengthwise. Wash well under running water, separating stalk sections to remove dirt. Select the tender, green inner section and cut into thin strips.

2. Arrange fish on a plate with thickest portions to the outside. Top with leeks. Drizzle with lime juice. Cover with plastic wrap, vented. MICROWAVE (high) 4–5 minutes until thickest portion of fish is almost opaque when tested with a fork. Let stand 5 minutes. Remove fish and leeks from plate and, if desired, swirl butter into juices. Stir in salt and pepper to taste. Spoon juices over fish.

⌣♥ MINT SCALLOPS

To double the amount of scallops, make the recipe twice; you get more even cooking results in the microwave if you cook ½ pound or less of scallops at a time. Scallops are edible raw, so minimal cooking is needed—overcooking would make them tough.

Preparation time: 2 minutes
Microwave time: 2 minutes
Servings: 2–3

½ **pound bay scallops**
1 **tablespoon fresh lemon juice**
1 **tablespoon chopped fresh mint**

Spread scallops on a plate. Drizzle with lemon juice. Sprinkle with mint. Cover with plastic wrap, vented. MICROWAVE (high) 1½–2 minutes, rearranging scallops once to push uncooked ones from the center to the outside. Scallops are done when the center is almost opaque. Let stand 3 minutes.

BIBLIOGRAPHY

Among the many books and publications used to research this book, these were particularly useful:

Beard, James. *James Beard's New Fish Cookery*. New York: Warner Books, 1987.

Cronin, Isaac, Jay Harlow, and Paul Johnson. *The California Seafood Cookbook*. Berkeley, California: Aris Books, 1983.

McClane, A. J. *The Encyclopedia of Fish Cookery*. New York: Holt, Rinehart and Winston, 1977.

Mosimann, Anton, and Holger Hofmann. *Shellfish*. New York: Hearst Books, 1987.

U.S. Department of Agriculture. *Composition of Foods: Finfish and Shellfish Products*. Washington, D.C.: *USDA Handbook No. 8-15*, rev. September 1987.

RECIPES LIST

APPETIZERS
Abalone in Ginger and Garlic Sauce
Cold Shrimp with Spiked Chili Sauce
Crab and Artichoke Dip
Crab Legs Maltaise
Crayfish-Stuffed Mirliton
Creamy Crab and Mushrooms
Fresh Bluefish Pâté
Ginger-Marinated Shrimp
Linguine with Cherrystones
Lobster Tail Mousseline
Mussels Steamed with Wine and Herbs
Mussels with Fresh Tomato Sauce
Oysters Steamed with Wine and Thyme
Oysters Stuffed with Mushrooms
Salmon Quenelles
Scallops with Passion Fruit Sauce
Shrimp-Stuffed Wontons
Snails de Jonghe
Snails Simmered in Wine and Herbs
Spicy Shrimp Boil
Squid Stuffed with Pine Nuts

Steamed Crayfish
Steamers in Natural Broth with Dipping Butter
Sweet Pickled Squid

SALADS
Catfish and Red Cabbage Salad
Char and Black Bean Salad
Crayfish and Asparagus Salad
Fresh Tuna Niçoise Salad
Hot German Cod Salad
Kingclip Salad with Rosemary Vinaigrette
Lobster Tail and Grapefruit Salad
Mahimahi and Wild Mushroom Salad
Monk Caesar Salad
Multi-Lettuce Flounder Salad
Octopus and Celeriac Salad
Ono Salad with Mango Chutney
Oreo-Shrimp Salad
Pike and Vegetable Vinaigrette Salad
Red Snapper and Orange Salad
Scallop and Cilantro Salad
Sweet-and-Sour Buffalofish Salad
Sweet Pickled Squid Salad
Sesame Shrimp Salad
Walleye-and-Walnut Salad
Warm Abalone and Artichoke Salad

SOUPS
Black Monk Soup
Bouillabaisse
Cod and Broccoli Soup
Eel and Leek Broth
Fish Stock
Lemon-Crab Soup
Monterey Squid Chowder
Oyster and Artichoke Soup
Perch-and-Potato Soup
Pollack-and-Lentil Soup
Quick Cajun Fish Stew
Red Snapper and Tortilla-Lime Soup
Roughy-and-Rice Soup
Scallops in Scallion-Flavored Broth
Squid Soup with Spinach

ENTREES

Abalone with Lemon Juice
Amberjack Chunks with Anchovy Sauce
Amberjack with Tomato-Dill Sauce
Bluefish with Caper Veloute
Bluefish with Honey-Mustard Sauce
Buffalofish with Mustard Veloute
Buttercrumb Amberjack
Catfish with Leek and Lemon
Catfish with Orange-Spiked Sweet Potatoes
Char with Apples and Cider
Char with Lemon-Almond Rice
Chervil Chunks
Chili-Marinated Shark with Avocado Topping
Chilled Whole Trout with Cumin-Mayonnaise Sauce
Cod Smothered in Mushrooms
Cod with Fresh Tomato
Crayfish Etoufée
Crayfish-Stuffed Mirliton
Crayfish with Orange Veloute
Creamy Crab and Mushrooms
Curried Kingclip and Rice
Dilled Peas and Fish
Double-Pepper Fish
Eel in Green Sauce
Eel with Ale and Black Bread
Fettuccine with Shrimp Sauce
Fettuccine with White Clam Sauce
Fish with Grainy Mustard and Pepper
Flounder and Beurre Blanc with Herbs
Flounder Rolls with Shallot Butter
Flounder with Lemon-Thyme
Fresh Tuna with Homemade Teriyaki Sauce
Garlic-Rubbed Monkfish
Ginger-Garlic Steaks
Grouper with Black Olive and Tomato Topping
Grouper with Buttery Crumbs
Grouper with Roasted Red Pepper and Cucumber
Haddock with Mediterranean Olive Sauce
Haddock with Plantain and Lime
Haddock with Wine and Capers
Halibut Kabob with Yellow Pepper Puree
Halibut with Basil and Bay

Halibut with Brandied Mushrooms
Honey-Mustard Carrots and Fish
Hot Marinated Buffalofish with Peppers
Hot Tuna Muffins
Indian-Spiced Orange Roughy
Indian-Spiced Smelts and Zucchini
Juicy Mushroom Fish
Kingclip with Dijon Mustard
Leeks and Lime Steaks
Linguine with Cherrystones
Lobster Tail Mousseline
Lobster Tails with Clarified Butter
Mackerel on Tangy Napa
Mahimahi with Bernaise
Mahimahi with Tangy, Low-Fat Cucumber Sauce
Marinated Smelts
Mint Scallops
Monkfish with Napa-Walnut Rolls
Mullet with Garlic-Tomato Topping
Mullet with Mustard
Mustard-Marinated Shark
Octopus over Green Rice
Ono with Fresh Dill and Mustard
Opah with Homemade Hollandaise
Opah with Lemon and a Touch of Butter
Opah with Warm Raspberry Vinaigrette
Orange-Orange Roughy
Orange Roughy with White Wine and Mushrooms
Oreo Dory with Julienned Vegetables
Oreo Dory with Lemon Veloute
Oriental Lobster Tails
Pacific Rockfish with Avocado Topping
Pacific Rockfish Marinated in Orange Brandy
Pacific Rockfish with Basil and Thyme
Perch in Tangy Mustard Sauce
Perch Meunière
Perch with Lemon and Chives
Pike and Pea Pods
Pike Beurre Blanc
Pine Nut-Stuffed Squid
Poached Whole Salmon
Pollack with Bloody Mary Topping
Pollack with Fish Veloute

Pompano in Parchment
Pompano with Skinny Asparagus
Poor Man's Lobster
Red Snapper on Apple Slices
Red Snapper with Sesame-Ginger Marinade
Salmon Benedict with Orange Hollandaise
Salmon Quenelles
Salmon Steaks with Lemon-Dill Sauce
Salmon-Stuffed Potatoes
Scallops with Oyster Sauce
Shark with Shiitake Mushrooms and Spinach
Shrimp-and-Crab-Topped Potatoes
Shrimp and Pea Pods
Shrimp Mousse with Beurre Rouge
Simmered Octopus
Skewered Ono with Red Pepper Puree
Smelts with Sharp Texas Barbecue Sauce
Snails with Sun-Dried Tomatoes on Linguine
Sole with Dill
Sole with Lemon-Lime Veloute
Sole with Tangy Spinach Sauce
Spicy Shrimp Boil
Spring Asparagus and Fillet Dinner
Striped Bass with Beurre Rouge
Swordfish Kabobs with Sweet-and-Sour Sauce
Swordfish with Dark Oyster Sauce
Swordfish with Hot Sake
Swordfish with Smashed Garlic
Tomato-Chive Fillets
Trout and Shrimp Quenelles
Trout in Saffron Wine
Trout with Bay and Lime
Tuna with Citrus Sauce
Tuna with Sweet Pepper Puree
Turbot with Buttery Shallots
Turbot with Lemon and Tarragon
Walleye Polonaise
Walleye with Honey-Papaya Sauce
Whitefish Fillets with Grainy Mustard and Pepper
Whitefish with Creamy Spinach Sauce
Whole Buffalofish with Barbecue Sauce
Whole Catfish with Butter-Pecan Sauce
Whole Grouper with Leek and Ginger

Whole Mackerel with Spanish Olive Topping
Whole Porgy with Fennel Seeds
Whole Striped Bass with Basil
Whole Stuffed Pike with Leek
Whole Whitefish Stuffed with Celery and Mushrooms
Wisconsin Fish Boil

INDEX

* marks a recipe with no added fat